ALL ROADS
—LEAD—
HOME

BETTE PRATT

Copyright © 2020 by Bette Pratt.

ISBN   Softcover   978-1-953537-14-0

All Scripture Quoted is taken from the New International Version of the Bible.

All rights reserved. No part of this book may be reproduced or transmitted in any form or by any means, electronic or mechanical, including photocopying, recording, or by any information storage and retrieval system without express written permission from the author, except in the case of brief quotations embodied in critical reviews and certain other non-commercial uses permitted by copyright law.

Printed in the United States of America.

To order additional copies of this book, contact:
Bookwhip
1-855-339-3589
https://www.bookwhip.com

One

It seemed like Grand Central station, but it was Isabel's house in Vansville, Georgia. Moments before Isabel's daughter had answered the phone. They'd found out that Pastor Roger of the Vansville church was stopping for lunch. He was driving his fiancée car with a trailer and her little girl was along, of course. Before they arrived, Isabel's renter, Duncan Roads, returned home early from his Christmas visit to his sister's. Somehow, Isabel's kitchen table must hold them all for lunch.

After introductions and some cheerful chatter, Roger recruited Duncan to unload the trailer that Roger had driven from Michigan on to his house in the country. Heidi happily stayed with her great-grandma, whom she loved dearly. They would fix supper for everyone, while the other adults left to fill Roger's house to over-flowing with Raylyn's things.

When they arrived at Roger's house, Ruth started helping her daughter unload the boxes and smaller things from the trailer and at the same time try to find places for all her things in Roger's house that was already fairly well stocked. Roger and Duncan brought in Raylyn's furniture. The loveseat-sleeper was the last thing and Duncan was on the back end of it. Roger reached the door into his smallest bedroom where it was to reside. It was the first time they'd been alone since Roger had brought Raylyn and Heidi to Isabel's for lunch.

"So," Duncan said, "how's come you deserted me?"

"Deserted you?" Roger asked, perplexed. "How can you say I deserted you? You're the one who left for a month."

As he cleared the door, Duncan shook his head and exclaimed, "Of course! I left here for my sister's place and you, bachelor Roger, are a week away from conducting some meeting in your church for Thanksgiving. I come back a few days after Christmas and you've got a woman and child hanging on you! And, the lady has a sparkling ring on her finger!"

"Well, yeah." He shrugged, moving backwards across the floor toward the wall under the window. "The first I saw them was with Isabel at that service you mentioned. That child truly looked like an angel and her mom wrapped her web around me at Sandy's while we ate Thanksgiving dinner at her table." He grinned at his friend. "You know, it happens to the best of us, Duncan. Even you might fall one of these days."

Vehemently, Duncan shook his head. "Oh, no! Not me! No woman, except my sister will ever get the time of day from me!" Instead of setting the heavy piece of furniture down carefully, he nearly dropped it from two inches up.

"You think so?"

"I'll never let it happen! I swore off women after I left home," he declared.

Roger chuckled, as he dropped his end of the sofa. "Never's a very long time, Duncan. I've heard it from a very reliable source, 'Never say never' almost always you have to eat your words sometime down the line."

Continuing to deny Roger's statement, Duncan said, "Not this guy! No sir, it'll never happen to me. I got a padlock on my heart and the key's hidden too well."

"We'll see!" Roger said, with a grin.

Anxious to change the subject, Duncan asked, "So when's the big day? You're moving furniture in your place here like she's gonna live here real soon."

Leading the way back to the hallway, he said, "Yeah, we see no reason to wait. My folks can get away a whale of a lot easier this time of year, so they're flying in next Thursday. They're staying for ten days in Isabel's cabins and our wedding's the Saturday before they leave. We've already talked to Ramon and Sandy, Ramon's going to be my best man and Sandy's playing and being our soloist. Would you be my groomsman?"

Making a face at his friend and making his whole body shudder, Duncan asked, "Who's the lady I escort? I suppose it's somebody I never met."

"My sister. I can see the question on your face. Heidi's Raylyn's maid of honor and the flower girl rolled into one."

Pulling his hand down his face and holding the end of his beard, Duncan asked, "I gotta shave this off and wear a tux?"

Roger shrugged. "Kinda hoped you would."

"Not askin' much, are you?" Duncan grumbled.

"It's a long time till hiking time, it'll grow back."

"Yeah, but the tux?"

"It's only one time and doesn't last all day, nobody'll make fun."

Duncan let out a long sigh, "You drive a hard bargain, but for you, I'll do it."

Roger stepped up beside his friend and slapped him on the back. "Thanks a heap, man! I'm much obliged."

"Yeah, well, it isn't every day a buddy of mine falls." They were in the kitchen now. Of course both Raylyn and Ruth heard him and Raylyn scowled at him, but didn't comment.

Still grinning at his friend, Roger said, "I'll remember that."

Duncan chuckled. "Not too hard, man."

It was the Friday after New Year's, Duncan had spent most of his time in Ramon's office with him and Sandy working their computer and his laptop. Since last summer, when Ramon had worked the trails around Vansville alone and then had his accident and Duncan had taken over the trips alone during the fall, they had worked hard to find other trails so they could expand their business now that Duncan would be working along with Ramon and leading hikes as well. They had found another area on the topographical map that had some trails. However, they knew they had to shut down, because today, this evening, they were meeting at Casbah's huge house for a catered rehearsal dinner before the wedding rehearsal at the little community church.

"Duncan, get on out of here and back to your cabin so Ramon and I can get dressed and not be late," Sandy said, as she wheeled herself from the desk.

Duncan sighed, "Sandy, you know what this means?"

"Sure, Roger's getting married tomorrow!"

"It means that my two friends got hitched within a year. That's what!" Thumbing his fist over his shoulder, he said, "That guy bit the dust when you sailed into town and now my other friend found himself another northerner to tie him in knots. I swear, who's a guy got to talk to?"

Bestowing her beautiful smile on him, Sandy said, "I know, Duncan, it happens to the best of men. You know what it says, 'It is not good for man to be alone. I will make a helper suitable for him.' (Genesis 2:18) so God made the woman so she could be a helpmate for the man. It's all there in the first book of the Bible, Duncan, in Genesis. There's a lady out there just for you, you be patient, God'll bring her to you."

Duncan blew out a long breath, grunted himself from the desk chair and slammed the top down on his laptop. Glaring at the lady, he said, "Sandy, you will be the death of me! Every time I'm here you shove that Bible stuff down my throat! Furthermore, I don't care, I will *never* be caught in any woman's sights, I will be a bachelor till I die! Haven't you heard me say that enough times to understand I'm single and I'll stay single?"

Her eyes laughing, Sandy said, "Oh, I've heard you say that most every time you say it, I'm sure. But you know, never's a very long time and I've heard it from several reliable sources, 'Never say never.' Haven't you ever heard that?" Sandy pushed the control on her chair and headed for the door into the rest of their house.

He didn't even take the time to put on his coat, he just grabbed it and slammed out the door, computer in hand and said, "Yeah, I heard it!"

Four long strides later, Duncan slouched in his SUV behind the wheel. He nearly threw his laptop and his parka onto the passenger seat and slammed his door. Only moments later he roared from the parking lot, leaving black marks behind him. Since it was such a small town and the other end of town was only a few blocks away, Duncan wasn't cooled down when he pulled onto Isabel's parking lot. He roared to his parking place and slammed on his brakes. The SUV rocked back and forth as he jammed the stick into park.

He threw his parka over his arm, grabbed up his laptop and jerked the door open. But when he stepped out, a blast of cold air hit him and with the cold came a dampness on his face. "Snow! Just what Roger and Raylyn need to get out of town for their honeymoon. Maybe it'll warm up and be sunny tomorrow for their wedding. I'm sure they hope so. It's a ways to the airport in Atlanta."

Since he was carrying his coat, Duncan wasted no time getting in his cabin. He dropped what he was carrying onto the nearest piece of furniture and went straight to his bathroom. He'd gotten steamed off enough at Sandy, he needed a shower. Before he stripped, he looked in the mirror at his face. He'd had this beard for three years and had never cut or trimmed it. He had to admit it made him look a bit scruffy. Roger had asked him to cut it off for the wedding. He was the groomsman and neither of the other two had beards.

In fact, come to think of it, Roger's face was clean shaven. He sighed, should he take it off now and get a bit used to it or wait until in the morning to shave? He left the bathroom and went to the kitchen for his scissors. With them in hand, he went back to the mirror in the bathroom and with a big sigh, began cutting the hair that covered his face.

"Everybody better appreciate the sacrifice I'm making! First of all, I'm going in a church, something I vowed I'd never do again, once I left home and my mother behind and I'm cutting off my beard," he grumbled.

You won't have anything to hide behind, will you? an insolent little voice goaded him from his shoulder.

He didn't give the little voice the satisfaction of an answer, just kept snipping away at the long hairs that nearly hit the plaid flannel shirt. Some time later he had the hair all cut short so that the hair that was left curled under his chin. He put the scissors on the counter, stripped and started the water in the shower. While the water hit his skin he decided to leave his face the way it was and shave the rest of it in the morning. This change was drastic enough for one day.

As he shut off the water, his phone rang, so he hurried to the bedroom and picked up his extension. "Roads," he said.

"Duncan," his landlady said, "could I ask a favor, could I ride with you this evening? It's snowing, you know and Ruth made me promise that when she's not here I won't drive in snow."

Surprised, Duncan asked, "You're going to the rehearsal dinner?"

"Yes, Raylyn and Heidi want me there, but you see, Roger has already come for them and it's just started snowing."

"I'll get you Isabel, give me about ten minutes, okay?"

"That's fine, young fella, dinner's not for another forty minutes or so and with your good SUV we'll make it just fine."

"No matter, I'll be there, watch for me."

Duncan dressed in a clean pair of jeans and another clean flannel shirt. He pulled on a pair of wool socks and his dress boots. After he stood up from his bed, he combed his hair and as he looked in the mirror, he wondered if he should trim it, too. It had been three years since he'd cut his hair. Even if he cut the split ends off it would be better. He sighed and looked at the clock by his bed and pulled his hair back into a tail down his back. If he was going to cut it it would be tomorrow, he'd promised to pick up Isabel and if he didn't grab his coat and be out the door, his phone would be ringing. Again.

He slid his arms into his parka, grabbed his keys and opened the door. A cold gust of wind hit his chest, since his coat was still open. Quickly, he pulled the door closed and reached for the zipper of his parka. He pulled the zipper-pull up as he jogged down the walk to his Jeep. The light came on on Isabel's porch and when he started his car, her front door opened. She was an old lady, but she dressed very well and always looked nice. He wished his mom would take better care of herself, she was much younger, but she looked disheveled all the time. Actually, it wasn't hard to admit, his mom looked a wreck. He would know he'd seen her over Christmas. She had come to his sister's house for Christmas Day EMPTY HANDED!! She had no gifts, not for her children or her grandchildren! And to look at her, he remembered seeing her wear that same housedress when he came home from high school.

He pulled closer to Isabel's walk and the old lady made her way carefully down her steps to his car. He left the SUV running, but hurried to meet her and walk with her to the SUV. "Isabel, why don't you wait on your porch until I come up there for you? You know you could fall and break a hip! The snow's covering the ground now and it's getting slippery."

Isabel gave a loud huff and said, "Sonny, I navigated these steps before you was even born. Now let me look at you. I kind of like that beard thing you got there now. A body can even see what you look like a bit."

Duncan chuckled. "Thanks, Isabel, Roger wants it all off for the wedding. I thought I'd start off easy and work into it."

"Downright good. You gonna do that to your hair, too?"

"I'm thinking about it, Isabel."

In her no-nonsense voice, Isabel said, "Well, think a bit harder, it'll make ya look more like a man than a beast."

Duncan opened the passenger door for the lady and laughed. "Thanks, Isabel, you've made my day, you know?" He helped her in and closed the door.

Snow was coming down at a steady pace and Duncan wondered how Ramon and Sandy's van would do. Actually, the van would do fine, it wasn't even a year old, so the tires were good, but would Sandy drive it in the snow? He slid behind the wheel of the SUV and headed across the gravel parking lot for Main Street. A mile out of town, he turned on a county road that led him back behind the town to the small mansion where Ramon's mom and step-dad lived. Derek Casbah had become a regular attendee at Roger's church, but his wife still refused to have anything to do with religion.

"So, will Millie be at her own house?" Duncan asked.

"Humph!" Isabel exclaimed, "I have my doubts! But if she's not there, I have no good ideas where she'll be. She's a law unto herself, that's for sure. Believe me, if she's not there, this dinner'll go a lot better."

"Tell me, Isabel, how do they work it when a man of the cloth gets married?"

Isabel shrugged. "Simple, he gets a minister friend to do the service. He stands there like any other man and takes his wife."

"I guess I never thought of that."

"You been here before, Sonny?"

Duncan looked over at the lady and said, "Isabel, just because Ramon and I are working associates doesn't mean I'm on good terms with his relatives. There's no love lost between Ramon and his mom and step-dad."

Isabel nodded, as they saw the large mailbox come into view. "I know that. Sandy's tried to get them to make peace and I think Ramon and Derek are pretty close to drawing up a peace treaty, but Millie is another matter."

The snow was a bit heavier out in the country, so Duncan slowed a little. "I know that's a fact! So how is it Roger's rehearsal dinner's here?"

"Well, Sonny, if you ever darkened the door of this church here in town, you'd know that Derek Casbah is one of the regulars now and he's the biggest giver in the church. He's taken a real shine to my granddaughter and great granddaughter as well as the preacher."

"I can see why that would be! That little shaver is a heart-stopper."

Beaming happily, Isabel said, "I love her to death!"

Duncan pulled up onto the snow-covered driveway of the huge house and cut the engine. He sighed and said, "Isabel, don't you start with that church stuff. Sandy got me before I left their place earlier. I was so mad I nearly saw red instead of white when I left their place. I've about had all I can take of this God stuff." Duncan pulled the keys from the ignition.

Isabel gave him her brightest smile. "Sonny, we'll win, you'll see!"

Shaking his head as he slid from the high seat. "I'm not holding my breath, Isabel. We might have this snow on July Fourth before that happens."

As he closed his door, Duncan heard her cackle. When he opened her door, she said, "Sonny, it'll happen, maybe sooner than you think."

Duncan snapped his lips together and glared at the old lady.

As he closed Isabel's door, lights shone on the road and soon Sandy's van turned onto Casbah's driveway. Duncan looked a bit more closely and saw that Ramon was behind the wheel. Obviously, Isabel had been watching, too, because she let out a sigh, as she slid her hand around Duncan's elbow. "I'm glad she didn't drive in this stuff! I know she's not comfortable with snow. She told me she didn't get to drive much before she left Philadelphia. Sonny, hurry and walk me to the door and then come back to help Ramon get Sandy's chair up to the door."

"Yes, Ma'am!"

They had reached the pillars holding the two story roof over a large porch when the door opened and a man with a full head of white hair stood in the doorway. He held out his hand to Isabel and smiled when she took it. "Ms. Isabel Isaacson, it's good to see you! You're as pretty as ever! Get yourself in out of that cold."

"Derek, I'll do that. Duncan's going back to help Ramon with Sandy's chair. In this snow it may prove a problem."

"Yes, it might." Derek stood looking out the door for a minute, then closed it on the cold and took Isabel's coat. "Isabel, go down the hall to the sitting room. Roger, Raylyn and Heidi are there greeting folks. Ruth's helping my housekeeper get things together."

"Thank you, I'll do that. No housekeeper needs my help with any dinner preparations. I've done my share, believe me."

Duncan turned from the door and went back to the van. Ramon was at the back and had the door open and the lift out when the front door opened and Derek stood, back-lit in the opening. "Hey, wait a minute!" he called. "Millie's car's not here and I'll move mine out. You close that back up and drive in the garage so she won't have to get onto that slippery pavement."

"That's a great idea, Derek, thanks!" Ramon said, as he pushed the control to put the lift back inside and close the door.

Soon, the garage door went up and the light came on inside, Derek got in his car and at the same time, Ramon slid behind the wheel of the van. Duncan realized they wouldn't need his help, so he walked into the garage into the empty space where there was no car. He could wait for the men to head inside. Soon the switch was made and Sandy was on the dry floor of the garage and wheeling herself toward the open door into the house that Derek was pointing her to.

She gave Derek a big smile and said, "Derek, I do appreciate your thoughtfulness, it made it much easier for everybody."

He held the door open and Sandy wheeled herself past him. "That's fine. I'm glad I thought of it before you got out."

"So, where's Mom," Ramon asked, knowing that if her car was gone, so was she. That car was her pride and joy.

Derek shrugged and put the garage door down, as he said, "I'm not sure. She told me before I left for work that she wouldn't be here. That's all I know and I'm sure you know I wouldn't ask. We're waiting for Roger's family, they should be here soon. They surely know how to drive in snow."

Ramon and Duncan both chuckled and Ramon said, "If they don't, they haven't lived in those Rockies very long."

"To hear Roger tell it, they had one whale of a storm the day Raylyn arrived out there."

Sandy had barely wheeled her chair through the door that Derek had held open when they heard another car outside. "That must be them," Derek said. "I'll get the door for them so they don't have to wait out in the cold. Go on down the hall to the sitting room. I'm sure you can hear the talking down there."

Soon, they were all seated around the huge table in the dining room and the housekeeper was serving them a delicious meal. There was plenty of food and desert was out of this world. The lady surely knew how to make a mouth-watering desert, even to follow a lovely dinner. Even though everyone ate until they were stuffed, they all had desert. Roger looked up from his empty plate and noticed Duncan putting a full fork into his mouth. His face broke into a huge grin, as he said, "Hey, everybody! Look at Duncan, he's cut his beard, a body can actually see he's a fairly handsome bloke."

Of course, Duncan was at a disadvantage, he had a mouthful and couldn't answer his friend's jibe. "Yeah," Ramon added, "I never knew he had a chin, I thought it was all hair."

Heidi was the only child in the room. She hadn't said too much during the meal, but now she looked around at all the adults, then at Duncan and said, "Mr. Duncan had a chin, Mr. Ramon, you didn't look hard enough."

"You think so, Heidi? Well, if you say so."

Nodding, Heidi added, "Oh, yes, but he still gots a tail down his back."

"Maybe that'll come off tomorrow," Isabel added.

Duncan swallowed and waved his hands. "Hey, everybody! I'm here in person you don't have to talk about me like I'm out of the body, or something."

Shaking her head solemnly, Heidi said, "You not out of your body, Mr. Duncan, you be right there. But you still gots a tail."

"Yeah, he does, Heidi," Roger said. "You're right."

Heidi looked at Duncan and asked, "Is you gonna cut off your tail, Mr. Duncan? You know Daddy Roger not got a tail and Mr. Ramon don't either."

Smiling at the little girl, Duncan said, "You don't think it'd hurt?"

"Uh uh, you not like a cat or chickens. You cut it and it don't hurt."

"I'll think about it, Heidi."

"Good, it be off tomorrow." That brought out several snickers around the table.

However, Isabel cackled. "Guess she told you, Sonny. I'll call Ted Lankaster tomorrow morning. I have a job for him, but he'll give you a right good haircut if I ask him."

Duncan looked around at his friends and also those he didn't know. He gave a long sigh, "Seems I'm out numbered."

After Isabel wiped her mouth, she said, "That you are, Sonny, that you are."

By the time dinner was over and it was time to leave for the church and the rehearsal, the snow had stopped, but the roads were slippery. Sandy and Ramon hurried into the van and Duncan helped Isabel into his SUV. Everyone else went back to the vehicles they had come in and left the mansion for town. They had had an excellent meal and good fellowship.

Derek closed the door after the last person had left and wondered briefly when his wife would be home. He went to the garage and pulled his car back in its place and hit the garage door opener. He didn't have long to wait because those on the road back to town met the little sports car on its way. Of course, Millie wouldn't have acknowledged anyone from the group, even if she'd known it was them. The garage door had barely reached the floor when the motor started again and it started up. Derek sighed and went in the house, hoping to reach the kitchen to help the housekeeper before his wife made her presence known.

The pastor from Isabel's church in Blairsville hadn't been able to come for the dinner, but he met the group at the little church in town. Everyone parked and then several walked with Sandy up the slippery ramp, while Duncan walked Isabel up the snow covered steps to the front door. Roger had come to the church on his way to pick up Raylyn and Heidi and turned up the heat, so that the building was warm for their rehearsal. Isabel went immediately to the front seat, because Ruth was walking her daughter in and giving her away. Several of Roger's family had been invited to the rehearsal dinner, but had no part in the rehearsal, so most of them stopped at Isabel's cabins. Isabel was the only one who didn't have a part in the actual ceremony, but no one expected her to leave.

Heidi was in heaven! She danced around the little church she was so excited that she was getting a daddy. She loved Roger and he had a special place in his heart for her, of course. She knew her part very well, but she wouldn't get her basket of flower petals until right before the ceremony, because the florist from Blairsville wouldn't be there until the next day. Even so, when it was her turn up the aisle, she pretended to be scattering petals as she went. Isabel decided she was the most precious child in all the world.

Duncan had been introduced to the lady he was to escort at dinner. She was an older, female version of Roger. She was married, but Roger had wanted Duncan in the wedding rather than Lonnie. Compared to his country bumpkin qualities, she was a total city slicker. He was back woods Georgia and she was suburbia St. Louis. Even if Heidi hadn't mentioned his 'tail,' the minute he was introduced, he decided that his hair would be cut when he walked her down the aisle. The question he'd had about his beard earlier was also answered it would be gone in the morning. No wonder Raylyn had expected that he and Ramon would wear tuxes. He had never felt so uncomfortable in his life.

After everyone was satisfied with how the wedding would work on Saturday, Duncan put his arm out for Isabel and walked her from the building. The wind was cold and even though the snow had stopped the dampness was penetrating. Isabel shivered as they hurried to the SUV. Immediately, even before Duncan started the car for the short ride, Isabel said, "So when should I have Ted come by to cut your hair?"

"He'll do a good job?"

"Of course! He used to be a barber in Blairsville before he retired and moved here and took on some handyman jobs. He used to cut my dear husband's hair every month and when he needed one, Ted would give him a good shave."

"It doesn't matter, Isabel. You know I'm up with the dawn. I don't have anything really planned until the wedding."

"Good. I'll fix a thermos of coffee and send it over with him about nine. Is that good?"

Duncan turned the heater blower to high to help take off the chill. "It'll be fine, Isabel. Walking that woman down the aisle is giving me the willies."

Fiercely, Isabel said, "Listen here, Sonny! She's no better or worse than you or me. In God's eyes we're all sinners only some of us have been saved by grace."

Duncan shut off the car and muttered, "Here we go again."

Before he could open his door, she said, "That's right, Duncan, it's only by the grace of God we have life and breath."

Duncan didn't say anything as he walked Isabel to her door. He decided if he kept quiet that maybe the subject would die a natural death. As she opened her door, she said, "You be watching for Ted about nine, now."

"Yes, Isabel. I'll be ready."

Duncan usually fixed his own morning pot of coffee, but Isabel's was so much better that he pulled out his orange juice and poured a glassful to drink with his cereal and toast for breakfast. He had barely washed up his dishes when there was a knock on the door and Duncan called, "Come on in, Ted, the door's unlocked."

Carrying a small satchel and a quart thermos, Ted walked in the small cabin. "So, I get to do some barbering today?"

Duncan sighed, "Yes, Ted, I found out yesterday that I'm to be paired up with some city slicker from St. Louis this afternoon. It's got me quaking in my boots. You know, I haven't worn shoes in years, they had to rent me some for today."

"Yeah, I always knew that preacher was more citified than's good for this little town."

Duncan shook his head. "Ted, it's not the preacher, he was raised on a big ranch in Montana, along with his sister, but she married a city guy. Roger stuck more to his roots."

Ted shrugged. "Okay, I'll give you that. The preacher seems like a good soul, but I can see why you want that tail off. So, you want it cut off or you want it styled?"

Putting his thumb in his chest, Duncan said, "Me? Have my hair styled? You have got to be kidding! Last I checked, I was that typical country bumpkin."

Ted set the satchel and thermos down on the table and said, "Now let me tell you a little something I learned while I picked up that coffee I brought over." Duncan pulled two mugs from his clean dishes and started pouring Isabel's coffee in them. "While you pour that coffee in them mugs, I gotta tell you that Miss Isabel told me to make you look right smart, that you was escortin' some highbrow lady this afternoon in that weddin'. She said she saw the lady."

"She did? She told you to style my hair?" He put the top back on the thermos and took a sip from his mug.

"Well, she didn't say that word, but it's possible she didn't know that was the word us barbers use for these new fangled haircuts we give men in the city. Even Blairsville had its share of critters wanted that!"

Duncan brought the two mugs to the table and set one beside Ted's satchel, then sat down in the chair closest to the sink. He took another mouthful and let it swirl around in his mouth for a few seconds. After he swallowed, he said, "Ted, you cut it how you want. If it's styled, I'll live with it, it'll look good today. That's what's important, anyway. By the time our hikes take up in the spring, nobody'll know my beard was gone or my hair was styled in January."

Ted chuckled. "I hear that. Cuttin' a man's hair is his choice, I always say." He took a long swallow from his mug, set it back on the table and opened his satchel. He pulled out a plastic cape and shook it out. "You sit right there. Take a big slug of coffee and then I'll put this around your neck. Even though Miss Isabel's coffee's good, it don't mix well with hair cuttin's fallin' into it."

Duncan chuckled. "I hear ya, Ted. I never did like it much when I took my drink in the bathroom and then had to dump it out when foreign stuff fell in it." Duncan drained half the mug, then set it on the table and leaned back in the chair.

Ted put the large cape around Duncan's neck and fastened it behind his neck, then pulled out the long tail. He pulled the rubber band from the tail and combed the mass of hair until it lay soft and untangled down Duncan's back. Before he picked up his scissors, Ted grinned and asked, "You want this stuff saved for somethin'?"

Duncan let a shudder go down his back. "No, I don't have a girl to send it to and my sister doesn't care."

"Okay then, here it goes!" Duncan tried very hard to sit still as the sheers started to work.

About half an hour later Ted pulled out a mirror from his satchel and held it in front of Duncan. "Whacha think, fella?"

"It looks good, Ted. Do you do shaves, too?"

Nodding, Ted said, "I used to be the best in Blairsville."

Duncan shrugged. "Might as well get the works. Somehow, it doesn't seem right with a fancy do on my head to let the face go."

"You'll get it, fella. I never emptied my satchel, so I got my shaving cream. I'll get you spiffed up in no time. So when did you start to grow your hair? It's been a while, huh?"

Duncan sat for a minute, before he said, "Off and on I let it grow from when I graduated from high school, but my mom hated it, so I'd cut it every so often. When I moved away from home for good was the last time I had it cut and that was about three years ago. I don't see her much any more and when I do she knows not to say anything about my hair."

The cream went on his face and soon the beard was only a memory. When he finished, Ted held up the mirror. "So, what you think?"

Duncan swallowed as he saw his face. He hadn't seen it without the hair in three years. Actually, he hadn't been a man when he'd last had a clean face. "I'd say I'd better not wear my plaid flannel shirts and my coveralls for a while. You've done a fine job, Ted. Thanks."

Ted chuckled. "Are sort of handsome, if I do say so myself."

Another shudder went down Duncan's back. "I wouldn't go that far, Ted."

The barber undid the snap and wadded up the plastic drape. He went to Duncan's large kitchen wastebasket and dumped the whiskers into it, then took a paper towel and wiped off the shaving cream. As he folded his cape and pushed it into his satchel, Duncan held out a bill and said, "You did me a great job, Ted. I don't know if this is enough, but that's all I had on me."

Ted shook his head. "I don't barber for a livin', not anymore, anyways."

He pushed Duncan's hand away, but Duncan pushed the bill into Ted's hand and said, "No matter, you did me a fine job and I want to pay you for it."

"Well, this is plenty." Nodding to the coffee in Duncan's mug, he said, "You best warm that up, Isabel's coffee is too good to waste."

"Don't worry. I'll send it through the microwave. I'll take her thermos back later, 'cause I'll drink the rest of it after a while."

Ted picked up his satchel, saluted Duncan and said, "Good luck at that weddin' today. Wish that preacher well for me, would ya? I don't plan to go."

"Will do, Ted and thanks."

The older man left and Duncan sent his mug through the microwave. He sat back in his chair with his warmed up coffee and pulled out a letter he'd gotten the day before from his sister. He liked to read her letters, they were newsy, telling all the things his nephew and nieces were doing. They'd been off for Christmas vacation and now they were back in school. His nephew was a star on the basketball team and his older niece was a cheerleader for their school.

By the time Duncan looked out his window the sun was out and the ground was bare of snow. That meant it was a warmer day than yesterday. He was glad it meant that Roger and Raylyn would have no trouble getting down the road a good ways after the reception. Roger had told him he was taking his bride to several Florida theme parks. He was happy for them.

When it was one o'clock, he picked up the thermos and walked out. He didn't plan to drive to the church it was only two blocks away. He knocked on Isabel's door and waited for her to answer. She came dressed for the wedding, but her hair was still up in curlers. "Sonny! I'd'a never guessed you was so handsome! Ted told me to hold onto my hat when I saw you, I'd be plumb bowled over. He wasn't kiddin'!"

Uncomfortable with her compliment, he could feel the warmth creeping up his neck, Duncan said, "Thanks for the coffee, Isabel, here's your thermos, it was good coffee, as usual. I'm walking over now, I was told that because I'm part of the wedding party I have to be there a bit earlier, so I'm on my way. I'll see you later."

"That's fine. Ruth and I are going in a few minutes, too." As she closed the door, Duncan heard her say, "Woo-woo! Yes-sir-re-bob, some girl might look at him now."

Duncan sighed, a good reason to have long hair and a beard. He wished he had a hood on his parka, his face and head felt cold in the wind. Duncan had been told to come into the church through the door into the pastor's study. The men would meet there and the tux would be there for him. He walked in and Ramon, Roger and the pastor were already there, they all turned as the door opened. As Duncan entered their mouths fell open and there was silence for a minute.

Finally, Roger said, "Is that really you, Duncan? If I'd have known what you really looked like I'm not sure I'd have wanted you to get that hair cut off. My lady might think you're more handsome than me."

Very uncomfortable, Duncan said, "Roger, cut it out! Raylyn has no interest in me and I'm not interested in taking her away from you. This is all Isabel's doing, she sent Ted Lankaster over with his scissors to make a new man of me."

"Believe me, he succeeded!"

"I suppose," Duncan sighed.

Soon, the four men were ready. They knew they couldn't leave the room until Sandy began playing the wedding march. The church was so small that the girls were dressing in Raylyn's cabin and being escorted to the church by Roger's dad when it was time. He was driving a big van that could get the ladies to the church without disturbing their stunning dresses. Sandy would get her cue when Mr. Clemens walked his wife down the aisle.

Roger began pacing his office, glancing out the window and then walked back to the solid door into the sanctuary. Finally, Duncan grabbed the end of his tux jacket and made him stop. "What has got you all stirred up, man?"

"I've never done this before."

Ramon laughed. "Who has? So you've never been in love before and you've never been married. It's something that grows on you. Believe me, you think you love her all you can now, but wait, you'll soon realize you love her even more!"

"But I'm gonna be an instant daddy, too!"

"The kid loves you!" Duncan exclaimed. "What's your worry? Man, she calls you daddy already, what's to worry?"

Collapsing into his desk chair, he said, "I don't wanna mess up!"

The pastor came over and held out his hand. "Come on, Roger, let's pray. You know God's there with all the answers."

"Yeah, go ahead."

Duncan joined the circle, but he didn't close his eyes, as the pastor said, "Father, God, we invite You to today's gathering. We are matching this man, who is Your man with the lady he feels is Your choice. Bless this marriage, bless the home he will head and may they have a long and happy life together with You as their Guide and Leader. We pray in Christ's Name, amen."

Roger let out a breath he hadn't known he'd been holding. "Thanks, Pastor." Only a few minutes later Sandy started playing the wedding march. It was not hard to recognize the traditional entrance music even through the closed office door.

It was March. Ramon's office phone had been ringing off the hook since January and Sandy had most of March booked for one, two or three day hikes for both Ramon and Duncan. They had had a mild winter and trees were already showing a bit of green if you looked close enough, even in the higher elevations around Vansville. People seemed to have cabin fever early this year, wanting to get out into God's out-of-doors early. Ramon and Sandy didn't like it much for him to be gone so soon in the year, but it paid the bills, so he was taking his share. Duncan, of course, didn't care about anything except being in the wilderness he had no close ties and liked it like that. He'd stay unshackled to the next millennium, if he lived that long.

Liking it or not, Ramon had his gear ready for tomorrow's hike, but realized he needed something from the basement and had gone for it. Sandy was in the office taking care of some business. It seemed once the season started, there was always something. When the business line rang in the office, Sandy answered, but the young woman's sultry voice said, "Could I speak with *Ramon*, please? This is very important and I must speak with him."

Since that line didn't ring downstairs, and hearing the 'I've-got-a-crush-on-Ramon' lilt to the voice, Sandy answered, "He's not available, I can take a message or perhaps I can help you?"

A longsuffering sigh, breathed out and the sultry voice said, "Oh, no, I need to talk with him." Definitely I've-got-a-crush-on-Ramon

Sandy persisted, "I set up the hikes, I could probably help you, since he's not available."

The woman sighed again and said, "Well, this is Lily White. I booked a hike for my brother and his wife and me and two girlfriends."

Sandy found the name in the appointment book and said, "Yes, you folks are on for Monday. Is there a problem?"

"Well, see, it's like this. My brother and his wife just found out they can't go, so it'd be me and my girl friends. Your literature says you only take groups of five or more. The three of us girls really want to go and we were hoping to convince *Ramon* to take us. We have the time all scheduled and everything, you know?"

Slowly, Sandy drew a line through the first hike of the season. However, she couldn't be too upset, after all, it was Ramon's and he would stay home! "I'm sorry Ms White, but we have our rules for a reason. If there are no longer five in your group, then we'll have to cancel. At this time, we have other slots open that could work better for you, unless, of course, you can come up with two more people between now and Monday, but as it stands now, your hike is off."

The girl sounded love-sick when she sighed and said, "I was hoping *Ramon* would make an exception and take us anyway. It would be just this once, you know."

"No, I'm afraid that won't happen, Ms White. We have too many requests to make an exception. If you want to reschedule, you'll need to call soon for a new date. If you do come up with two more people between now and tomorrow morning, let us know as soon as possible. Thanks for calling and telling us about this." The voice never said, 'goodbye,' the disconnect crashed loudly in Sandy's ear.

Sandy couldn't even say 'goodbye.' She pulled the receiver from her ear and looked at it as the dial tone hummed at her. "Now, that was interesting! I wonder how she knew who Ramon was to be so besotted with him?" The name was new no one by that name was in last year's book. Slowly, she replaced the receiver in the cradle and finished the line through Ramon's Monday hike.

She had just closed the book when she remembered that another group had wanted tomorrow's slot, but then took their second choice, so she looked up that group leader and called. "Hello, Mr. Banks, this is Sandy DeLord with DeLord's Hiking Service. I just had a cancellation for tomorrow's hike and since that was your first choice I wondered if you'd want to go tomorrow rather than in three weeks. We'd be happy to make that change for you."

The man hesitated, probably looking at the clock. "Well…no, I guess not. It would be too hard to contact all our people and get there by tomorrow morning. It's too bad they waited so long to cancel, though."

"Yes, I agree with you on that, Mr. Banks. We'll see you in three weeks."

"Thanks, Mrs. DeLord, we'll go with that. Besides, it's warmer then, that'll be better."

Two

Ramon came in the office, laid his hand on Sandy's shoulder as she hung up and asked, "Why'd the business phone ring today, Love?"

Mimicking the little wretch, Sandy sighed and said, "The love-sick Lilly White called to see if you'd take her group even though there will be only three, because her brother and his wife backed out. I told her there wouldn't be a chance, so I called Mr. Banks, since that was his first choice. He said he couldn't round up his people that quickly, so I guess you're not out of here tomorrow morning."

Ramon wrapped his arms around his wife and hugged her tightly. "I can't say I'm mad about that, Love. Three more days to spend with you." A minute later he sat down in the chair close by and scowled. "Did you say the caller was *love-sick*?"

Chuckling, her eyes twinkling, Sandy said, "Oh, yes! She specifically asked for *Ramon* and didn't want to speak to anyone else. She sighed a lot and very reluctantly spoke to me, but then she said she hoped she could convince you to take three of them on this hike tomorrow."

"Who was it?"

"She said she was Lilly White and that's the name I had in the book."

Shaking his head, Ramon said, "Can't place that name."

"I know, I can't place a voice like that from last year, either." Her eyes twinkling, Sandy said, "How did she know you're so devastatingly handsome?"

Now it was his eyes that twinkled. "Mmm, I wonder."

Monday morning, at seven o'clock there was a knock at the door. Sandy was whirling around the kitchen fixing breakfast. Duncan was known for how much he could put away at breakfast and she was continuing the tradition that they had started last year. Duncan came for breakfast, the guides did a last minute check of their route, so when the group came at eight he was there and had the route outlined, so they were ready to shoulder their packs and head out. They had found it worked really well and as the old adage goes: 'Don't fix it if it ain't broke.' It hadn't 'broke' last year, so why fix it now?

Ramon answered the door. Duncan's SUV sat on the parking lot in his usual place with his huge backpack leaning up against it. Ramon gave him a grin and said, "Come on in, Sandy's got coffee ready and the eggs are sizzling along with the bacon."

Duncan stepped inside, raising his head to sniff appreciatively, but as Ramon closed the door, he scowled and asked, "So where's your pack?"

"Mine cancelled yesterday, they only had three. They may show up anyway."

"Oh?"

Ramon's grin broadened, as he said, "Sandy said the girl who called was besotted with me and wanted me to take them out anyway."

Duncan chuckled. "Three girls?"

"Mmm."

"I'll take 'em, you take my group." Duncan's full laugh echoed through the house. "You won't hear me complain about only three, **girls**."

Ramon chuckled with him. "No can do, man. Can't change the rules on the literature. If we did it for one, news would get out and others would want the privilege, you know. Besides, the group you have didn't want me, they wanted you."

"Aw, come on, they'd take you if you'd have them."

Ramon shrugged. "Mmm, maybe, maybe not. Besides, I get to stay home with my wife for another few days – which, of course, you couldn't do."

Shaking his head, Duncan said, "I can do without that." Duncan put his hand up like a stop sign. "That's no offence to your wife, mind you!"

"Aw, never know, man, she may grab you one day."

By now, the men were in the kitchen and Sandy placed the huge bowl of scrambled eggs on the table that was already groaning with bacon, toast, two kinds of jelly, butter and huge mugs of coffee. Duncan put his hand on the back of his chair, then looked at the table, then at Sandy and finally at Ramon. "You said your mumbo prayer thing yet?"

Smiling, Sandy's eyes twinkled as she took his hand. She pulled enough that he lost his balance and sank onto his chair. Ramon quickly fell into his and Sandy was in the middle. Still smiling, her eyes dancing, she said, "As a matter of fact, we haven't. Father, we thank You for this day You've given us. Our first group of this busy season comes today and we pray that no mishaps happen while Duncan's out with them. Bless this food, we pray, amen."

Duncan hadn't closed his eyes, even though the other two did. Even before Sandy could pull her hand back, he grumbled, "Why'd you do that?"

She did pull her hand from his and said, "What, make you guys breakfast? Breakfast's a tradition around here."

Giving a loud huff, Duncan waved his hand and growled, "'Course not! I didn't want to be here when you said those words!"

"But Duncan, all the food on the table would have been blessed, even if you hadn't been here. What difference would it make if you weren't sitting at the table?"

Glaring at the beautiful young woman, Duncan declared, "Ms Sandy, you know I don't do God! He's never been a friend of mine!"

"Why is that, Duncan?" sincerely, Sandy asked.

His eyes still angry, he said, "Leave it! I don't want to start out on a hike in a fowl mood and I'm about to!"

Not matching his tone of voice, Sandy smiled a sad smile and said, "Whether you want to believe in Him or not, makes no difference, Duncan. God is here in this room and out on that trail. He's made and controls everything that is visible or invisible. It doesn't matter how we believe, Duncan, God has created us in His image and put us on this planet for one purpose and that's to bring Him glory. He's told us that in His Word, the Bible."

Without taking that first bit of food from the serving dishes, Duncan threw his fork down on his plate and scraped his chair back from the table. Surging from his chair, he gave Ramon a hard look. "Listen, man, I'll be outside waiting for my group to come. If you have anything to say **about this hike**, you can come out there to talk about it. I won't be here for breakfast ever again!" He directed his last sentence to Sandy then he turned and nearly ran from the room.

"I'm sorry to hear that, Duncan. Have a good hike, I'll be praying for you," Sandy said.

Ramon knew better than to chastise his wife, so he laid his fork down on his plate and smiled at her. "I'll come back and we can nuke ours after they're gone, Love."

"Okay, that's fine, Honey."

They both heard the office door slam.

Ramon left the kitchen much more slowly, giving his wife a sad smile, but Sandy stayed at the table and bowed her head. Duncan had never shared with them why he was such a staunch atheist, but that didn't mean she wouldn't pray for him. She didn't move from the spot at the table for a very long time, her heart was heavy for Duncan. Some people just didn't realize how much they needed the Lord.

Out on the parking lot, Duncan paced as if the dogs were nipping at his heals. His fists were clenched at his sides, his face set like granite, but the color on his cheeks was a bright red and he looked at nothing in particular. To say he was angry would be an understatement. If looks could kill, even through several walls, Sandy would be dead now. He continued to pace until Ramon came outside and closed the door.

Duncan whirled around and bore down on Ramon until he stood right in front of him. Angrily, he asked, "Why'd she have to do that?"

"Her faith's important to her. As far as she's concerned, we have only two choices in life, we choose God's way or we choose our own way. God's way takes us to His presence when we die, our own way takes us to a terrible place called Hell when we die. Sandy doesn't want to see anyone go to Hell. As I'm sure you know, we have no input in how long our lives last, we could live to be a ripe old age, or we could die on the trail or here in the parking lot."

Shuddering, Duncan said, "You believe that stuff?"

"If I didn't, we wouldn't be married," Ramon stated bluntly.

Duncan gasped, "She wouldn't have you if you didn't?"

"No! When she first came I also had no use for God. Through her life and witness, God did a number on me, so much that I had to believe. Once I accepted Christ as my Savior, then I asked her to be my wife."

Muttering under his breath, "And Roger fell, too. I'd better get out of here!"

Ramon shrugged. "You can run, but you can't hide."

Duncan had turned away, but he whirled around and glared at Ramon. "Don't ever say that to me again!"

Duncan had turned away again and was nearly across the parking lot when three cars drove from the street onto the lot. Both Ramon and Duncan knew that the group Duncan was leading was made up of four couples. The first two cars each had two men and two women, the other had three women. The two guides looked at each other. "Uh oh," Ramon grumbled, "I'll bet that car's got the three women whom Sandy told couldn't go."

"Might be. What'll you do?"

"Send them with you or if they won't do that, send them home."

Duncan peered into the car and shook his head. "Don't do me any favors, man. I can do without some love-sick females."

Ramon grinned at his friend. "Are you sure?"

"Oh, yeah! I'm real sure!"

The driver of one car of couples came up to the two men and looked first at Ramon, then at Duncan. "I assume one of you's Duncan Roads?"

Duncan held out his hand. "Yes, that would be me."

Nodding back toward the cars, he said, "I'm Charles Harman, I'm the one who made reservations for the three day hike. We've got our stuff ready to pull from the cars. Do we leave from here or drive to some trail head?"

"No, we leave from here. Let's shoulder our packs and get on the move!"

Another door slammed and a very blond, possibly bleached blond, shapely young woman, dressed in anything but hiking gear, hurried as fast as her platform sandals let her, over to the men. Giving the men her most winsome smile, she said, "I'm Lilly White. My group's here for our hike with *Ramon*."

Winking at Ramon, but in such a way Lilly couldn't see him Duncan turned and walked to his SUV to pick up his pack. However, Ramon crossed his arms over his chest and looked at the woman with narrowed eyes, his upper lip almost curled with disgust. As far as he was concerned, she was not attractive. After a minute of silence, he said, "I only see two others in your car, Ms White. My wife told me you'd called and said there were only three of you. She informed you very specifically that we don't do hikes unless there are at least five."

Waving her hand to dismiss his words, she batted her long, made up eyelashes at him and said, "I was sure I could convince you to take us, but she wouldn't let me talk to you yesterday, even though I was sure you were there. We came today and since we're here, you'll take us, won't you? I mean, a hike's a hike, right?" Sighing dramatically, she said, "We **really** wanted so very much to go on this hike with you, surely you can make an exception, can't you?"

Moving away from her toward the house, Ramon said, "No, Ms White, I won't! One of the rules in our literature is that there must be at least five for the group to leave the parking lot. We do that for a very good reason. You only have three, therefore, your group isn't going. Further-more, our literature states you must have hiking boots – those are not!"

She pulled an envelop from the back pocket of her jeans that looked like she'd put them on wet and held it out to him. Her voice changed to a whine, as she said, "But here's our money, it's for all five of us. Please take us!"

Stuffing his hands in his pockets and shaking his head, he said, "If you must go on today's hike, you'll join Duncan's group that's about to leave." He nodded toward the group who all had their packs on their backs already. "Otherwise you'll head on home. As I said, my wife informed you of our rules. They haven't changed over night."

Two large tears welled up and slid slowly down the blonde's cheeks. "But we wanted **you** to take us!"

Turning on his heel, not letting the tears effect him at all, he shook his head and said, "No, it won't happen, Ms White."

Trailing after him, she stretched her hand out to grasp his arm or shirt, or anything else she could latch onto, but she lost ground because of her fancy shoes, Lilly said, "But you can't be married! You own a hiking service. All guides I've ever known are single."

Over his shoulder, as he continued across the parking lot, he said, "There are always exceptions and I'm one of them."

"Ditch her!" she snarled, her tears completely dry.

Ramon swung around and was in the woman's face. "Not on your life, woman! I love my wife. Go on home or join Duncan's group. Now leave me alone!"

Ramon nearly ran to his office door and closed it firmly behind him. He was pushing the lock in the knob when he felt the door move a fraction against his hand, but it didn't open, since he had it firmly closed. When the woman realized he'd managed to get the door locked, she began beating on it with both fists. Ramon leaned against it and let out a sigh of relief, surely she'd give up soon.

After a minute, he straightened, left the office and the knocking and went down the hall to the kitchen. Sandy looked up and asked, "Who's knocking, Honey? Shouldn't you answer?"

"Lilly White will not take 'no' for an answer. She's determined that I'll take her and her two friends for a hike. I guess she thinks her charm will convince me. Not only that she is very inappropriately dressed for the trail."

"She's still knocking. Shall I go?"

Nodding, Ramon said, "Maybe you should, but I'll be right behind you."

Sandy wheeled herself into the office, straight to the door onto the parking lot. She turned the lock and pulled the door open. The young woman's fist was raised and she nearly fell onto her. Lilly straightened quickly and said, "Oh!"

Before she could say anything else, Sandy said, "I presume you're Lilly White? I talked with you yesterday afternoon and told you we'd be glad to reschedule your hike for later on this spring. You only have three people today, so you'll need to find two more and you'll need to call soon, our open slots are dwindling rapidly."

The woman straightened from her near fall onto Sandy and looked disdainfully at her, then up at Ramon, who stood behind her with his hands on her shoulders. "Who's this **cripple** think she is? This isn't **your** wife! Not..." Lilly didn't know what hit her! One minute she stood facing

Sandy and Ramon, the next she'd been whirled around in the doorway and was being propelled faster than her feet would move across the parking lot toward her car. She stumbled with nearly every step, but Ramon kept her moving.

Before she could speak, Ramon, holding her by the shoulders and taking long strides, said, "You are not welcome on this lot again! Do not call for another date for a hike! My wife is no cripple! I will not have you speaking to my wife that way ever again!"

The two women from her car were standing beside it as Ramon propelled Lilly across the lot. When they saw his intent, one of them opened the driver's door and Ramon nearly threw her onto the seat. Nodding to the other two, he said, "Goodbye, Ms White! Don't ever call again." He slammed her door and turned away, refusing to even look at the young woman.

Duncan hadn't waited for the women to go with him. He and his group had disappeared. Silently, the two women climbed back into the car and watched as Ramon took long strides back to the office door, where Sandy sat in the doorway. Ramon didn't see the gesture Lilly made, but Sandy did, however, she wouldn't comment. The car started and tires squealed. It was good Ramon had hurried across the lot, because the woman backed much too far around, but when she saw that no one was on the lot, she yanked the stick into drive and gunned the car out of the lot, leaving black marks behind.

Oblivious to the woman's show of temper, when Ramon reached Sandy, he put his hands on her armrests and leaned over to kiss her. Only seconds later, one hand circled her control and pushed it so the chair would back up. When they were both inside, he kicked the door closed behind him, leaned forward and kissed her a second time. This time, Sandy's arms circled Ramon's neck and they savored a long kiss.

Into the silence, he said, "What a morning! We've both had a confrontation already and it's not even nine o'clock!"

"I know, Honey and I'm sorry. That woman was not a nice person. I can imagine what you would have gone through if there had been five for you to take."

"Mmm, I can too, Love. Let's go eat."

Sandy grinned. "I'm with you on that!" Only moments later they were back in the kitchen and the microwave was whining.

Once Lilly reached the street, she only had black words for Ramon. Her knuckles were white as she gripped the steering wheel. Her friends sat silently and let her rant and rave. They knew the woman was twenty-five, but she'd never been denied anything in her life, she wasn't used to being turned down. She'd never been treated as Ramon had done and she didn't like it.

"The nerve of that man!" Of course, it didn't matter that it was her words that caused Ramon to act as he did.

Nancy sat quietly in the back seat, but she didn't like Lilly's words. She was certainly shocked at the gesture she made, so she asked, "What did you do or say to him?"

Lilly had to swallow the awful taste in her mouth before she answered, "That… that um, person…" she swallowed, "that, um, woman in the doorway was his wife! Umm, I called her a cripple. I guess he didn't like that."

Nancy gasped, looked at the woman, her eyes wide. "You what! You called her a cripple? What is wrong with you?"

"Nothing," Lilly said, sullenly and slammed her hand on the steering wheel. "Nothing at all! Nothin's wrong with me! She's a cripple! I can't believe I talked with her and made that reservation with her. I'll never do that again!" She muttered to herself, "The nerve of him! What a louse!"

Nancy was a nurse and worked at a facility in Blairsville that specialized in rehabilitating accident victims. She scowled at Lilly's reflection in the rearview mirror and said, "So? What has talking with her and making a reservation have to do with anything, Lilly?"

"She's **crippled**!"

Looking at the young woman intently, she asked, "Is that supposed to mean something? So she's a paraplegic, that has nothing to do with her mind!"

Slamming her hand against her steering wheel again, she exclaimed, "'Course it does! They're not all there! Something's missing if they can't walk!"

Getting angry at the self-centered, arrogant young woman, Nancy said, "Oh, yes, she is! Probably she's more there than you are, woman! I'd lay odds that she's had a much harder life than you'll ever think of having! I can't believe you lied to us! You told us it made no difference there were only three of us! Of course it mattered. You're the louse, woman! Don't bother running me to my place, just stop at the corner, I'll get my rig and be gone."

"Well, fine!" Lilly yelled and slammed on the brakes. Nancy grabbed the straps to her rig and scrambled from the car. Again, Lilly left black marks.

Vansville hadn't seen the last of Lilly. Duncan's group was scheduled to return on Wednesday. When she had first made the appointment for her hike, Sandy had told her that the groups this early in the season only took up to three day hikes. Taking the chance that Duncan's group had taken a three day hike; Lilly came back on Wednesday and parked on the street until she saw the bedraggled group come onto DeLord's parking lot late that afternoon. She watched as the four couples put their packs in their cars and Duncan shoved his into the back of his SUV. He was very ready to go home.

She was about to get out when she saw the door open and Ramon came out of his office saluting Duncan. The two men talked briefly, then Ramon went back inside and Duncan walked back to his vehicle. Lilly waited until he was almost to his door, where he was out of sight from the house and no one from the house would see her, then hurried from her car toward him.

Still dressed very provocatively, Lily raised her hand to get his attention. Still realizing that she hadn't brought his eyes to her, she called, "Wait!"

Scowling, Duncan turned toward her and tried to remember where he'd seen this woman before. "Yes? What is it?" he spoke rather impatiently. The soft seat in his SUV and a warm shower in his cabin sounded extremely good right then. It was March after all. Even walking as she did because of the shoes she had on made no difference to Duncan.

She sighed dramatically and batted her eyelashes at him while she said, "You're Duncan, aren't you?" When he nodded, she said, "I'm Lilly White." She held out her hand, as if she were a queen and her subject should take it and kiss her fingers. Duncan didn't even raise his hand. "The receptionist there said we could have gone with you on your hike, but when that man got done talking, you'd left already. Are you going on another hike soon? Could I get to be part of it? I know my friend and I would really like to go on a hike this spring."

As soon as the woman said her name he remembered her from Monday. He wasn't interested in talking to her. "You'd have to check with Sandy, she's the one who sets things up. She'd be the one who'd know who you could contact to see if you could join some group."

"I'd have to talk to *her*?" she whined. "You couldn't just say?"

"Sandy makes all the reservations. I have no say in the matter." *Thank goodness!* "You'll have to talk with her." He began inching toward the door of his Jeep.

"So you couldn't just say my next group goes tomorrow, I'll squeeze you in?"

"Nope, can't do that!"

"Well!" she huffed and tossed her long hair over her shoulder dramatically. With as much sway as her hips would do in her very tight jeans and her very tall heels, she marched back to her car. Her sporty car roared to life, she pulled her steering wheel in a tight circle and made a U-turn on the street. Her tires squealing, she roared out of town.

Duncan had his hand on the door handle, but didn't open his car door. He sighed and turned back toward the house, deciding to eat crow while he was here, rather than go back to his cabin and mope about it for another two days until it was time to get packed up for another three day hike. He pocketed his car keys and walked back across the lot to the door to the office.

The light on the desk was on and Sandy had the phone to her ear. Duncan gave three short knocks, but opened the door and let himself in. He closed the door as Sandy said, "Thanks for calling we'll see you in three weeks."

The lovely young woman looked up and said, "Duncan! What's up?"

He slouched into the chair across the desk, pulled his hand down his face and said, "I came in to eat crow. I didn't get to eat my breakfast the other morning, so crow's about the only thing left for this time of day."

Sandy laughed and closed the appointment book. "Ramon'll bring some iced tea in a minute. That's better than crow."

"Yeah, but I really need to apologize for the other morning. I'm sorry for how I acted, Sandy. It's just that your talking about God really makes me mad!"

Compassion spilling from the lovely woman, she asked, "Why, Duncan? Why does the whole subject of spiritual things upset you?"

"My mother is a fanatic about such things," he said, but didn't add anything else to explain himself. Didn't that explain it all?

Sandy smiled at the man and said, "My folks are dedicated Christians. If she's a *Christian*, it can't be a bad thing, Duncan."

He sat forward in his chair and pounded his fist on the desk. "She ran my dad off with her fanatic ideas! She forced me to church and all that… umm, stuff all my growing up years! Dad couldn't stand it any more and he left. When I was old enough, I left too and decided I never wanted any part of something like that."

"What did you learn at church, Duncan?"

"Nuthun!" he said, emphatically. "Anybody who worked there wore black, gown-like things. They mumbled words I couldn't understand, in a language I didn't know and Mom had to give money every time. After Dad left, it didn't stop she gave money, even when she didn't have extra, so I didn't get shoes when my feet stuck out of the old ones. While I was growing, I had to wear jeans way too small and much too short because we didn't have the money to buy such things, but she always gave money to the church! You know that happened a lot, I shot up in a short time. I absolutely hated just the mention of the word."

As Ramon served the tea, Sandy said, "Duncan, that's not how the Bible says the Christian life is. Do you have a Bible of your own?"

Duncan took several long swallows before he said, "No, but Isabel has one in every one of her cabins. When I saw it, I shoved it in a drawer so I didn't have to see it."

"After we drink our tea and you go back there, you pull it back out and find the book of John in it. It's listed in the index in the front. Read every word of that book, Duncan, I'm sure you'll come away thinking differently about who God really is, who Jesus is and what the Christian life is all about."

Duncan gulped down the last three swallows of his tea, set the glass on the desk and said, "I'll give it some thought, Sandy. Thanks for accepting my apology."

"Not a problem, Duncan. You'll be here Sunday for breakfast?"

He grinned at her. "I'll make the effort."

"That's great! We'll look for you."

Ramon watched as the door closed behind Duncan, then turned to his wife and asked, "He came to apologize?"

"Yes, and he'll be here for breakfast on Sunday."

Ramon shook his head, then took the lady in his arms and kissed her tenderly. "You are something else, Love! You really are! I believe and have for a long time that you don't know an enemy! You love everyone regardless of how they treat you!"

Sandy shrugged. "Jesus said to love our enemies and to pray for those who speak evil of you. I try to do that always. While you were on the parking lot the other day I prayed for him." Thinking about the salesman at the car dealership when she got her van she added, "Well, for the most part I do. Sometimes my words get the better of me."

Ramon nodded. "I was sure you were praying for him."

Duncan left Ramon's parking lot and only minutes later pulled onto Isabel's parking lot. Where there was usually only one car, he noticed that there were three vehicles parked in front of her house/office. One, of course, was her car, the truck was her handyman's and the other car had Michigan plates. That only meant that Ruth was back for another visit. What was the deal? The woman hadn't been here in years, so Isabel said and now she was back for the second time in three months. He guessed she was being serious about her pledge to come often to see her daughter and grand-daughter.

Duncan drove on and parked closer to his cabin, then walked up the walkway to the cabin he rented from Isabel. He expected the door to be locked. Whenever he went away for more than a few hours he locked up, but the door wasn't quite shut and a light was on as he walked in.

"Hello?" his voice boomed.

"Hey!" the voice called from the bathroom.

"Hey, Ted, you fixin' that leak?"

His voice sounding like he was in a cave, Ted said, "Sure am, Duncan. Meant to have it done before you got back, but things happen, you know? Only got to it this afternoon, but it'll be done here in a minute or two."

Grinning, Duncan came to the bathroom door and saw Ted on his back with his head stuck under the sink. "Umm, that wouldn't have anything to do with the younger lady who's at Isabel's house now, would it?"

Ted gave the wrench one last twist, then pulled the tool off and looked up at Duncan. Ignoring Duncan's last question, Ted said, "Son, could ya give that handle a twist, so's I can see if the leak's fixed or not?"

Grinning at the older man, Duncan said, "Not a problem, Ted." He did as he asked and turned the cold water tap to full. There was silence under the sink and Duncan knew if there was still a leak, Ted would be hollering. "Guess you fixed it, man! I'm sure grateful."

"Guess I did." As he moved slowly from under the sink, he dropped his wrench beside his other tools and said, "Now to answer your other question. Ruth Harland and me ain't an item. Just you remember that."

"I'll keep that in mind, Ted, I'll keep that in mind."

"So why don't you have some lovely girl on your arm?"

"I guess my beard and stuff keep 'em away."

Nodding, Ted said, "So you like to hide, is that it?"

Duncan shrugged. "You could say that. Me, I'm a free agent. I visit family on rare occasions, but I don't want ties. I love the out-of-doors, that's why I took the job with Ramon."

"Well, I'm outta here See you again, young fella."

"Yeah, thanks for fixing that leak."

"Not a problem," he said, before he closed the door.

Duncan watched the older man as he trotted down the steps of his cabin and went to his truck to put his tools in the toolbox he had fastened to the bed. After he closed the lid, he never even touched the door handle to get in, but turned and walked up the walk to Isabel's house. Duncan smiled, sure, he could be collecting money for his work, but Duncan was pretty sure that wasn't the only reason for the trip up the walk, especially when Ruth answered the knock and Ted followed her in and closed the door behind him.

"Just as I thought," Duncan mumbled. He grinned, maybe the man didn't have a thing for the lady, but she definitely did for him.

Later that afternoon, the phone rang in DeLord's office. Sandy finally heard the office phone, left her piano and buzzed down the hall at a fast clip and reached the office as the answering machine clicked on. After its speech, even before Sandy could reach the receiver, a voice said, "Hi, I'm Nancy Southerland…"

Sandy picked up the phone before Nancy could say more and said, "Hi, Nancy, this is Sandy DeLord, could I help you with something?"

Surprised by the real voice, she swallowed before she said, "Absolutely! First of all, I want to apologize for the awful way my former friend, Lilly White treated you the other day. That was absolutely awful! If I had known before your husband escorted her to her car, I'd have apologized for her. I know she'd never do it herself."

Sandy smiled, Nancy could hear it in her voice. "Nancy, I've forgotten about it, so don't worry. It's something that happens a lot to people with handicaps."

"I know that's so true, Mrs. DeLord, I work at Blairsville Rehab, but it was not kind and I want to apologize for her."

"Thank you for that, Nancy. Is there something else?"

"As a matter of fact there is. Definitely something else. Lily misrepresented herself to me. She came across when we met at the mailboxes as a very nice person and I was gullible. Anyway, my other reason is to ask if there's a group going out soon that I could latch onto. I'm by myself and I definitely need a break from work. I feel like if I don't take one, I'll burn out and getting out in God's out-of-doors sounds like it's my cup of tea."

"Let me get my appointment book open, Nancy and see what I can do." A minute later, she said, "It looks like there's a group that Duncan's leading that leaves next Thursday at eight that'll return on Saturday evening that you could join. It's a group from Blairsville." After a second, Sandy said, "Are you sure you don't know this group? It says they're from the Blairsville Rehab Center."

"Huh. Maybe I do. Is one of them Dillon Marshall?"

"Yes, that's the contact name."

"Great! Perfect!" she exclaimed. "Add one more to that group and I'll get with Dillon about the details for the hike. Thanks so much, Sandy. I look forward to meeting you and going on that hike on Thursday."

"I'm glad that worked out, Nancy. Come in the office and say hi, won't you?"

"Sure, I'll do that." Nancy hung up from talking to Sandy.

When she'd come with Lilly, she'd caught a glimpse of Sandy as she sat in the doorway. Of course, she'd been too far away to see any features, but she was sure, just from how she spoke, that she was a lovely young woman. Now that the invitation had been extended, she was anxious to meet her and she would at the earliest possible time. She would make sure of it.

She glanced at the calendar, knowing she was to work in the morning, but she looked more closely to see what time. She was pretty sure Dillon was to work, too, so she'd wait until then to ask if she could join his hike. She wondered why he hadn't asked her when he set up the hike, he knew she liked out-of-door activities and had done some hiking in the past.

She looked around her efficiency and wondered what to do until the next morning when she was scheduled to work at eight o'clock. She decided that work wasn't the only reason she wanted to go on a hike. When you ate, slept and breathed in one room, you didn't have much to clean up or put away, but one room could get awfully stale and definitely didn't supply much fresh air or exercise. She looked out the only window she had, knowing that it also didn't open and saw that dusk was coming on, she'd better get some supper, then a shower, or maybe the shower first, then she could wear her comfortable sweats while she microwaved her frozen dinner. She didn't mind cooking, but for one, it was too much mess to clean up, besides, she was tired after a day on the ward.

On the way to the window to draw the drapes, she decided that maybe on the hike she'd help cook some decent meals. She wondered how many women were going. Probably Dillon's girlfriend. She shed her shoes in her closet then padded in her socks to the tiny bath. A hike in the great out-of-doors sounded like a wonderful get-away.

The next morning, Nancy arrived early and headed for the offices that were all grouped on one wing of the rehab center. Dillon had an office, since he was part of the administration. He was a nice guy she wished all the men of the administration were as nice as he was. The door wasn't closed, but she couldn't see him, so she knocked. A chair squeaked and a nicely modulated baritone voice said, "Come on in!"

Wearing a scowl, Nancy pushed the door open and strode purposefully to the desk. Before Dillon could say anything, Nancy put her hands on her hips and asked, "And why didn't you ask me if I wanted to join the hike you scheduled for next week?"

Hitting himself in the head, he exclaimed, "Nancy! I completely forgot that you like to hike! But since I didn't ask you, how do you know we're going on one?"

Shrugging, as if it was common knowledge, she said, "A group I tried to go with had to cancel, so I called DeLord's myself because I really want to go on a hike this spring and Sandy told me about your hike. I told her to add one more to your group and I'd get with you. So I'm part of your group whether you like it or not," she scolded.

Dillon chuckled. "Don't worry, you're welcome. If I'd have thought with more than my big toe, I'd have remembered. That's good, you'll make eight. A couple of the group were a bit tentative, but if you're sure, then we'll be sure to have our five in case they cancel."

"I'm sure, so who all's going?"

After he told her, he wagged his finger at her and said, a smirk on his face, knowing Nancy's work ethic was awesome, "We must be there by eight, no sleeping in that morning, Miss Southerland. I know it's early...."

Giving him another scowl, Nancy said, "Dillon, you know me better than that! I'm not one to sleep in, I'll be ready. Can I ride with anyone?"

"I'll go through the list and get back with you, Nancy. Can you pay your fee now? We'll need to buy supplies for our meals before we go and then the rest will go for the hiking fee."

"Sure, I came prepared."

"Great! I can't imagine why I never gave you a thought when I started asking around! I know you've hiked before, in fact, wasn't it last year you went visiting someone and went on a hike while you were gone?"

"Yes, I did and had a great time. Believe me, if I didn't have to work to make a living I'd go hiking a lot more."

After Nancy gave Dillon her money, he said, "Thanks, Nancy, I'll get back with you real soon on the particulars. If you're anything like me, you're looking forward to this hike. I feel like I've been cooped up all winter and it's time to stretch my legs and expand my lungs in the mountains for a change. Don't forget your hiking boots and a rain slicker."

"Don't worry. I think March around here is the wet season. I'll really be glad to get into those hills, too! God's matchless out-of-doors is calling and I surely can't wait to answer."

Nancy left Dillon's office and turned toward the patient wing. She knew she had three people to work with today; one was a twelve year old boy who'd been thrown from a horse about three months ago. The doctor was holding out for a complete recovery once he was in therapy. The kid, however, was another story. Another, was a man who'd been pinned in a semi cab, they weren't so optimistic about him, although he was much more determined than the twelve year old to get back on his feet. Her third was a twenty-eight year old woman who'd had a Caesarean and for some reason, her right leg had gone numb, or rather, had never regained the feeling in it once the anesthesia wore off. The doctor had no idea why, but they were working with her to get her back on her feet. The last she'd known, which was two days ago, the woman still had no feeling in her leg. Nancy suspected that the doctor had nicked the nerve when he'd done the surgery. If that was so, she might never regain its use, but Nancy was a lowly nurse and that doctor was a royal pain in the petuty, so no one argued with him. Of course, the young woman wanted her leg working so she could care for her baby properly.

With fear in his heart, Duncan arrived early at DeLord's house on Sunday for the next hike he was to lead. He wasn't worried about the hike; he and Ramon had met in his office yesterday to set out a route for him. He'd worked it through on his computer since then and had a map he'd printed, but what had him scared was what Sandy would say about his religion or lack of it. He sighed, he hadn't done the assignment she'd asked him to do, in fact, he hadn't even searched for the Bible he knew was in the cabin. Actually, he'd completely forgotten about finding the Bible, he'd been exhausted.

"What's the deal?" he grumbled, as he pulled onto the parking lot. "What does it matter what I do or don't believe? Everybody dies and goes in the ground." He sighed again, he really did know that wasn't true. Even his mom had told him a long time ago that there was a part of every person that lived forever. Ramon had said that while we live we have a choice where that part goes. He said it was either Heaven or Hell.

He parked in his spot on the lot, unlocked the back door of his SUV, then left the driver's seat and went to the back. Sandy must have a window open, the rich aroma of her coffee was coming to him from across the parking lot and immediately his stomach growled, letting him know supper had been small and a long time ago. He sniffed appreciatively as he pulled his huge pack from the back of the SUV and leaned it up against the back wheel. After slamming the door and hitting the remote to lock the vehicle, he strode across the asphalt toward the office door. It opened before he arrived.

"Yo, man! Sandy's got coffee brewed and pancakes going. She's got enough batter for an army! You ready for a hot one?" Ramon asked.

"My stomach growled on the way over and again when I opened my door and smelled the coffee. You know, she makes the best coffee!"

"You better believe it! Mine, I could take it or leave it, but when I started drinking hers, well, I'm a convert. Her pancakes are to die for, too, believe me! Maybe you knew she's from authentic German stock and Germans can cook!"

"Yeah, I'd heard that."

"Come on, Duncan!" a cheery voice called from the other end of the house. "Don't dawdle! Everything's hot and ready to eat."

"On my way, Sandy! I'm trying to get around this hulk that's trying to keep me from that delicious smell out there."

In response, Sandy called, "Honey, I need your help!"

Ramon sighed, "Duty calls, come on, follow along."

Duncan chuckled. "Sure, right behind you."

Duncan walked behind his friend. The man was a year younger than he, but he'd married a woman who had never walked and sat in a wheelchair eighteen hours a day. She was pretty, vivacious and talented, but she had limitations. On the other hand, Ramon was the epitome of male health, virile and strong and Duncan wondered how these two made their marriage work. However, it didn't take long to figure out that they did.

After filling the mugs from the carafe and setting the carafe back on the warmer, Ramon said, "Okay, so sit yourself down and let's pray."

Swallowing a sigh, Duncan pulled out his chair and slid onto it. Today, Sandy sat across from him, but she still reached across the table and held out her hand. Grudgingly, he took it and clasped Ramon's hand which he held out. Ramon voiced the prayer for the meal and Sandy squeezed his hand when Ramon finished. Duncan had to admit, by all appearances, Sandy knew no enemies. She was the most genuine person he'd ever met.

Immediately, before Sandy could ask him about reading his Bible, Duncan said, "I have a map on my laptop if we can hook it up and print it out."

"Good, we'll do that right after breakfast. I printed mine out a few minutes ago. I got a new ream of paper yesterday, so we're in good shape."

Three

Her eyes twinkling, Sandy asked, "So, did you find that Bible you know Isabel has in your cabin? Did you read what I told you?"

Duncan sighed, "Sandy, I didn't look for the Bible. Thursday I washed and dried my clothes before I got to the cabin. I was bushed and went straight to bed. Friday, I slept in and actually, I forgot. I answered some mail and went to Alex's store. Yesterday, I came and worked with Ramon all morning, working to see what we can open up this year and again I forgot in the afternoon. This morning, I didn't have time, but I remembered on the way over."

Chuckling, Sandy said, "I'm taking Isabel to her church this morning, so when I bring her back, I'll have her tape a note to your door reminding you to pull out that Bible and read the whole book of John. If you forget then, I'll have to decide that you're senile."

Earnestly, Duncan said, "Sandy, I'm not senile, but I can't get past what I remember from Mom as I grew up. It was a horrible place to live as a child and teen and I blame most of it on her church. I was never so glad as when I was old enough to get away from there. I've never gone back. If we meet, it's for a meal and I treat at a restaurant. I know Mom still faithfully goes to that church and I suspect she still gives all the money she can to it. Believe me, it still shows in what she wears when I take her out."

Nodding, Sandy said, "You probably can blame it on her church, there are some who say that only if you work and do good deeds will you get into heaven. Duncan, please don't lump all churches and Christians together and say they're all like that. Certainly not all Believers that go to church have any resemblance to that. It's easy to blame God for things that happen, but it's not God's fault, it's ours. We're the ones who sin. God loves us and wants the very best for each one of us. Remember, He's even got the hairs on your head all counted."

Duncan chuckled. "That's a feat!" Patting his head, covered with a thick thatch of blond curls, with one hand and stroking his beard with the other, he said, "You mean all of these?"

"Yes, I mean all of those."

Shaking his head, he said, "Hmm, that's something." He looked at Ramon and asked, "So why do you take hikes scheduled for Sunday, man?"

"It pays the bills. More important, Sandy and I read and pray together each morning, we have already this morning. I take a Bible with me and spend some time in it when camp's quiet. It was last year on the trail with several groups who had devotions each day that brought me to the point I saw my need to be a Christian. In fact, it was on that hike when you went for the first time that I accepted Christ as my Savior."

Duncan shuddered. "I remember that something happened to you that time. You think that'll happen to me?"

Sandy murmured, "I'm counting on it and praying for it, Duncan."

Duncan shuddered again and said, vehemently, "Don't!"

"Remember, you'll have a note on your door to remind you to read the book of John."

"Mmm, I'll remember," he answered, resigned.

Both Ramon's and Duncan's hikes went uneventfully and the weather was nice. Everyone came back on Tuesday evening; Duncan's only a half hour before Ramon's. Duncan went home to his cabin and found the note taped to his door. Taking it down, he smiled as he looked at it. Not only had Sandy left him a note about finding and reading the Bible, she'd incorporated it into a picture of the hills and valleys around the area. She'd done it with a pencil and he wondered how long it had taken her to do it. Probably only minutes, but it was beautiful and he would keep it, just for the lovely picture.

He unlocked his door and walked in, sighing, glad to be home. The place was spotless, as he knew Isabel would keep it. That was a perk of renting one of her cabins by the month, he didn't have to worry about keeping the place dusted, just had to make sure his clothes were put away. He'd forgotten the first time he wasn't there and she'd washed, pressed and folded his clothes! She was eighty years old and he only thirty. At that time he vowed he'd never give her a reason to do that again.

Only a few minutes after he'd emptied his backpack, Isabel came and knocked. He was still sorting out the things he'd dropped from his backpack onto the floor. When he answered, she asked, "So you got Sandy's note?"

"Yes," he said, looking mischievously at her and holding up the paper. "I got this beautiful *picture* that was taped to my door."

Scowling and shaking her finger at him, she said, "Humph! Sonny, that's a **note** to remind you to read that Bible. I know where I leave the Bible in each cabin, but I know you've put yours somewhere. You go find it and read it!"

"Isabel," he sighed. "I promise to find that Book. I think I remember where I stuffed it, so I'll get it out before I go to bed tonight."

"And read it!" she said, sternly, shaking her finger at him.

"I promise, Isabel!"

"Good!" she said, turning away. Obviously, her mission was accomplished, because she walked back out his door and closed it behind her.

He sighed, "She and Sandy are like dogs worrying a bone!" Hadn't he heard somewhere about the hounds of heaven?

While Duncan stood under hot water and showered for many minutes, he thought about what Sandy had told him there in the office. He had to admit that Sandy and Isabel, for that matter, were nothing like his mom. He had no idea how their church was, but he couldn't believe that their church was anything like the one his mom had forced him to go to. Maybe he was judging this religion thing unfairly after all.

After he dried off he put on his comfortable sweats and pulled a frozen dinner from his meager supply. After his microwave dinged, he ate the tasteless contents and threw away the waxed paper plate. After washing his mug and heating some more water for another cup of coffee, he went to the closet and reached to the back of the top shelf, easily lifting the Bible from the back. He took it back to the living area and put it on the stand next to the sofa where it had been when he came to the cabin.

The microwave dinged, so he put instant coffee into the mug and stirred it. Sighing, he set the mug beside the Bible, moved one of the throw pillows from the corner of the sofa to the middle to take advantage of the full seat, then plopped down beside the end table and switched on the light. He decided to settle in for a long read. He had no idea how long the 'book of John' was, but if it was a book, it couldn't be just three pages.

He took a sip from the mug then with a sigh, he picked up the Bible and opened it to the index. He easily found John, then turned to it and started to read. He was captivated from the very first verse and every word kept his attention.

> "In the beginning was the Word, and the Word was with God, and the Word was God. He was with God in the beginning." John 1: 1,2

The first half of the chapter was totally different from what he'd learned in school. He sat staring at the page and said, "If this is so, I got it all wrong!"

Absently, he drank the contents of his mug, but didn't leave the sofa to make any more. He was totally captivated by what he read, he hardly moved. He read for most of the night and only as the gray of dawn crept in his window did he lay the Book aside, turn out the light and stretch out on the too short sofa and close his eyes. There was another day to read and face the words he read. What he read was something like what his mom had told him years ago, but much of it was different – so much!

Nancy was excited about the hike she was going on with her colleagues the next day. Time dragged at work, but finally it was the evening before. She hurried home from work and dug out her backpack, sleeping bag and one-man tent from in the big walk-in closet. She started loading the backpack with things she needed. She knew she must save some space for the food she'd have to carry. Dillon had reminded her of that, but that was no problem. She put in her clothes, her necessities and last of all grabbed her Bible from the stand next to the daybed and put it on top. She sighed there was still room for some food. She ate supper soon after that then climbed into bed, she'd have to be up at four thirty. Again, no problem.

Dillon had promised her a ride for the morning and they'd be by about six. They'd go to the rehab parking lot and load up their packs with the food, then head out to Vansville to DeLord's place. Knowing the time element, she didn't think there'd be time to seek out Sandy DeLord to get to meet her, but even if she had to make a special trip, Nancy determined to meet the other young woman. She was sure she'd find a kindred spirit in the lady in the wheelchair.

Nancy was fairly tall, but not overweight, but because her work required her to work with bodies and extremities that didn't work correctly, she had strong muscles. She didn't consider herself a beautiful woman she had sandy brown hair and blue eyes and a ready smile. She loved her Savior, but she couldn't always attend church because often her schedule required her to work on Sundays. She was glad this hike ended on Saturday and that she'd asked for Sunday off along with these three days, she'd be able to go to church – well, not to mention she'd probably have to recover from some muscle soreness from using some she hadn't used all winter.

In the morning, Nancy hurried through breakfast, then grabbed her rig and headed out of the apartment at five minutes to six, because her apartment was on the back of the building. As she reached the main door that opened into a foyer with four apartment doors opening into it, she saw headlights come around the bend. She closed the door behind her and waved at the car as it stopped. She couldn't remember the last time she was this excited.

Dillon popped the trunk from the driver's seat then came to the back. "Hi, girl! You ready for this hike in the mountains?"

"Am I ever!" Nancy said, on a sigh. "There's only so much you can do in a one room apartment. Most of that's done from the daybed. Work is good, but sometimes it's frustrating when the results don't come as quickly as you'd like."

Dillon chuckled and helped her lift her pack into the trunk. "I hear you!" He slammed the trunk lid, then moved to the back door and opened it. "As you can see, four of us are in my car. We'll meet the others at Rehab."

Nancy climbed in and Dillon closed her door. "Hi, guys. Smells like somebody can't wake up without coffee."

In the dawn light the other occupant of the back seat raised his mug and groused, "You better believe it! It's six o'clock! Even for work I don't get up until six thirty!"

Cheerfully, Nancy said, "Goodness, Mel, you miss the best part of the day when you don't get up with the dawn to see the sunrise."

Mel threw his head back against the seat and groaned, "Mmm, well, I can easily do without sunrise." The young man took another slug from his mug.

The other occupant, who was in the front seat, turned and said, "Hi, Nancy, I'm sure glad you're going! You and I are the only women, Alisha was supposed to go, but she backed out yesterday, so it's you and me against all that testosterone."

Nancy grinned back. "I guess we'll have to stick together, then."

Another car turned right behind Dillon onto the Rehab building parking lot. All doors opened and the two trunk lids went up. Each person pulled out a backpack and Dillon began handing out the food from the grocery bags. When everyone's pack was full, nearly to overflowing, the men lifted the heavy packs back into the trunks. The lids slammed down and everyone scrambled for the doors. Nancy looked at her watch, if they left right now, they'd barely make it to Vansville by eight o'clock. She was disappointed she wouldn't be able to meet Sandy DeLord again today.

Duncan was at DeLord's place eating breakfast. Sandy said their blessing again this morning and Duncan sat quietly through it, but as at other times didn't close his eyes. Ramon passed him the bowl with the delicious scrambled eggs in them and he took a large helping. He handed the bowl on to Sandy, but didn't meet her eyes. Quickly he turned back to Ramon who was holding the plate of bacon and toast.

With a bit of laughter in her voice, Sandy asked, "Did you get my note?"

Duncan snapped his fingers and said, "I meant to thank you for the very pretty picture you left on my door, Sandy. Well, actually, I guess it was Isabel who put it there. I picked up a frame for it from Brad yesterday. I have it hung in my living room now."

Not taking the bacon plate from him until he looked at her, she said, "Duncan, did you find that Bible and read the book of John?"

Without a trace of a smile, he said, "Yes, I did, Sandy, I lost a whole night's sleep reading that book. It gives one something to think about."

Seriously, Sandy nodded and said, "Yes, I hope you do give it some serious thought in the days to come, Duncan."

Pushing a large mouthful of the eggs into his mouth, Duncan chewed and swallowed, then said to Ramon, "So this group I have today are from a rehab center in Blairsville, is that it?"

Ramon nodded and said, "That's what Sandy tells me. I saved you on this one I have a church group from a bit farther away."

"Whew! I sure am glad about that! The kind with the devotions each day I can do without, believe me! This time of year there still isn't much plant or animal life out to inspect."

The chime clock in the living room began its hour routine and all three people looked at the kitchen clock. "Good grief! We're not ready and here it's eight o'clock!" Ramon exclaimed. He grabbed his mug and stood up. Before he left the table, he swilled down the last mouthful.

"We'd better fire up your printer!"

Sandy knew that Nancy was part of Duncan's group. She wasn't dismayed a bit that the men were running behind. If the group arrived on time, there might be a minute to meet Nancy. She followed the men to the office and headed around the desk to the door. Only minutes later, as the computer went through its beeps and noises and finally the printer activated, two cars turned onto the parking lot and Sandy opened the door.

Sandy knew she wouldn't know Nancy. The only woman she'd seen from Lilly's group had been Lilly, but she sat in the doorway and watched the young people pull their packs from the trunks. They all looked so huge and heavy, she wondered how any of them, especially the women could walk with such a load on their backs. Only a few minutes later, she was rewarded when a young woman moved from her pack and started quickly across the lot toward her.

The young woman's smile was genuine as she approached. It broadened as she came closer to Sandy. "Hi," she said, from a few steps away, "I'm Nancy Southerland, I'm so glad to finally meet you!"

Sandy smiled at her and held out her hand. "I'm so glad to meet you! I'm Sandy DeLord." Conspiratorially, she continued, "My husband and Duncan got tied up talking over breakfast and didn't get their last minute paperwork done. That's why they aren't out here already. But it gives us a minute to chat."

Looking at the lovely lady, Nancy bit her bottom lip, but there was something she wanted to ask Sandy. Finally, she screwed up her courage and asked, "Sandy, are you a Christian?"

"Oh, yes! And you must be, too or you wouldn't ask if I am."

"Yes, I am. When I saw you last week and then talked with you I had a feeling you were. Are your husband and Duncan Christians? Will they be holding devotions on the trail?"

With a twinkle in her eyes, Sandy said, "My husband became a Christian last year on the trail because several of his groups held devotions, but Duncan isn't. His landlady and I've been working on him, but so far, he hasn't given in." She chuckled. "Maybe on this hike you can work on him, Nancy."

"I'll do what I can, Sandy."

There was movement behind Sandy and Nancy looked up from Sandy's face right into the eyes of the young giant who was coming toward her. She caught her breath as she looked into those blue eyes; they felt like lasers as they drilled into her. As they stared back at her, all coherent thought fled her mind and her knees felt like water.

Duncan stopped, as if he'd hit a brick wall, but Ramon behind him, said, "Hey, I guess your group's here already and mine isn't!"

That broke the spell and Duncan swallowed and turned quickly from Nancy to say, over his shoulder, "Yeah, looks that way. Surely, yours can't be far behind."

"I hope not, since it's already after eight o'clock."

Nancy swallowed and looked back at Sandy. "I guess I'd better get back to my backpack. It was good to meet you, Sandy."

Giving the other young woman a smile, Sandy said, "Hey, it was great to meet you! Could you come back for a visit sometime?"

"I have Sunday free..."

"Super! Come back for dinner after church."

"I'd love to, thanks. I'll see you then."

"Absolutely!"

While Nancy still spoke with Sandy, Duncan moved quickly around the women and stepped out onto the parking lot. He strode purposefully toward the group, momentarily detouring to his SUV to pick up his own backpack. He pulled in a deep breath and wanted to shake himself, but that would be too obvious. No one, no woman, had ever given him such a jolt before and he didn't know how to handle it. However, there was no mistake, that woman talking to Sandy had made it happen. He determined that if she was in his group, he knew he must keep as far away from her as possible.

As he reached the group, Dillon stepped up with his hand out. "Hi, I'm Dillon Marshall."

Taking his hand, he said, "Sure enough, I'm Duncan Roads. Are we ready to get started? I'm sorry I was delayed a bit. We had to print out our itinerary." Duncan started shouldering his backpack then buckled the waist strap.

Nodding toward the door to the office, Dillon said, "No problem, it's obvious that Nancy knows the lady in the wheelchair, but she's one of us."

Duncan didn't let it show, he didn't look back at Nancy, but his stomach knotted up and his breakfast felt like a hard lump. He'd have to deal with that woman for the whole hike? He nearly groaned out loud, but he swallowed it before it reached his vocal chords. He nodded as Nancy ran up to the group. "Let's get our packs in place."

"Are we ready?" Nancy asked, only seconds later.

"Seems so, Nan. This is our leader, Duncan Roads. Well, guys, it appears that Duncan doesn't waste any time, he expects us to not waste any time, I guess that means we'd better get our packs on if we're going with him."

"That's true, if we want to get as far as my map shows," Duncan said, looking purposefully at his waist as he adjusted the strap for comfort.

The sleepy young man groaned, put his mug back on the seat of Dillon's car and lifted his pack from the ground. "Is it noon yet?"

"Nope, but it's time to get on the trail. We have several hilly miles before we get a lunch break, so get yourselves together," Duncan said.

"I'm on it, man hold your horses," the young man grumbled. He turned to Nancy and said, "Now her, she's miss sunshine, she loves to watch the sunrise. Sunsets are my thing, that and a full moon."

Soon, the group started out. Duncan, of course, was in front and Dillon started out with him because the trail was wide that left DeLord's parking lot. Nancy was next and then the other woman started out walking with her. The other three fell in behind the women, but the sleepy young man found himself bringing up the rear, which suited him just fine.

"Hey, guys wait for me!" he called after them.

"Mel, move it, we can't watch over our shoulders to see if you're with us!" Dillon called.

"I'm on it, I'm on it," he grumbled and hurried to catch up. He took about five running steps then slid back to his slower pace.

Trying to ignore her initial reaction to Duncan, Nancy did more looking around than watching the leader. Of course, she had to glance back at the trail often, since she'd never been hiking in the area, but she didn't want to look at Duncan, at least not in the eyes However, it was as if her eyes had a mind of their own, after only a few minutes of looking at the breath-taking views, then back to the trail, she found her eyes riveted on their leader's broad shoulders.

She grumbled to herself, *Listen, woman, the man's not a Christian. It shouldn't be your place to show him his need, it should be another man. You **can't** show any interest in him, he's not for you!* A little invisible creature on her shoulder chuckled in her ear and said, *Yeah, right.*

The group made as good time as possible, since Mel still wasn't wide awake. Dillon looked back several times to see him off in the distance, moving along at a much slower pace than the rest of the group. Finally, he sighed and said to Duncan, "Man, that guy! Look at him again! I think I'd better drop back and put some hooks in Mel's nose to get him up to steam. We'll catch you at lunch, man."

Duncan nodded and looked back, purposefully over top of Nancy's head. "Yeah, better get him moving, it's still a ways to go before lunch."

With Dillon gone, Duncan looked back then quickly looked forward. The next hiker behind him was none other than the woman who'd put a stop to his forward motion at the office. He didn't even know her name, for goodness sake! She was a bit tall for a woman, but quite shapely, she didn't have an ounce of fat anywhere on her body. Well, he guessed since this group was staff of a **Rehab Center** maybe she threw bodies around.

She was pretty, in a homespun sort of way, he guessed, with blue eyes and light brown hair, but with hiking boots and a huge backpack putting her face in shadow, he didn't dwell on it. In fact, he couldn't. He would not be pulled into any woman's net! Hadn't his sister tried setting him up with a woman at Christmas? Of course she had and he'd determined then that he'd have none of it. He had no ties, no strings attached. He liked it that way and he was determined to keep himself that way.

He tried setting a faster pace, but after a few steps he realized he'd better not go any faster, one of the group still wasn't up to speed and he didn't want to lose anyone. Besides, he wasn't about to let on that this woman effected him in any way. So they'd had a stellar moment back at the office, but it wouldn't happen again, not on his watch! Besides, hadn't he heard her talking to Sandy about being a Believer? He had to stay clear of that! Sure, he'd read the book of John. Some of it was intriguing, but that didn't mean he was falling for any of that stuff. He looked back again. Dillon had the poke up to speed.

About noon, Duncan's stomach growled and Nancy was close enough to hear. She chuckled and asked, "Was that your stomach? Is that how we determine when we stop to eat?"

"Yes, it was my stomach!" he grumbled. "No, that's not the determining factor for lunch. It's noon, we have another fifteen minutes to go before we stop. That guy put us behind."

She stepped up beside him. "He's caught up now. Dillon's walking with Linda you could have gone a bit faster for the last half hour or so. You haven't looked back in longer than that to know he's up with us now."

Testily, he said, "I set the pace. I don't want to tire anyone out the first day."

"That's real kind of you, Duncan, thanks," she said.

"Yeah, well...." Several strides later, he turned, but didn't look at her and asked, "What's your name again?"

"Again? You never asked it before. I'm Nancy Southerland."

"And you work at the rehab center these guys come from?" he asked, looking anywhere but at her face.

Still with a bit of laughter in her voice, Nancy said, "That's right, Duncan. I'm a nurse from one of the wings. I work with some of the disabled people who come for long-term rehab. It's hard work, but it's good. Still I'm glad to get away."

"Good to know ya," he said, still not looking at her. "I never been in a hospital. Isn't it depressing to work with those people?"

"Sometimes it is, especially when the people give up before they make as much of a recovery as the doctors say they can make. Then other times some people have so much determination, but they still can't get back completely. Either one of those can be frustrating, not only for the therapist but also the patient."

"Yeah, that would frustrate me."

"So have you been hiking for several years?"

"In other parts of the country I have been, but my sister lives in Atlanta, so I looked for something that wasn't too far from her. She's the only family I really have. I saw an ad he put in a magazine last summer and started working with Ramon at the end of last season after he was hurt. How about you, from around here?"

"I'm from south Georgia, but I went to college and nurse's training in Atlanta, then found this job. I've liked it until recently. I decided getting away from it for a few days would change my outlook on the place. Believe me, I hope it works. I don't want to fall victim to burn-out."

Duncan began unbuckling his backpack and said, "I guess we've arrived at our lunch spot. Maybe we'll talk some again."

Yup, maybe we won't, too. She thought.

The men had insisted that the women carry the lightest food stuffs, which meant that the two women had all the dried packets and granola bars in their backpacks. As soon as Nancy had hers on the ground, Dillon came over and said, "How about getting some of those packets out so we can mix them with water and get this meal over with?"

Nancy unzipped the top of her pack and started pulling out packets. She grinned. "Not a problem, Dillon, this way I'll have a lighter pack right away." Everyone gathered around and as she held something up, someone grabbed it. Soon she had given out nearly half of what she had in her pack. However, Duncan hadn't been one of those who came for some powdered lunch.

Dillon noticed and said, "Duncan, come get stuff for lunch. It's here in Nancy's pack. Like the literature said, we brought enough for our guide."

"Anything's fine." He held up the bag he'd pulled from his pack, and said, "Actually, I have some trail mix from my pack and I ate big at Sandy's, so I'm cool for a few hours."

"As big a man as you are and you're not first in line?"

Pulling the edges of the bag of trail mix apart, he reached in for a handful. "Yeah, I've learned to pace myself."

Nancy realized Duncan was going to make every excuse possible not to come for anything from her pack, so she pulled two packets from her pack then zipped it closed. She smiled to herself and filtered some water to mix with her packets. She sat down on a rock not too far from Duncan, but without looking at him, she asked, "Wasn't it your stomach I heard growl back there on the trail?"

"Yeah, but it quit." He was studiously looking off toward the mountains, keeping his gaze steadfastly away from Nancy.

Nancy followed suit, she didn't look at Duncan either. "Mmm, and that small bag of trail mix will hold you until we stop for supper, right?"

His eyes flashing, he turned his head and glared at her, then realized that was a bad mistake it happened again, he couldn't look away. When his eyes locked with hers, it seemed all time stood still. He swallowed and with great difficulty pulled his eyes from hers. Still, he couldn't remember why he was mad and he truly couldn't remember what she'd asked him. That part was NOT GOOD!

The jolt had been the same as the first time, but when he pulled his eyes away, she remembered what she'd asked him and he hadn't answered, so she asked again, "So, you'll survive on trail mix until supper?"

"Yes!" he spat out.

She drank the last of the cupful that had been her lunch. "I'm glad. This mix I've had didn't look like much when I dumped it into the water and mixed it up, but it did make into a rather tasty lunch. I know Dillon expected you to eat from our supply."

Chewing another large mouthful of trail mix, he swallowed and said, "Maybe tomorrow I'll have some."

Chuckling, Nancy finished for him, "As long as it's not from my pack."

"I didn't say that," he grumbled, opened his mouth and shook the last of the mix in.

Now she was laughing, "No, but you didn't need to." He didn't acknowledge what she said. Looking away, he wadded up the empty bag and stuffed it into the side pocket of his pack.

"So we keep our trash and burn it at supper time?"

"Yup, that's the plan, no leaving stuff to go back to nature."

After everybody had their cups back in their packs and their packs in place on their backs, Duncan was annoyed to find that Nancy was still the next person behind him. He'd hoped that as soon as Dillon had gotten his colleague back on track that he'd rejoin him in the lead, but it didn't happen. Of course, he wouldn't ask him to join him, that would show his problem.

Duncan looked at everyone, including the woman beside him and said, "Everyone ready? Let's head out!" He hadn't even turned to start down the trail when his stomach growled.

Nancy heard and looked up with sparkles in her eyes. "That wasn't thunder, was it? The trail mix'll hold you?"

Pulling his canteen from his belt, he muttered, "Of course." He nearly emptied his canteen, then capped it ferociously, jammed it back on his belt and started down the trail, not mindful if the others were ready or following.

"Come on, guys," Nancy called. "Fearless leader's on the move! Since we don't know the trail, we'd better be on the move, too."

Mel grumbled from the back of the line. "Miss cheery sunshine at it again. Did that dried stuff have cheery granules in it?"

"Nope, mine had in it the same as yours. It's all in your outlook, Mel. You can either determine to have a great time or not."

Nancy turned back and saw that Duncan stood right in front of her. "Are you going to be like this all three days?"

"I hope to be cheerful, isn't that okay?"

Duncan let out a long sigh. "It'll be a trial, believe me."

Nancy chuckled. "I'll try to make it real easy and keep you out of prison as best I can."

His stomach growled again, as he turned around, but again Nancy heard it. "You know, Linda has some of those dried mix packets, I'm sure she'd be glad to give you a couple so you'd make it until we stop for supper."

"I'll make it!" he exclaimed and kept walking.

"Great!" Nancy exclaimed.

It was late afternoon and Duncan knew there were still two hills they must climb before they stopped for the night, but he felt almost faint from hunger. Why'd he been so stubborn to refuse the packets Nancy had offered him? So she was everything he'd always told himself he'd stay clear of, but it had been her pack they'd taken the food stuffs from and they were like any other. He'd been a fool! Besides, she'd known what he was doing and had goaded him about it. His stomach growled again, so he pulled his canteen from his belt and gulped down the last few swallows. Thank goodness there was a clear spring at the campsite where he could get a refreshing fill up. He almost speeded up, but then he knew that the group of seven were spread out and only one of them was close behind him. That one, of course, had to be Nancy!

He looked over his shoulder, there she was, not walking beside him, there wasn't room on the trail, but a few steps back. That's where she'd been all day! As soon as Dillon had left to round up the straggler, she'd been right on his back. When she saw him turn his head, she smiled and he saw the twinkle in her eyes. She was so close she'd probably heard his stomach growl. Acknowledging that she saw him, she put her hand to her forehead and saluted him. He didn't acknowledge her, but snapped his head back and kept putting one foot ahead of the other.

He heard her chuckle and her soft words, as she said, "I guess supper'll be soon?"

"Two hills to the campsite. You make it? Gotta get the fire going first," he snapped.

"Sure, I ate a decent lunch, remember?"

"Yeah," he said grudgingly.

She raised her voice a little and asked, "When we get there, Linda and I'll get supper going. Who build's the fire?"

His stomach growled again. He almost grabbed the belt of his backpack to tighten it, but then decided that would call too much attention to his problem. "I build the fire for the hot meals. I'll get it going as soon as we stop."

"That's great, Duncan! That'll give Linda and me time enough to get the food gathered and get things together. We'd planned on having stew. I guess the guys'll have to carry the cans, but they won't be as heavy." The path widened and Nancy stepped up beside him. "You know, I've enjoyed today a lot. You must really love these hills."

He shook his head and finally, did pull the strap tighter on his waistband before he said, "Actually, I'm not from around here. I came late last year and hired on with Ramon. We used the computer all winter to set up more hiking trails, so it's only been on the computer that I've seen these hills, but yes, I love the great out-of-doors."

Nancy sighed, "I do too, but I have so little time to get out. I work four tens in a week and by the time my shift ends, I'm about exhausted."

"I believe it!" Duncan exclaimed. "So with three days off are they usually together?"

"Yes, I get three days a week off unless, of course, someone's sick and they ask me to work overtime, which isn't too often, thank goodness. No, they aren't usually together. Sometimes I work two and get one off, then two more and two off, but just as often I work three together. I rarely get the same days off each week. Since lots of our residents are live in, we have a seven day schedule. I had to ask for these days specially."

He looked down at her and grinned. "So you get to throw people around a lot?"

She chuckled. "Yeah, some I'd like to throw around more and others I'd like to throw out. You know what I mean?"

"Mmm, I think I get it. Some patients aren't anxious to get back their mobility, I take it."

"Yes, that would be the crux of it. It's heart-breaking sometimes when people don't give a rip if they get out of that wheelchair again."

Duncan nodded. "I can see that! As active as I am, I can't imagine not wanting to get to use my limbs and to get back a hundred percent!"

"Sandy's in her chair twenty-four/seven, I bet she gets discouraged."

Duncan shook his head. "Not that I'm aware of! Never when I've been there has she ever been anything but positive, happy and vivacious."

Without any hesitation, Nancy said, "I'm sure that's the love of her Lord shining through, Duncan. Jesus Christ can give you joy in any situation."

"Possibly is," Duncan answered, thoughtfully.

While they talked, they'd moved from the trail to a large open area, the top the fair sized hill they'd climbed and they could look off across several miles of valley below. Quickly, Duncan unbuckled the waist belt from his pack and slid his arms from the shoulder straps. He was anxious to get the fire going for supper, but he wouldn't let on, of course. Nancy followed suit and soon their packs were side by side on the ground. As the others arrived, Duncan moved away from Nancy and began searching for kindling and larger pieces of wood for the fire. As soon as the first man had his pack on the ground, Nancy was beside him, waiting for him to bring out some of his food supplies. Her stomach hadn't grumbled, but she knew she could eat. She knew that by the time Duncan had the fire going they needed to have the stew ready to heat.

It wasn't long before Duncan's fire was going well. Nancy and Linda had washed their hands in the merry creek and had a delicious smelling stew cooking in a large kettle over the fire. Dillon, Mel and Steve had taken the tents from the gear and were setting them up in a large circle around the campfire. Don helped Duncan hunt for wood.

After everyone's bowl was filled to overflowing with the delicious stew and each person had found a seat near the glowing fire, Dillon asked, "So what time of day do you usually start in the morning, Duncan?"

Looking at Mel, but not showing any mercy for the non-morning person, Duncan said, "Dillon, I'd say if we're up by six and on the trail by seven thirty, it'll be good. Remember, we'll be on our way back tomorrow afternoon, since this is only a three day hike, but that's if we're moving right along."

Mel groaned. "Six! Seven thirty! You have got to be kidding, man! Today's the earliest I've gotten up in…. well, months and you're saying…"

"Nope, not me," Duncan answered. "Last I checked, most people haven't croaked because they had to get up early."

"There could always be a first," he grumbled.

"I suppose," Duncan replied, dubiously.

Since the days were heading toward the first day of spring, the light in the sky was lingering longer. After everything was cleaned up, Nancy noticed there was still quite a bit of light in the sky. She found her tent that the men had set up and her pack they'd set beside it. She opened the top and pushed the food packets to one side until she found her Bible. She carried it back to the fire, since the temperature was dropping, and dropped, cross-legged onto the grass. She opened the Book to her favorite book, the Psalms and silently began to read.

Duncan watched her leave the circle for her tent, but when he saw her return with a book, he looked more closely and saw that it was a Bible, or what he thought was a Bible. His breath caught in his throat, would she insist on devotions with the group? He'd just gotten comfortable near the fire, but only seconds after she returned and sat down, he was on his feet. Scrambling from his spot, he made his get-away, moving quickly between the tents and on to the trees. Dillon could do as he wished, but their hiking leader wouldn't be a part of it.

Nancy began reading silently, enjoying one Psalm after another. When she came to the end of one, she looked up at her surroundings. God truly was awesome! What they had traveled through all day and now sat in the middle of, was breath-taking! It was nearly dusk and the birds were twittering their night songs in the trees close by. The gurgling brook seemed to provide the accompaniment for the birds. She'd had a great time today, tomorrow should be super.

Nancy noticed that Duncan had vanished as soon as she returned to the campfire, but she hadn't let it bother her. She hadn't planned to make him part of her devotions, but she knew all too well that she must have no close dealings with him, since he wasn't a believer. Finally it was too dark to read, so she closed her Bible, left it on her lap and silently prayed.

The sky was molten with sunset colors and Dillon said, "Wow! Look at the sky! What an awesome sunset!"

Nancy opened her eyes and turned toward the west. "Wow! God sure does make His world beautiful for us!"

Duncan was creeping back, he was at the far end of his tent and heard Nancy's comment, but without the fire, the evening was quite chilly and he'd planned to come back to warm up. He stopped where he was to hear Dillon's reply. Waving his hand around, Dillon said, "You said something like that the other day in my office, Nancy. Do you really believe God made all this?"

Still smiling, but with as much sincerity as possible, she said, "Yes, I do, Dillon. I believe God made everything. You know, He's such an awesome Being that it only took Him six days to make everything we see and don't see, including single celled creatures."

"Aw, come on, Nancy!" Mel joked. "An intelligent person like you doesn't believe in that creation stuff, do you?"

"Sure I do, Mel! It's easier to believe in God creating everything in six days than it is to try and get my mind around billions of years for some muck in a swamp to turn into an intelligent being like Man."

"So how long ago do you think all this happened, if it wasn't billions of years?" Dillon asked, truly perplexed.

Holding up her Bible, she said, "According to the record given in here, it's been about six thousand or sixty-five hundred years ago."

Throwing his head back and laughing for several minutes, Mel finally got control enough to say, "Nancy, you've got to be kidding! God created this world in six days only six thousand years ago? That's the craziest thing I've ever heard!"

Not at all affected by Mel's laughter, Nancy answered seriously, "Yes, Mel, I firmly believe that. After all, God was there, since He was the one who told about it. You weren't and neither was anyone else who's living now."

After a moment's silence, Dillon said, "Yeah, I guess you have a point." Mel had stopped laughing and had nothing to say.

The sky was dark now, the only light, other than the campfire, were the billions of stars in the black sky. There were no large cities to send their glow skyward to mar the expanse. Nancy had said her last statement so clearly and forcefully that Mel had immediately sobered and now everything was quiet. The only noise was the cheery crackling of the fire. The gentle breeze stirred the flames and as one log fell through the ashes, some sparks flew up. Several of them caught on the tail end of the breeze and flew away before they burned out. It was a wonderful evening to spend in the out-of-doors.

Only moments later, Duncan came from between the two tents and said, "If we're to get an early start, I think we'd better be hitting the sack, folks."

"Oh, right," Mel sighed. "I guess there's not much to stay up for. We did see that sunset, but I don't see the moon yet."

Duncan answered, "Well, Mel, tonight happens to be new moon, I doubt we see it."

Nancy jumped up and ran to her tent, put her Bible back in her pack, then headed for the woods on her way to the stream with her toothbrush and a washcloth. She stopped by some rapids in the little stream and wet the cloth, then washed her face. She shivered the water was cascading down from higher in the hills and was really cold, but refreshing. Soon, she had paste on her brush and began scrubbing her teeth. While she was brushing, Linda came up and started her own bedtime procedure. Nancy waited until Linda finished and the two girls went back to camp together. They hadn't said much to each other all day, but just being with the other female on the hike made for good company.

Four

It was still dark when Nancy woke up to the jangling of an alarm clock the next morning. She reached out to where her clock usually sat on her bedside table, but instead her hand ran into the tent wall. Still being half asleep, she kept feeling around, but couldn't find anything. She opened her eyes and realized she wasn't in her apartment or in her bed and the jangling clock wasn't even in her tent. Finally, the noise went off, but not before she heard grumbling from several places around the circle of tents.

Only moments later, while she pulled out a clean T-shirt, she heard Duncan's baritone booming from close by, "Come on! Rise and shine! It's six o'clock. We don't have all day to get our camp dismantled and breakfast eaten."

"Yeah, we hear you," Dillon's muffled voice responded.

As soon as his alarm went off, Duncan left his tent to stretch in the clear, refreshing morning air. He enjoyed mornings, he always had. From where he stood, he saw movement in the tents, but there was one, and he was pretty sure it was Mel's, that wasn't moving at all. Others came from their tents, some were dressed for the day, but most of them left their tents and made a trip into the woods immediately.

A few minutes later, Dillon came from the woods into the clearing and Duncan motioned him over. "Is this the tent of that sackrat?" Duncan whispered, bending close to Dillon's ear.

Dillon nodded. "Yeah, what's your thought?"

Nodding toward the other side of the tent, Duncan said, "Give me a hand here."

Chuckling, Dillon nodded. "Sure, I'm with you!"

The two men grabbed the side seams of the tent and shook the canvas as hard as they could. From inside, everyone in the camp heard a blood-curdling scream. Dillon and Duncan let go of the seams and scrambled out of the way. Only seconds later, a zipper began moving on the front of the tent and before the opening was bigger than a fist, fingers appeared and forced the opening wider. Only seconds later, a head, then a body and feet that were going at a dead run already came through the opening. "Bears! Bears! Get me out a here! Some bear tried to get me and almost ripped up the place!"

Nancy had missed the shaking action, but as she came from the woods she heard Mel. Her eyes wide, she hurried into the circle and looked around. "Mel! What are you saying?" she exclaimed. "Did you say something about bears? Did they run off with all our noise? Goodness, I didn't know bears could move that fast!"

Mel's feet never stopped until he was inches from the fire that Duncan was calmly stirring up. Duncan looked up and asked calmly, "Bears? You've got to be kidding! There haven't been any reports of bears yet this spring, man! You must have been dreaming. Ramon never told me about any bears around here."

Mel looked around. Dillon and Steve were taking down two tents. The Don was gathering twigs and branches for the fire and Linda was still gone. He looked back at Duncan, chagrined, "That wasn't a bear that shook my... umm... tent?"

Still looking at the hot coals he was stirring, Duncan said, "Man, I was the first one up and out of my tent and I never saw a bear, but of course, my tent's over there and I could have had my back turned."

Looking around again, Mel asked, "Where's Linda?"

Duncan shrugged. "Who knows! I learned a long time ago not to try to keep track of any woman. They're a law unto themselves. Could be she's at the brook splashing that cold water on her face before she puts on makeup, I guess."

As Mel turned back to his tent, Duncan heard him say, "So if it wasn't bears, could an earthquake have shook the tents?"

Duncan smiled behind his beard, but he didn't answer.

Before Mel bent over to get in his tent, Linda walked between two other tents. Totally surprised, she exclaimed, "Mel! You're up! Wow! I can't believe it's happened this morning! Wow! I can't believe it! The coffee's not even started and you're up!"

Nancy came along side of Linda so they could start breakfast. The gray before dawn was giving way to a few bright rays on the eastern horizon, so there was enough light for Nancy to look him up and down. Mel still stood beside his tent like he wasn't sure what to do with himself. With a broad grin, Nancy asked, "Is that what you're wearing on the trail today, Mel? It's sort of cute, you know?"

The young man looked down at his Pugh Bear pajama bottoms, shivered, because it was all he had on and dove into his tent. From inside, the voice said, "No! Some giant shook my tent! I had to get out before he shook it to pieces!"

Nancy looked around the quiet camp, watching the men take down the tents and Duncan silently adding wood to the fire. She looked at Linda with a grin and said loudly, "Did you see a giant, Linda? I didn't see one or hear one over at the creek, did you? It was so pleasant there."

Duncan jammed the end of the iron hook in the ground close to the hottest part of the fire and as Linda gave him the large pot full of water, she said, "No, it was really quiet where I was by the creek. Duncan, did you see any giant around here?"

Standing up to his full height of six foot three inches, he said, his eyes twinkling, "Nope, but these are tall trees, maybe there's a beanstalk in the branches and he ran up it real quick."

"Yeah, maybe that was it."

Dillon was chuckling as he and Steve moved to another tent. "Get a move on, Mel, we could use some help taking down these tents. The girls have water on for coffee, so it won't be long before breakfast's ready. Seven thirty isn't too far away."

"Yeah, Mel, everybody else is working around here," Steve added. "Giant or not, time's a wastin', you know."

Only a few minutes later, Mel came grumbling from his tent, pulling his backpack behind him, dressed in his hiking gear then zipped down the door zipper. He muttered, as he looked around at the others, "I'm here.

I bet you never had a bear shake you out of a sound sleep! Where's that coffee you promised?"

"Nope, never did have a bear shake me out of a sound sleep. It's usually my clock-radio that plays soft music that gets me going in the morning."

Mel raised his nose and took a big sniff of the fresh morning air, then looked at the two women busily working close to the fire. His voice clearly showing his disappointment, he asked, "Where's the coffee?"

Linda clucked her tongue and said, "Mel, there's no Starbucks out here, you gotta wait for the water to heat before you add the hot water to the instant coffee. I guess, if you get your cup and open one of those packs into it the water'll be hot enough to dissolve it by then."

As Mel headed for his backpack, he muttered, "I can't function without coffee."

Dishes were put away, Duncan was dumping water on the coals and Mel was swilling down the last mouthful of coffee from his cup that he had filled twice since leaving his tent. Dillon looked at his watch and said, "I do believe we've made it! Even with all the excitement of bears and giants, we've still gotten everything done and we're ready to go by seven thirty."

"Don't forget the earthquake," Steve added.

"Earthquake!" Linda exclaimed. "What earthquake? I really must have missed something while I washed my face!"

"Just a figure of speech," Mel grumbled.

Dillon wouldn't let that rest. He said, "When Mel came screeching from his tent claiming bears were getting him, and then didn't see any, he thought maybe an earthquake had shaken the campsite. By the time you girls came back, he'd tamed it down to a giant."

"I swear, I'm not sure you guys are any friends of mine!"

"Aw, 'course we are, Mel!" Steve said, shrugging into his backpack.

Because Nancy was putting away the remains of their meal, she was the last to get her backpack. Dillon was holding Linda's pack for her while she threaded her arms through the straps. Duncan had vowed ever since he'd seen her for the first time back at DeLord's that he was not going to touch the woman or make any move to single her out in anyway, but everyone else stood around while she went to the last pack sitting forlornly where her tent had been. She picked it up and came toward the group, holding it in front of her.

She started to turn the large pack around, but before she could push an arm between the strap and the bag, Duncan reached out and snagged it. "Here," he said, gruffly, "we're waiting on you it'll be faster if I help."

Just before she turned her back to him to put her arms through, she gave him her most merry sunshine smile and said, "Why, thank you, Duncan! That's so kind of you."

"Think nothing of it," he grumbled.

Smiling at him, she said, "Well, I will! You were a big help, thanks!"

As soon as he let go of the pack, even while Nancy buckled the waist strap, Duncan started down the trail. The others turned to follow, but since Nancy had been closest to him yesterday, she turned quickly in front of them and fell in right behind Duncan. Nancy pulled in a deep breath and exclaimed, "Oh, what a beautiful morning! Oh, what a wonderful day!"

Over his shoulder, Duncan said, "Hold your applause on that until supper."

"Why, what'll happen the rest of the day?"

Nodding toward the red clouds in the eastern sky, he asked, "Did you notice how red it was in the east, how the clouds were all red?"

"Sure! It was all so beautiful, it still is. I was busy or I'd have taken a picture of the sunrise, but maybe I can get a copy of Dillon's."

Duncan nodded and asked, "You ever heard of the saying, 'Red sky in the morning, sailors take warning.'?"

"Oh, sure. So you're saying we could get wet?"

Nancy could see one massive shoulder raise, then lower, as the big man said, "It is March, you know, Mother Nature doesn't need anyone's permission to send change and of course that could include a shower."

"Nope, I guess not. I've never melted in rain before, so I don't figure I will today. I guess this dirt can get a bit slippery if it rains, can't it?"

"You better believe it! It's not just the trail that gets soggy, either, but if there's shale, the going can be a bear! I mean, not like what Mel's talking about. Things in the backpacks collect dampness, it's hard to start a fire for supper, tents become hard to raise and believe it or not, people get cranky, too."

"Would that include our fearless leader?"

Glancing over his shoulder at her and seeing her smile, he scowled and said, "I have on occasion. You might want to keep that in mind."

"I'll remember that. I sure will!" she exclaimed.

As they walked along enjoying the perfect day, the sun shone down on them and Nancy opened the buttons of her flannel shirt. Several hours later, the beautiful blue dome above them began to slowly gather clouds. At first they were just wisps, but by lunch time they were more substantial. The sun was peaking through the haze when Duncan stopped them for lunch. It still wasn't bad until the wind picked up, but of course, it was March, the group should have expected that it would. Nancy was glad she'd packed her plaid flannel shirt and that she'd decided to wear it over her T-shirt this morning. She'd thought there might be a possibility she'd shed it later on. She noticed that Duncan looked up at the sky several times.

Remembering the stupid move he'd pulled yesterday, Duncan was in line when they stopped for lunch and took his usual four packs of dried food to mix with water to fill his empty stomach. He'd eaten heartily at breakfast, but it was long gone. After they had both filtered water into their cups, Nancy sat beside him and in a quiet voice said, "What is this, don't you have another bag of trail mix to gobble down today?"

Duncan took a large swallow from his cup, but then in as quiet a voice as he could muster, he said, "Listen, woman, I only had one bag of trail mix. That was supposed to last me for a snack this whole hike."

With a grin, Nancy said, "And you ate it all yesterday for lunch! Was that your fourth pack you emptied into your cup just now?"

"Yeah, it was." Duncan grudgingly admitted.

"No wonder I heard thunder before we hit camp last night!"

His eyes were slits, as he looked at her, but he said, "No thunder yesterday, but it's a good possibility today."

"What if it rains tonight when we're in our tents?"

Duncan shrugged and said, as if it was common knowledge, "The outside gets wet and if you keep everything from touching the sides, nothing inside'll get wet."

Nancy made a face. "My backpack's so big that when I'm in my sleeping bag the pack has to lean against the side."

"You'll get wet, then," he said, as if it was a foregone conclusion.

"Thanks for being so optimistic!"

He turned back to look at her and grinned. "That's my specialty, Ma'am."

"Mmm, thanks."

After the group had their cups put away and everything cleaned up, Duncan stood up and started down the trail. Nancy, of course, fell in behind him and the others straggled along behind. They came to a clearing and Duncan motioned for Nancy to come up beside him. He even stopped for a minute so she could catch up. When they were both walking again, he said, "I heard you tell somebody, maybe Mel, last night that you think the earth's only six thousand years old. How can that be? What about all the dating devices, what about the fossils? Don't they insure that the world is billions of years old?"

Shaking her head, Nancy answered, "There is no totally accurate dating device, Duncan. I was looking on the internet not too long ago and read about a scientist who took a blade of grass that had sprung up in the spring. He put it through one of those dating experiments and it showed that it was a billion years old. Lava that poured out of Mount St. Helens was put through one of those tests. The result said it was millions of years old. It doesn't take a scientist to know that lava wasn't billions of years old!"

"You're serious!"

"Yes, I am."

From behind them they heard, "Hey, guys! Dillon's gotta round up Mel again he's lagged behind since lunch."

Duncan turned around letting out a long sigh. Linda was stopped several yards back sitting on a rock beside the trail. Steve and Don were also stopped, but both of them were looking behind them. Dillon and Mel were not in sight. Duncan sighed and motioned for Nancy to sit on a large rock beside him. Shaking his head, he said, "I should have kept better track of that lazy critter! What kind of work does he do at that rehab center?"

Nancy shrugged. "I really don't know. He works in the administrative wing and I'm on the patient floor."

"You mean, 'Never the twain shall meet'?"

"Yeah, something like that. Dillon comes onto the patient floor occasionally and so does the director of nurses, but the rest of them come and go from their offices."

In his booming voice, Duncan called out, "Come on, guys! It's going to rain any time soon and we have a good ways to go! No one should be lagging behind, it puts us all off and we need to get to our camping site before dark."

A few minutes later, Dillon came striding into view and on his heals came a panting Mel. Duncan and Nancy still sat on the rock until all those in the group were together around them, then Mel, looking very uncomfortable, said, "I…had…to…um…you… know." His cheeks growing pink with each word.

Nancy could tell that if there had been no women present that Mel would have been more specific and Duncan would have made a comment, but he only nodded and stood up. Facing down the trail, he said, "From now on, if anybody needs to stop at least give a holler. I'm not in the habit of losing my hikers and I don't want this to be a first."

Nancy trudged behind Duncan for quite a while. The trail was narrow and rocky. Dillon and Linda were close behind them and the three men came along, but Don made sure that Mel was in front of him. If he saw that Mel started to lag, he goaded him and cajoled him into catching up. Mel did fairly well for a time.

It was about five o'clock and the stopping place was close, but Duncan could feel the air getting more humid and he knew the others were also feeling the dampness and the pressure that humidity presents in higher elevations. Those in the group with him were slowing down, even marginally in Nancy's case. The others were lagging noticeably.

Nancy came up beside him and said, "It'll rain soon, won't it? I can see the mist."

"Yes, I'm afraid so. We're almost to our spot, but we need to get there. If we don't, it'll be after dark when we get back to DeLord's. It may still be, if it rains much."

"Are we making a big circle? Is there no way to shorten the return trip?"

"Not really. There isn't a good way back except by this trail we're on. Ramon and I researched all these trails over the winter."

"I guess we'll just have to keep plugging along."

"For a little ways we can walk together. So you'll tell me your views on the fossils?"

"Sure. As for the fossils, how do you think they come to be?"

Duncan shrugged. "Come to be? They're animals or plants buried in rocks. Stuff covers them, they rot after the stuff hardens."

"Yes, that's right. How do you suppose a perfectly preserved skeleton or the outline and veins of a leave were preserved in those rocks?"

After some thought, Duncan admitted. "I guess I never gave it much thought, Nancy. They didn't decompose before the rock hardened or get eaten by scavengers, that's sure."

"That's right, they didn't they didn't have a chance. In the very first book of the Bible is the account of a world-wide, catastrophic flood."

"A world-wide, catastrophic flood?" Duncan asked skeptically. "And this has to do with fossils, how?"

"Yeah, listen up. According to the account, fifteen hundred years after God created the world, the earth was well populated with humans, animals, plants and trees. But according to God's account, those humans were very wicked and God was disgusted by the evil people were doing constantly. However, He found one man, his wife and his family, made up of his three sons and their wives, who pleased Him. He gave them instructions to build a huge boat."

Duncan looked down at the young woman beside him and with a grin, he said, "You're talking about Noah and the Ark!"

Very seriously, Nancy said, "Yes! Remember the boat didn't look like the cute pictures that come out every once in a while with giraffes grinning and their long necks sticking up above this little house boat and silly looking monkeys jumping around the deck. It was huge, about the size of a football field and plenty big enough for all the animals to be inside."

"Really? I had no idea."

"It took Noah a whole year to build that boat according to the specs. When it was done, God sent a pair of every kind of air breathing creature on earth to that boat. When they were all inside, God told Noah and his family to get on board, too, then He shut the door behind them."

"You believe all this," Duncan said, skeptically.

"Absolutely!"

Her one word answer was nearly drowned out by a snap of lightening and a clap of thunder so loud that Nancy jumped and Linda, behind them screamed. Quickly, everyone threw off his backpack and pulled out rain slickers. Nancy and Linda were pulling on the hoods when the leaden clouds opened up, but it didn't fall on the two couples. Instead the three men who had been straggling behind them got wet. That gave them the incentive to hurry and join the two couples. Astonished, the couples looked behind them to see the trail they had just hiked on, that had been sending up puffs of dust with each step turn into a quagmire of mud.

"What do we do now?" Mel whined, shaking off the few drops on him.

Duncan shrugged. "We keep moving perhaps we'll stay ahead of it. No helicopter will be swooping down to airlift us out of here."

Looking around at the trail he'd never seen before, he said, "You said we'd be heading back after lunch. How come we're still going this way and not turned back the way we came?"

Duncan sighed. "Mel, we are going back. Just because we aren't covering the same ground we did yesterday and this morning doesn't mean we aren't closer to your car than we were at lunch time."

"Oh. I didn't think about that."

"Yeah, Mel, give the man some semblance of intelligence!"

"Besides, we've made it to our camping site for tonight."

"We're camping tonight? In stuff like this?" Mel held up his hand and it got wet.

"Yeah, DeLord's parking lot is not around the next corner."

Looking up the trail that only showed virgin timber on both sides, then looking back to see a muddy path, Mel sighed, "Yeah, I guess that's true."

Duncan looked at the hikers, all in their bright slickers. "So, are we ready to set up?"

"There's not much else to do, is there?" Dillon asked.

"Nope, not that I know of," Duncan said.

Duncan was glad they'd arrived. He shed his backpack and started in quickly gathering what dry wood he could find. What Nancy told him pretty much lined up with the stories he'd heard as a kid, but he'd always put them in a slot marked '*stories* from the Bible' and never let them make any difference in his life. After all, didn't his science teachers in school tell them the true story of the earth? He needed time to think about what Nancy had told him, since it was almost the opposite to what he'd been led to believe all his life.

Nancy had followed Duncan, but once the rain started, she kept her head down, but finally it registered he'd shed his pack. She reached inside the hood and pulled the collar of her shirt tightly around her neck and buttoned it so that the wind wouldn't go down her back, but her jeans were damp and she was cold through to her skin. As she unbuckled her backpack, she listened and counted the time between the snaps of lightening and the claps of thunder. It sounded like the storm was already upon them.

Linda and Dillon came into the clearing and Steve and Dillon immediately shed their packs. Dillon detached his and Linda's tents from the bottom of their backpacks. As soon as their packs were on the ground, Linda set off looking for dry wood. Her quest was not very satisfying. Nancy joined her, but in a different part of the woods. Her quest wasn't any more successful. Everything was damp. Soon the three men joined them in the clearing. They each knew their jobs so they started in right away. If they could set up camp without the rain that was most acceptable.

It took Duncan a long time to get a fire going that was hot enough to heat water for some warm drinks. Fortunately, some of the provisions could be fixed in filtered water, so the soggy people sat around the smoking campfire and ate their rations in silence. Just as they finished eating, a brisk wind sailed through the meadow and as it left, the sun burst through the clouds.

"Yes!" Nancy exclaimed. "*Thank You, Lord*!"

After cleaning up from supper, Nancy didn't pull out her Bible. After her tent was up, she'd put her pack inside. After they ate, it was too early to bed down, so she pulled her sleeping bag from its waterproof cover and left it inside then took the cover back to the fire. After spreading out the cover, she sank onto it and hoped the feeble fire would help her dry out.

Duncan came close and stirred up the coals. He'd found a dead branch that had been hung up in the lower branches of a tree. There was enough protection from the rest of the tree that the big limb was dry. After stirring the fire, he jumped on the big limb in several places and broke it then put the dry pieces on the fire. In only minutes the flames were eating at the dry wood. When he saw that the wood had caught, he took a step back and hunkered down.

Keeping his feet under him, he crouched beside Nancy and said, "So, we were talking about fossils. What's your take?"

"Fossils. Where were we? Oh, yeah." She looked at him and asked, "If it was a world-wide, catastrophic flood, what do you think happened to everything that wasn't on that boat?"

"Lots of them drowned, I suppose."

"All of them, Duncan, there wasn't a spot on earth that wasn't covered by water. After the rain it took months for dry ground to appear. What happens to a carcass when it dies?"

"It'll sit there and rot, if it's not buried or eaten by some other creature."

"If it's in water?"

"It'll fall to the bottom and scavenger fish'll eat it."

As soon as he answered, she asked another question, "How does a river change course?"

Duncan shrugged and using his hands to show what he meant, he said, "The water finds a weak place and erodes away the rocks."

"All your answers are right. Now suppose all those things are happening at once. There is so much water that it drowns all the creatures and it's moving with such fury that it carves the rocks in only days and hours instead of months and years. Do you think there'll be time for flesh to rot or scavengers to eat it before the sand that the water's made from the rocks will cover those creatures with many, many layers?"

"No, probably not. But that's all subject to believing the story."

"Duncan, I haven't called it a story. People today call things stories when they think it's something like a fairytale, fictitious. The account in Genesis is true because God was there He's the eye witness, the Author of the first book of the Bible. He's the only One who can tell what really happened and say it with certainty. Yes, fossils were made during the world-wide flood. They were made by layers of sand, dirt and rock fragments covering the bodies in only seconds, then those layers covered by more layers that later became hard rocks when all the water drained away into the oceans and lakes. These fossils are world-wide. Do you see what I'm saying?"

"Well, yeah, I think I do, Nancy."

Even though the sun came out from behind the clouds while they set up camp, it only stayed a short time. They hadn't even finished supper when the clouds covered the sun and soon the mist and fog moved in around the hikers, making them miserable again. The meadow where they had set up camp was large and soon they couldn't see the trees surrounding it. Not long after they'd finished their supper, a cool breeze went through the meadow, leaving a shivering group of people in its wake. This kind of weather drove most people inside. Of course, the only 'inside' was a flimsy tent.

After Linda and Nancy had finished cleaning up from supper, Duncan and Nancy stayed by the fire. The others did other things for a while, but finally everyone gravitated to the warmth of the fire. It burned brightly while the large pieces of the limb that Duncan had found burned. However, as they turned to ash, the fire started to die. No one else had found any more dry wood, so there was no way to keep the fire going into the evening. They all knew that when the wood was gone, only the coals, then only ash would be left and it would get colder and colder.

Nancy stared at the fire, watching it die and become dull embers. Smoke was rising from the pile of ash, but it wasn't going far, the fog and mist were so oppressive and put the smoke in people's eyes. Also at about that time the breeze picked up, it was a cold dampness, but it took with it what heat there was coming from the coals. None of those around the fire had dried out completely and Nancy shivered, she couldn't help herself. Duncan was sitting next to her and noticed. It felt like something on the breeze came and sat on his shoulder, then tapped his ear and whispered, *You're a chickenheart, old man, she's cold, put your arm around her, why don't you? I mean, will it really hurt you?*

It sounded so real and the urge was so strong, that he nearly gave his ear a flick and answered out loud, *I'm no chickenheart!*

Prove it! Instead he pulled at his beard and wrapped his arms around his knees. He wasn't ready to give up his 'bachelor to the next millennium' status yet.

He clasped his hands together and said, "That breeze is a bit cold. Since there's no more dry wood and the fire's dying, I think I'll call it a night and crawl in my bag." Putting action to his words, he stood up, looked anywhere but at Nancy and took a step away from the fire.

Despite her discomfort, Nancy smiled and said, "Good night, Duncan."

"Yup, back atcha." *Oh, great, Roads! Leave the scene!*

This time, since he was on his way to his tent, he did swat his left shoulder, wishing he could get rid of that pesky voice. He never looked back, Nancy knew he wouldn't, but quickly grabbed a strap from his backpack and hauled it into his tent. It was much darker inside the canvas, so he pulled out his flashlight to hunt for some clean, dry clothes to sleep in.

With his size it was hard to change all of his clothes in the little one man tent, but there wasn't any choice, the only dry place to change was inside his tent. He knew that in the morning even inside the tent would feel damp. After he changed he lay down on top of his sleeping bag and stared at the ceiling. He sighed and decided he really was a chicken-livered dunce. It was still quite early, not everyone was in his tent and he was sure he'd wake up long before his alarm. Instead, he lay there awake for quite some time until he heard the voices around the fire say goodnight and silence descend on the campsite. He had to concede, he'd saved his hide once more from falling for a woman. *Oh, yeah?* that insolent whisper said.

Nancy sat shivering, watching silently as Duncan left the fire. His big body had blocked a lot of the breeze, she realized after he was gone. He hadn't touched her in any way and she hadn't leaned into him, but she realized his bulk had cut down the wind that reached her. Until he left she hadn't been aware how much and how cold the wind had become since darkness fell.

She looked around the circle Dillon had his arm around Linda and they talked quietly. She knew they weren't engaged, but from the way they'd been acting on the hike, she was sure it would happen soon. The three men were like islands around the far side of the fire. Mel looked like he was cold, he sat as she did, hugging his legs to his body. The other two were leaning back on their elbows with their feet stretched out toward the fire. None of them were talking.

Still shivering, Nancy decided that Duncan hadn't had a bad idea. She scrambled from the circle and headed into the fog. Before she reached the trees, she looked back and realized she couldn't see the camp, so she quickly took care of some business then rushed back to the tiny glow of the fire. She found her tent, reached in for her backpack that stood inside the door. She remembered what Duncan had said. She shook her head, there wasn't any choice, if it rained she wanted to be dry in her sleeping bag, let the dampness seep into her backpack, it would dry out at home. She opened the pack and pulled out what she knew she'd need then zipped it closed, pulled it outside of her tent to stand by itself overnight and crawled into her tent.

It was dry in the tent and the wind wasn't inside. She sighed, glad for the relief and quickly zipped the door down. She rolled out her sleeping bag then crouched beside it to pull down her wet pants before she sat on it to take off her wet shoes. The strings were soggy and gave her a very hard time, especially when she couldn't really see what she was doing. Finally, she stripped out of her wet slicker and clothes, then left them in a heap next to her sleeping bag, but not close to a side then quickly pulled on her dry things. Her shoes were wet, but she could do nothing about them, she left them inside the door at the foot of her sleeping bag and hoped they'd be a bit dryer in the morning. She did try to wring out the laces, but only a drop or two came out. Crawling inside her bag, she turned on her side and adjusted her hip away from a root, then closed her eyes and fell fast asleep. She didn't hear the rest of them say goodnight or their tent zippers close.

Much later, Duncan woke to a long, mournful sound. He lay still and soon heard an answering sound across the meadow. He lay there, mentally picturing their campsite, satisfied that they had left nothing of their provisions out. Usually, this time of year the wolves weren't scavenging, but one couldn't be too careful. He pulled his bag up under his chin and waited for the pack to move across the clearing. He could tell that the pack was skittish because of all the foreign objects that covered part of their domain. As they crossed the meadow, Duncan heard some of them sniffing close by, but eventually, they moved on and all was quiet again.

Later, Duncan had a dream. It was raining, raining harder than he could ever remember being in before. With the rain streaming down around him, he stood in front of a huge boat. He couldn't see either end in his peripheral vision; he had to turn his head first one way, then the other to see the stem and the stern of the massive, three story ship. He scowled, as he looked more closely, there was no water under the boat, it rested completely on dry ground. He'd never seen a ship in dry-dock, but this wasn't any dry-dock he'd ever seen either, even in pictures. The ship sat there on the dry ground. All around him were tracks of many different animals, all of them leading to the long, wide ramp that led up to the door. For the size of the ship, it was a small door. He knew if the rain kept up like this those tracks would soon be obliterated.

As he stood on the ground several yards back from the bottom of the ramp, someone came to the door and began beckoning to him. The voice that came clearly to him, said, "Duncan, come up the ramp quickly. You'll be safe inside, but the door will shut soon, then you can't get in. Come now!" He knew that voice, he'd heard it all day yesterday, as they'd talked. He looked toward the little door and saw her.

Before he could make up his mind in the dream whether to go up the ramp or stay on the ground, there was a jangling beside his head. Like a jack-in-the-box, he shot to a sitting position, his sleeping bag sliding down to his waist and his hair brushed the top of his tent. Only after he opened his eyes did he realize that his alarm had woken him from his dream. He punched the clock and the noise went off. He listened, but there was only silence, it wasn't raining. As hard as it rained in his dream, he was glad it was only a dream.

He picked up his flashlight, since it was so dark, but he knew his alarm was set for six o'clock. It meant it was time to get a move on. He sighed another day to deal with Nancy's talking and Mel's constant grumbling. With his flashlight on, he looked at himself and knowing that he was dressed for the day, he pushed his sleeping bag down and pulled out his legs, then rolled up his bag and fastened it to his backpack. He took one of the straps and zipped down the door. It wasn't raining, but the fog was so thick, he couldn't see anything. All he knew for sure was that the tent pegs had fastened his tent to the ground. He made a face; this was not a good day to try to find a trail he'd never been on, in an area of the country where he'd never hiked.

As he stepped out, he heard soft sounds coming from other places around the circle, so he dropped his pack outside his tent and walked out into the fog. He didn't have to go far to feel entirely alone. For all the noise coming from the woods around him, he could be totally alone on the planet. None of the forest creatures had ventured out yet. He decided they were smart, especially those who had homes in the trees.

As he came back, the fog lifted enough to see a faint outline of a few of the other tents and the people milling around inside the circle that they made. Two of those men were taking down one of the tents. He looked around and counted five other people beside himself. He sighed, he knew who was missing. He was not surprised, not with the way the man had acted and grumbled all day yesterday.

Dillon saw him and came over. "Mel hasn't moved yet. We can't leave him, can we?"

"No, he'd be lost before he left the clearing."

Dillon sighed, "I kind of figured that. I guess we'd better try that trick again this morning that rousted him out yesterday."

"Yeah, you're right, let's do it," he said, without much enthusiasm.

The two men went to either side of the door to Mel's tent and grabbed two seams each then they began shaking the tent as hard as they could, up and down and side to side. From inside a muffled voice said, "Can't you bears leave a guy to sleep in peace?" But there was no movement from inside.

Several minutes went by, while everyone watched the silent tent. Dillon looked at the tent and grunted, "Now what do we do?"

Duncan grumbled, "Haven't a clue!"

Finally, Nancy stepped forward and said, "Linda, do you have that water pan full from the creek? It's still cold, isn't it?"

"Yeah, it's right here. Why?"

As she stepped forward and took hold of the zipper to Mel's tent, she said, "Bring it over here, would you? We can't make a fire in this weather anyway."

"I... I guess," she said, tentatively. "What are you going to do?"

As everyone stood watching her, Nancy zipped up the zipper on Mel's tent as far as it would go, then her head, shoulders and arms disappeared inside. Only moments later, she backed up, pulling a large, blue piece of cloth. Inside it, everyone could clearly see was a sleeping Mel.

Pulling the bag all the way out, so they could all see the peaceful face of their hiking companion, Nancy said, "Okay, everybody, back up and Linda, dump the whole panfull on his head, then get out of there."

Dillon, Duncan and Nancy stepped back, but the other men scooted up close, of course, wanting to see what would happen. Their eyes were glued to Mel as Linda upended the large pan, letting the water splash on Mel's face and head. As soon as the pan was empty, she stepped back into

Dillon's arms and the body in the bag shot to a sitting position. Sputtering and wiping his eyes furiously, Mel screeched, "What's going on! Can't a body get any peaceful sleep?"

Calmly, Nancy said, "No, Mel, not any longer, we're to be on the trail by seven thirty. Get a move on! We'd leave you behind if we could, but the fog's too thick and you'd be lost."

Grumbling, Mel stopped rubbing his eyes. One hand swiped the water from his face the other pushed his hair from his eyes and forehead. Looking around at the faces silently watching him, he started to get out of his sleeping bag and grumbled, "This was the worst idea anybody ever came up with! I could be home in my own bed and not have to deal with any of you!"

"No matter, get a move on!" Dillon said.

The words were barely out of his mouth when they clearly heard off in the distance a long roll of thunder. Mel nearly tore his bag getting out of it the rest of the way. He shook his head to get the excess water out of his hair, then grabbed the wet end of his bag and pulled it to the door to his tent then he vanished inside. The other men scrambled toward the other tents to take them down and the women rifled through the backpacks to find something for a quick breakfast. They heard another roll of thunder, much closer. Duncan only sighed, spring was for showers, so he guessed they had it coming.

The fog was lifting, but that was small consolation, they'd soon be in the middle of a thunderstorm. Quickly, as the last tent came down and got fastened to Mel's pack, the others shouldered their packs and grabbed the cold packets of food the women held out for them. There was no hot water for coffee. They needed to move, but Mel was grumbling the entire time.

They quickly walked across the rest of the meadow, headed for the limited shelter of the trees that only had partially developed leaves on the branches. They all knew they'd get wetter before they got dryer this morning. Just as they all reached the trees, the storm broke over them and sent down a deluge. Between the noise of the lightning cracks and the roaring of the thunder, the rain itself sounded like steam coming from a boiling teakettle. It pelted them with ice cold drops, of course, their rain slickers shielded them, but even with the hoods, some drops made it down their necks.

Most of it ran down their backs between their slickers and their backpacks. Soon, their shoes filled with water, too. Their feet squished in their shoes as their shoes squished in the mud. The fog that had lifted became sheets of rain. Lightning cracked, with an instantaneous roar of thunder. Of course the slickers kept out a lot of the rain, but they didn't keep their lower legs dry. As the rain came harder, the wind whipped it into their faces like tiny knife points poking them. It was a nasty way to start a day.

Regardless of her resolve of the night before, Nancy found herself behind Duncan. No one moved until she took her place behind him, then they all fell into their usual spots, single file down the trail. She sighed she must avoid the temptation, even though she was strongly attracted to him. She was pretty sure he wasn't nearly as attracted to her as she was to him. He'd certainly never let on. Besides, his actions the night before spoke louder than any words. He'd seen her shivering, but he'd gotten up and left. He'd seen Dillon and Linda, but he'd walked away. That told her volumes.

When he knew she was behind him, he turned and said, over the noise of the storm "Think that rain you were telling me about yesterday was like this? This sure is coming down."

Waiting for another clap of thunder to die, because she knew her voice wouldn't overpower it, she said, "No, I'm sure it wasn't. It was something so much worse that we can't even imagine. Besides, the Bible says that the rain not only came down for forty days, but the fountains of the deep were opened. I'm not sure what that means, but I've always thought that it meant that something like geysers sprayed water on the land from an underground water source. I suspect that water could have been hot, too, like the geysers we know about today are."

After another snap of lightning and clap of thunder, Duncan said, "Wow! I bet the people on the outside wanted in right then!"

Nodding, Nancy said, "Yes, it says that the people cried to Noah to open the door, but God had shut them in and they couldn't open it, even if they'd wanted to."

Duncan didn't say anything for several minutes, he remembered his dream. In his dream he'd been standing in rain like they were experiencing right now and he'd been drenched to the skin in only seconds. Nancy had called him from the door, but like a fool he'd stood there getting wetter and debating with himself if he'd walk up the ramp and go in or stay outside in the rain. He would have been like millions of other people.

In his mind's eye he pictured what Nancy had said, a geyser could have sprouted right there beside him! He'd been to see Old Faithful and knew how hot water from geysers could be, the guide had encouraged them to put out their hands and test the temperature. He remembered it had been hotter than body temperature. He'd only felt the spray and it was hot! He sighed, he still didn't know all there was to know and he wouldn't make a foolish decision.

They slipped and slid down an incline, mud everywhere. Duncan's hiking shoes kept him from sliding much, but Nancy's didn't find the same purchase and she slid into him, her head hitting the side of his pack. "Oh," she grunted, his solid body instantly stopped her. "Oh, my! I'm sorry!" she exclaimed instantly.

He'd vowed not to touch her. Between the shock at Ramon's office when he'd seen her for the first time and he'd helped her with her pack and felt the current from her shoulders to his hands, he knew he had to keep away from her. Once he'd helped her into her pack the other day, he'd determined not to touch her again. Until that moment he'd kept his resolve.

Five

However, as he felt her much smaller body thump into him, his arm came up instantly and instinctively he put it around her and pulled her against his side. When she felt herself falling, she'd thrown her arms out to her sides and as his arm went around her, hers wrapped around his waist. They stood like that for several minutes while Nancy pulled in several gulps of air. Her heart was beating furiously, like she'd run a two mile sprint. The warmth of his body felt good for an instant, her teeth stopped chattering.

When she finally realized where she was, her arms dropped and she took a step away from him. His hand instantly dropped from her back, but if he hadn't given himself a quick tongue-lashing, he'd have pulled her back to his side. From mere inches from his solid body, she looked up at him and said, "I'm so sorry, Duncan! I completely lost my balance when I tripped over that root and slipped in the mud."

The look in his eyes that she thought she saw, he quickly masked, but his voice was a bit husky, when he said, "It's okay, the trail's really slippery and with this rain, it's hard to see the roots." He cleared his throat and continued, "The roots don't look much different than the mud in this light." The hand that had been around her clenched into a fist. Even with the cold rain, it felt like his hand had been singed.

Her face turning bright red, she stepped away from him completely as fast as possible and said, "Yeah, that's true. Still, thanks for catching me." Duncan only grunted, took his canteen and swilled down a mouthful of cold water.

The other hikers had caught up, so before Nancy could say anything else, Duncan turned and started down the trail. He wasn't about to let this woman get to him or throw him off his determined course. Nancy swallowed and shook herself, took in a deep breath, then put one foot ahead of the other and followed him. No one said anything, they had seen her nearly fall, so they'd been more careful on the incline and none of them had tripped or slipped in the mud. Nancy felt really stupid, here she'd been trying to stay away from Duncan, but instead, she'd fallen into him and, of all things, she'd wrapped her arms around him. What must he think of her? What must the others think of her, too?

Sometime later, the storm moved on, the thunder grumbled in the distance and the rain tapered off, but as it did, it pulled the blanket of fog in behind it, so thick that the seven hikers were enclosed in it. They were practically walking on each other's heels making sure they wouldn't lose sight of the person in front of them. Now that the rain had stopped, they could hear the drops falling from the branches and the tiny leaves. Even though it wasn't raining, they were still getting wet from the water dripping off the trees. Nancy wondered how Duncan knew where he was. He'd told her that he'd never hiked this trail before, that all he'd had to go by was a map he'd printed off his computer.

Duncan brought himself to task. He walked along, peering into the dense fog, hoping he wasn't losing his way, but his arm still felt the shards of awareness that had attacked it the minute he'd put it around Nancy. What was the matter with him? He had determined long ago that he was a free agent he'd never tie himself to any woman. Essentially, he didn't like women, look what his mom had done to him! His sister was an exception he'd always loved his older sister. But this spitfire was not his sister! And he'd put his arm around her, for goodness sake! How was he going to look at himself in the mirror when he got back to his cabin?

Of course, he rationalized, she'd fallen against him, so he had to keep her from falling to the ground, didn't he? He sighed, why didn't any of the other men latch onto her? She was pretty enough and intelligent enough. After all, she was a nurse. Why had she picked that spot right behind him, anyway? He didn't dwell on the fact that the others expected her to.

To get his mind off the woman behind him, he conjured up a picture of his cabin waiting quietly back at Isabel's. He knew it would be dry and cozy. He turned the heat down when he left for his hikes, but she always kept a calendar of his absences and before he got home, she'd have his heat turned up to take off the chill in the place. Today he'd be grateful for the warmth. He sighed, before he went to his cabin he must stop at Alex's store, he was about out of most of his staples and also at the Laundromat. The clothes in his backpack had to be washed and he had a basket in the SUV of most of the rest of his clothes. He might as well stop and put them in before going home to change clothes. That pesky little creature that sat on his shoulder every once in a while tapped his ear, *Hey, Ramon has a wife who'll be waiting for him with open arms. She'll gladly wash his wet clothes and she'll probably have a delicious dinner waiting. You sure could use some of that TLC, couldn't you?*

By the time they stopped for lunch the rain had moved on and so had the fog. The clouds still hung over them and some of them were low enough they couldn't see the tops of some of the higher peaks in the distance. Duncan led them onto another high meadow and since the fog had lifted, they could see for quite a distance. They could see the rainstorm that had left them was still pelting the valley off to their right. Because of the heavy clouds it wasn't the beautiful scene they'd experienced when they'd left DeLord's the other day, but it was awesome.

"Wow! That's some view!" Nancy exclaimed. "Look at that rainstorm, no wonder it stayed over us so long, it's huge!"

"Yes, it is. The way it's going it'll be over Vansville really soon."

"Did Mr. DeLord have a hike this time, too?"

"Yeah, he had a group of five, but they drove to a different trail head. I'm sure they got wet, too. It may seem like we've been far from civilization, but we really haven't been that far."

"Sure seemed like it with those wolves last night," Dillon said.

"Wolves!" Nancy exclaimed, "There were wolves around our camp?"

"Yeah, I heard them sniffing around, but they moved off without doing anything."

"I'm glad I slept through that!"

This was their last meal together and Duncan stopped close to a gurgling stream so they could filter water for their dry rations. Remembering how Duncan had acted for their first lunch, Nancy smiled silently to herself as she opened her pack to bring out the rest of the dry packets for their meal. She silently looked up at Duncan and grinned. Knowing what she was thinking, he gave her a salute and stood up to reach in for some of the packets she held in her hands. He was glad he wouldn't be seeing her any more, he knew she'd never let him live that down. But the thought of never seeing her again put a strange feeling in his chest. After he'd filtered the water into his cup he rubbed his chest to make that feeling go away. It didn't.

"Eat up, guys," she said, "tonight you can all eat at home in a dry place."

"Can't come too soon for me," Mel grumbled. "Get me out of this wet, dismal place right now! I have seen enough rain to last me for centuries!" He looked at Nancy and said, "So, where was your 'be-u-ti-ful' sunrise this morning, Sunshine?"

"Aw, Mel," Nancy answered, "you mean you haven't enjoyed this time of togetherness with your friends? It's been great being in God's out-of-doors!"

He glared at her. "Speak for yourself, woman!" Holding his cup in one hand and letting the spoon slide into it, he held up his other hand with his index finger and his pinky pointing to both her and Linda. He said, "You are no friends of mine! You especially with your cheery miss sunshine!" Scowling, he said, "That's twice now you've embarrassed me completely! Believe me, I will never look you up again!"

Nancy shrugged, knowing he wouldn't have anyway. "We can't do anything about the weather, Mel. God sends the rain on the just and the unjust exactly the same."

"Doesn't mean I gotta like it."

"No, it doesn't, Mel."

Linda swallowed her last mouthful from her cup, scowled and asked, "What do you mean the just and the unjust, Nancy? What's that mean?"

"Linda, God in heaven says that everyone who is born into the world is a sinner, each one is unjust, but He's supplied a way for every sinner to become right with God, to get rid of his sin and become just in God's eyes."

"There you go again," Mel grumbled. "You're spouting off that religion stuff again. Keep it to yourself, woman, we don't want to hear it!"

"I'm sorry you feel that way, Mel, but Linda asked. Eternity's a long time to spend in such a place called Hell and that's where God says the unjust go."

"Mmm, yeah," he murmured.

After they finished eating, they shouldered their heavy, wet, backpacks. Nancy had been so relieved to be shed of it while they ate, she nearly groaned as she picked it up. She looked around at the other hikers and watched them struggle into theirs, but she was sure she'd never get it high enough to put her arms behind the straps and get the pack in the right place on her back, it was too heavy. She squatted down in front of it, intent to do her best, but her arms wouldn't cooperate and she felt the hot, scratching feeling of tears forming behind her eyes. She squeezed her lids shut, intent on keeping them from falling.

Duncan saw her and walked over, his was already on his back, but gruffly, he said, "Give me that! I lifted it when it was dry, you'll never get it on the right way now that it's soaked."

"I know. Thanks for your help, Duncan. I know it's against your principles to help a woman, but I'm truly grateful," she whispered.

"Think nothing of it," he muttered. She only had the straps over her shoulders when he turned and started down the trail. Her eyes were still scratchy, but she blinked them several times and wiped her sleeve across her nose. It was really chilly no one would suspect that she was trying not to cry, they'd think her nose was running because of the cold. Nancy looked at the others, hoping that they had set out, but none of them had moved.

Dillon motioned to her and winked. "After you, ma'am, doesn't feel right if you're not in your place, you know."

"Dillon, come on! You know that's no more my place than anyone else's." she said, but he only grinned. "Besides, I haven't gotten all strapped in yet."

"Not a problem."

She quickly buckled her waist strap and hurried after the long legged guide who was several yards down the trail by now. She found she couldn't run, the pack was too heavy, but she did hurry as fast as she could. She didn't want to be the cause of the hikers getting lost when they were this close to the end of the trail.

Duncan was well aware of Nancy. He'd intentionally left before she had her pack secured. He'd hoped that someone would take her place, since the others all had their packs on. In the stillness, however, he heard Dillon's words and sighed. It wasn't Nancy who had decided to walk behind him it was the others who wouldn't get between them. He sighed again, however, he wouldn't make a scene he'd ignore her as best he could. After all, she was a woman and a pesky woman at that.

Some time later, since nothing had passed between them, Duncan swallowed a sigh and asked, "So, do you go back to work tomorrow?"

"No, I asked for four days off. I figured I'd need tomorrow to rest up before I went back to throwing bodies around. Actually, I planned to go to church tomorrow, since I don't always get the chance. When I met Sandy the other day there at your office, she invited me for dinner after church. I gladly accepted her invitation. That one room of my apartment becomes mighty small and eating alone isn't something I really love to do. Do you live with the DeLord's?"

"God forbid!" Duncan exclaimed, shaking his head and turned to look at her. "I couldn't stand that always positive, always cheerful Sandy! No, I live in a cabin at the edge of town. They're nice and the old lady who owns them keeps it spotless. I supply my own food and wash my own clothes. If I didn't, she would. I figure at thirty I'm a lot more able to do my own wash than she is at eighty."

"How big are these cabins?"

"The one I have has a large porch across the whole front. Inside the front door is a really large living area with a kitchen to one side. Across the back is the bathroom to one side and a bedroom with a large closet between the bathroom and the bedroom. It suits me just fine."

"That sounds bigger than my place. I eat, sleep and everything in one room. There's one window that doesn't open. The couch is really a daybed that I pull the cushions off each night."

Looking up at the still dripping trees, Duncan said, "It's dry, though. Don't have to worry about leaning your backpack against the side and having it get you wet."

"Yes, it is. I'll be really glad to shed this heavy pack and get into some dry clothes. March can be so unpredictable."

"Yes, it sure can."

"So when's your next group come for a hike?"

"We'll leave again on Monday."

"When the weather's like this don't you ever wish you were doing something else? Will you ever go into some other type of work?"

"I wouldn't have minded if the hikes hadn't started already this year, but the phone started ringing asking for hikes in January! At least for now, hiking and being on a trail are in my blood. Will I ever go into some other type of work? Right now, I can't think of anything I'd rather do. Will you always be a nurse in that rehab facility?"

She needed to mull that over for several minutes, before she said, "No, I don't think so. I've seen a lot of nurses come and go in the three years I've been there. It's hard work and it's not like a regular hospital where the patients come and go with only a short stay. These people are long term and many of them don't make a full recovery. Some of them can't, but many of them come with the attitude that they're washed up, they've reached their potential. Believe me that's discouraging for those of us who work with them. I plan to be a nurse for a good long time, but I'm sure I'll move on before I get burned out from working in rehab."

Duncan shrugged. "I think that's the way I feel."

The sun had never come out, even after the storm passed. The trees continued to drip on them all afternoon and as the hours slipped by, the clouds hung heavy over them. It was getting darker and Nancy looked at her watch as they came down out of the hills. Her stomach made a noise and she pushed her hand against it, then pulled her canteen from the belt of her backpack and let several swallows slide down her throat. Hopefully, it wasn't too much farther, carrying the heavy pack had zapped all her strength, she couldn't wait to reach DeLord's parking lot so she could shed the pack into Dillon's trunk. She hoped Dillon didn't mind wet seats in his car none of the other hikers was any dryer than she was. There was no way to avoid the drops coming from the trees.

It was a few minutes later when the trail widened out and Nancy was sure that their hike was about to end, so she hurried up to Duncan's side. She looked up at him and grinned. "So Duncan, since your next hike isn't until Monday, why don't you come to Blairsville to church tomorrow? It'd do you good and you'll have time tonight to get your laundry done."

The man turned toward her. His eyes slits, as he said, vehemently, "Woman, I don't do church! I don't do God! It's all I can do to stomach Sandy's mumbled words over breakfast I eat with them each time there's a new hike going out. God and I do not coexist! Do you hear?"

"Yes, Duncan, I hear you." After a pause, she continued, "So I guess if Noah lived today that you'd be happy to be one of those on the outside of the great ship."

"I'd take my lumps," he said decisively.

Nancy's heart sank the things she'd said really hadn't made any difference to Duncan. "You know, while he built that ship, Noah preached to all those people. Thousands of them, day after day. God had told him that when the ship was finished he was going to send a flood that would wipe out civilization as he knew it. He told the people this, he begged them to turn from their wickedness, but they essentially said to him what you said to me. While it rained the people took their lumps, but they cried for entrance into the Ark. Noah and his family were the only ones safe and dry in the Ark and God had shut the door."

"Okay, so tell me how could I get on that ship." Again he remembered his dream, but he wasn't about to tell her about it.

Nancy's smile was like the sunshine breaking through the clouds, as she said, "Duncan, it's very simple. Today, God's safe ship is His Son, Jesus Christ. About two thousand years ago God sent His Son to this earth to become that safe ship. Jesus died on the cross for your sins. When you believe He did that for you and you tell God you want the blood of Christ to wash your sins away, you can go through the door of the ship and be safe from the storm of life. That also makes sure that you will be with God in heaven when you die."

"That's too simple."

"It is simple, but it's the only way. It's God's way and that's how it has to be."

Looking at her, he said earnestly, "You don't have to give money? You don't have to do stuff and try to be good?"

Nancy shook her head. "No, none of that. You must believe that Christ died for your sin and tell God that you accept his free gift of life eternal, which means that when you die your soul goes to live in heaven. It says in the Bible, 'For God so loved the world that he gave his one and only

Son, that whoever believes in him shall not perish but have eternal life.' (John 3: 16)"

"I read those words recently. Sandy told me to read the book of John and my landlady made sure I found the Bible she'd put in my cabin before I came. I remember reading that."

"Duncan, it's that simple. When I was a little girl, Mom quoted that verse to me, but instead of 'world' she used my name. It goes something like this, 'For God so loved' Duncan, 'that he gave his one and only Son, that' Duncan 'who believes in him shall not perish but have eternal life.' What do you think?"

"I'll have to think about that. This is all new to me." Duncan said quietly. *No, it isn't really,* that little voice said.

Up ahead both he and Nancy could see DeLord's parking lot. It was a matter of putting one foot in front of the other for a few more yards and he would be home free. He looked down at the pretty girl at his side. She was wet, her slicker was shiny and drops still slid off it, there was a mud streak on her cheek where she'd pushed her hair off her face when her hand was muddy. Her hair hung in wet curls down her neck and on her forehead. It looked the color of mud, not the pretty dark blond he'd seen when he first met her, but her eyes sparkled and her smile was genuine as she looked up at him. The realization hit him that he had never seen a more beautiful woman as Nancy Southerland.

He pulled his eyes away from her with great difficulty and took a long step down the trail. He knew that the parking lot was a few strides away and he could escape from those eyes and that smile in only a few minutes. He would, he had to. It had everything to do with his free agent status - his hatred of women. He would not be pulled into the crushing web of any female. He had very good reasons to keep away from women. Didn't he? Of course he did! The best reason of all was his mother.

Nancy felt him withdraw, watched him take that extra long stride and knew it was to leave her behind. She'd heard him say he didn't like women, he'd said he'd never get involved and she had to agree, she couldn't get involved with a non-believer, but it still hurt. She'd laid everything out for him, she wondered if in laying everything out she'd laid her heart out as well. She swallowed a sigh as he took another long stride, she'd let him go, he had to come to terms with life's issues himself. Right now he wasn't ready. She'd laid the ground work perhaps someone else could cultivate and water what she'd planted. She'd hope and pray to that end.

The thought came to her that Sandy fed him breakfast every day that a hike left. She would pray that Sandy had the opportunity to reach this stubborn man. Of course, he'd had thirty years to build his resistance, why did she think she could tear it all down in only three days? Well, God could do anything she had to be the vessel He wanted her to be. Right now, she knew she'd done everything she could to show him his need to be in that Ark when the flood waters of life battered him.

Only a few steps behind Duncan Nancy stepped onto the blacktop of DeLord's parking lot. She was still drawing her second foot up to take another step and the clouds burst apart in the west. The sun was not far above the horizon, but it shone brilliantly upon them. She'd been thinking some sad, heavy thoughts, but with the sun, a smile burst across her face. She was sure it was a sign of God's blessing.

"Thank You, Jesus!" she murmured, as she turned her face toward the warming sun. "Thank You for life and health and even a good time in the rain. Bless this man who really is seeking. Show him who You are and show him he needs to climb on board and walk through the door into Your Ark of safety."

She threw her arms out, forgetting the heavy load on her back. "Oh, look!" she exclaimed, "The sun came out, isn't it wonderful?"

"So the sun came out!" Mel grumbled, also stepping onto the blacktop. However, he didn't crack a smile as Nancy had. "Where's it been while we were hiking? Why'd it wait until now to show up?"

"It's been there all along, Mel, the clouds were too thick for the sun to shine on us, but now it's out. Feel how much it's warmed us? You can't be grumpy, Mel, we're back safe and sound at the parking lot. There's Dillon's car over there and we can get in it and go home to dry places. Remember when the Tsunami hit over in the Far East? Those poor people didn't have a place to go to get out of the terrible things that were happening to them."

Exasperated, Mel exclaimed, "Woman, I swear, your mind must always be thinking up stuff to remind a body about tragedies and such things. Give it a rest! I'm beat, I want to go home, but I still have to sit in the backseat with you on the way!"

"I know, but just think when you get there you'll be able to have that hot cup or two of coffee you didn't get to have this morning. Won't you be glad of that?"

Mel sighed, "I think I'll go to bed, I lost plenty of sleep these three days."

"True but there's always tomorrow!" Nancy exclaimed.

Duncan was enough ahead of the hikers that he'd taken his backpack off and had it leaning up against his SUV. He came back to the hikers and much to his own surprise he put his hands around the two sides of Nancy's pack. She felt it lighten and turned her head. Of course, a giant of a man was looking over the top of her pack down at her. Quickly, she released the clasp on the belt around her waist and slid her arms out from behind the straps.

"Duncan! Thanks so much! You've shed your pack already!"

"Sure, I don't carry it any longer than I must."

"Believe me, I don't either, but it's easier to carry it on my back than in my arms and I still had to get to Dillon's car to put it in." She walked with him as he headed for Dillon's car and said, "Duncan, it's been a great hike. Thanks for taking us and putting up with us."

"Hey, you've answered a lot of questions."

Earnestly, Nancy said, "Duncan, I really hope and pray you'll remember what we talked about and let God work in your life."

"Like I say, I gotta think about it. But I'll give it some thought, Nancy, I promise you."

"Thanks, Duncan, that's all I ask." Her smile rivaled the sun and put a knot in his belly. She said, "Maybe, since Sandy told you to read the book of John, she'll help you along the way."

Duncan groaned. "I was afraid you'd think of her!" Nancy grinned, as Dillon, Linda and Mel walked up with their packs.

"Whew! What an experience!" Dillon exclaimed. He searched in the side pocket of his backpack and found his keys. Minutes later, instead of using the key fob, he used the key to open the trunk and four packs thudded in.

"Yeah, it was something else," Mel groused.

The only cars on the parking lot were Duncan's, Dillon's and Steve's. All the hikers went to the cars and put their backpacks into the trunks, but since Duncan had Nancy's pack, she wasn't looking into the trunk as the others were. Movement caught her eye off to the side of the house. Quickly she looked and saw a magnificent buck with a huge rack of horns standing at the edge of the woods they'd just left.

Dillon was about to slam his trunk lid, but Nancy whispered loudly, "Wait! Look! Look, over there!" and pointed toward where they'd just come.

Everyone on the parking lot looked where she pointed and saw the deer, then as they watched silently a doe and a tiny fawn came cautiously up beside him. "Oh, my!" Linda gasped. "Aren't they beautiful! I wish we'd seen some on the hike."

Dillon wasn't wasting time talking, he had the zipper to his side pocket on his backpack open and quickly snagged out his camera. Before the trio moved he'd snapped off several pictures on his digital camera. Before any of the other hikers could think to reach for their cameras, however, Ramon opened the office door and the doe and fawn scampered away. Then, since he was oblivious to the animals, Ramon closed the door behind him. The noise startled the buck so he turned and bounded after the others.

Ramon looked at the bedraggled hikers and said, "Sorry about the weather, but, hey, it's March, after all."

Dillon shrugged. "You couldn't help it, Ramon we had a decent time, really. The inside of our tents was dry, so we slept okay. The sun's out now and we can go home to a dry place."

"Yes, that's true. What were you looking at over there?"

"Oh!" Nancy exclaimed. "There was a beautiful deer family that came to the edge of the woods and watched us for a little. We didn't see any deer on the hike, but now that we've seen these we can remember them. Dillon got some pictures before they ran back into the woods. I'm sure he'll let me have a copy."

"You didn't see any on the hike? I'm surprised."

"No, but last night we were visited by a pack of wolves," Duncan said.

"Wolves! Did they bother you?"

"No, we were all in our tents. They sniffed around but didn't find anything to interest them, so they wandered off."

"Wolves, no bears or skunks?"

Mel made a noise in his throat, but turned away and wouldn't look at the other hikers. However, Dillon grinned and said, "No, no bears or skunks. We did have a really sound sleeper among us who claimed that bears tried to rip up his tent both nights, but none of the rest of us saw any evidence."

"I'm glad to hear that."

"How long have you been back?" Duncan asked, looking around the parking lot. "Ramon, you're dry."

"Not long, really. Remember we started at a different trailhead, so I drove with the others and they left for home from the trailhead. I barely parked my truck in the garage a few minutes ago, but I ran in and changed. So nobody got lost or hurt?"

"Nope, we almost left a body this morning, though."

Ramon scowled. "Why?"

Nodding toward Mel, Duncan said, "Sleepyhead wouldn't get out of his tent. When we shook it, he told the bears to go away and let him sleep."

Ramon looked around, at the seven in the group. "So, how'd you get him moving?"

"Umm, well, one of us was ingenious and got him up by another method."

Ramon grinned, "And that would be?"

Thumbing over his shoulder, Mel grumbled, "That woman dumped a pan full of ice water on me, after that one pulled me out of my tent!"

Ramon threw his head back and laughed. "Great! Super! I'll remember that one."

"Yeah, you do that! I guarantee it won't be me it's used on again!"

Only a few minutes later, the hikers had climbed into the cars and as they left the parking lot, most of them waved at Duncan. Chagrined, Duncan caught himself looking into Dillon's car. Sure enough, Nancy was waving to him. Not to show much enthusiasm, Duncan raised his hand in a salute, as he stood with Ramon.

After the lot was quiet and the cars out of sight, Duncan turned to his buddy and said, "So, we're off tomorrow and back on for Monday, right?"

Ramon turned toward the house and said, "You got it! Unless you really like being chilled to the bone, come on in the office, why don't you?"

Following, Duncan said, "You don't have to convince me! I've been cold since the rain started yesterday."

As Duncan closed the door, Ramon slouched into the desk chair. "Got some other news."

"What's that?"

"While we were gone, Sandy took a call from another guy who's from around here. He wants to work with us, for DeLord's Hiking Service."

Scowling, Duncan said, "What does that mean for us?"

Ramon shrugged. "Since Sandy's got most of the summer scheduled for two hikes at a time we can alternate and one of us get a few days off, or if more calls come in, she can schedule more hikes. I think it'll make us pretty flexible. Neal wants to start as soon as possible, so I'll take him with me on Monday and then we'll send him with you on the next hike so he gets an idea of how we want the groups conducted then we'll play it from there."

"I don't want much time off," Duncan grumbled.

"I'm sure times'll fill up and there won't be much down time for any of us. So, he's coming tomorrow afternoon to see how we work these hikes on the computer, you'll come for lunch and the afternoon, won't you?"

"I guess since we're going out again on Monday that's the way it'll have to be. I need to get to Alex's before he closes, so I'll see you then."

Chuckling at the wet giant, Ramon said, "Sure, keep dry!"

"Thanks!" Duncan grumbled and headed out the door again. His SUV was the only vehicle on the parking lot now.

He breathed a sigh of relief, the little spitfire was gone. She lived in Blairsville and worked a lot, he lived in Vansville and led hikes going the opposite way from Blairsville and was gone most of the time, so he was sure they wouldn't meet again. He could put her out of his mind and get on with life as it had been. 'He got along without her before he met her, he could get along without her now.' He was determined that was the way his life would be.

Duncan hurriedly threw his soaked backpack into the back of his SUV. He'd shed his slicker while the hikers did, so he climbed behind the wheel and drove quickly down the few blocks to Alex's store, because the clock on the dash said it was nearly five o'clock and his cupboards and his refrigerator freezer were nearly bare of anything that resembled edibles.

Just to emphasize the problem, his stomach grumbled as he left the SUV at the curb.

Alex was on his way to the front window to change the sign from open to closed as Duncan pushed the door open. Alex turned the sign, but gave him a grin and said, "I had a feeling you'd be in today."

Wiping his hand down his still wet jeans, Duncan nodded and pulled a basket from the bunch beside the door. He said, "Yeah, it's good the Laundromat stays open until nine, I don't have a clean, dry thing at my cabin. The trail wasn't very cooperative since dinner time yesterday with that first shower."

"Don't I know it! Sandy called me and had me deliver a huge order. She tells me a new guide's joining you folks and she's having a bunch of company for dinner tomorrow. I guess you'll be in on that, too."

"I suspect so. Ramon asked me just now and this new guide's coming."

His eyes twinkling, Alex added, "She tells me a girlfriend of hers is coming, too."

With Alex following, Duncan had gone to the frozen food section and pulled a door open to get out his frozen dinners, he had one in his hand and nearly dropped it when he whirled around and let the door close. Again, he nearly dropped it when the door closing caught the corner, as he said, "A girlfriend of Sandy's?"

"Yeah, she said they'd talked about her coming after church for dinner tomorrow when they'd talked on Thursday."

To cover his groan, Duncan turned back to the freezer and pulled the door open. "Oh, yeah, I guess I do remember that." Duncan pulled out several different frozen dinners and let the door close behind him. "I guess I'll take these. I'm going back out on Monday, so I won't need much before then."

As Alex rang up the prices, Duncan asked, "How much rain did we get today?"

"My rain gauge out back registered two inches. Not a nice day to be on a hike."

"You could say that. In my tent last night was the last time I felt dry. Even that was relative, though, you know how fog and mist can dampen things inside your pack."

"I never was on a hike, not like you lead, but I know what you mean. We've had our share of fog and mist these last couple of days. On an open trail I'm sure that's almost as bad as the downpour we had today. I mean, it came down pretty hard there for a good hour." Alex looked his customer up and down. "You're still wet!"

Following Duncan to the door to lock it behind him, Alex said, "I'll see you again, Duncan. Hope you dry out soon."

"Yeah, that dry cabin will be welcome, believe me."

Duncan walked out to his SUV, thinking about his talks with Nancy. They'd gotten two inches of rain. It hadn't rained for more than an hour and a half. Nancy believed it had rained for forty days and forty nights straight and geysers had erupted during a world-wide flood. Two inches in an hour and a half was a lot of rain. He shuddered as he climbed into his vehicle. The clouds were back, darkening the sky again. Maybe he'd go home now and wash his clothes in the morning. No, he couldn't, the Laundromat wasn't open on Sunday.

Duncan hurried to the gas station/hardware store to the only Laundromat in town that faced the same parking lot. He jumped out and took his basket and his backpack inside. He was the only person there at this time, but he was glad. He'd put the latest copy of his camping magazine in the car before he left home, so he planned to read it while he waited.

However, that was not to be. He had the three washers going when the door opened and Brad Thomas walked in. He'd closed his business and come to see who was washing clothes on a Saturday evening. Nodding, he said, "Howdy, son. Guess you got wet on the trail today?"

"Drenched," Duncan groused. "Alex told me his rain gauge said it rained two inches."

"I'll bet that's the truth! It came down in a torrent! I was really glad to be inside during that storm. Say, did you see the excavation going on on the country side of Isabel's cabins?"

"I haven't been there yet, but there wasn't anything going on when I left Thursday morning. They're digging up the place?"

"Yep! They had to stop Friday afternoon because it started raining, but first thing Thursday and again on Friday they moved in some big equipment. Vansville's gettin' on the map, it seems. We're scheduled to get a health clinic by the end of summer."

Duncan shrugged and said, "I guess that's good for the village. It won't help us much, I don't guess. If somebody's hurt on a hike, they'll still have to be airlifted and the helicopter comes from Blairsville."

"Yeah, that's true, but it'll be a branch of the Blairsville Hospital. I think it'll bring some new blood to town, though."

Sighing, Duncan wasn't excited about that give him the wide open spaces! He said, "I guess it's in how you look at it."

Brad shrugged. "More people, more business, that's how I see it. This'll be the first new building in ten years, I think. I'd hate to see Vansville die."

"Yeah, it's a nice little town."

Brad turned toward the door, then turned back and said, "So, Duncan, when you leave, pick up that phone and dial six. I'll come lock up after you're gone. I can't see there'll be much business after you leave on a Saturday night. The way the day's been people won't be coming out to wash clothes, ya know?"

Duncan nodded. "I'll give you a call, Brad."

After the door closed behind the older man, Duncan picked up his magazine, but didn't open it. When he'd first come to town, he'd met Brad Thomas in much the same way, here at the Laundromat. He was a grouch to put it mildly and then he'd heard how he'd tried to run Roger out of town. It hadn't been too many weeks later, though, that the old man had a change of heart and went to the preacher to apologize. He'd come away from there a changed man.

Shifting in the uncomfortable chair, Duncan jumped up and checked his machines, then sighed and sat back down. It had only been a few minutes, the water had filled up the tubs and the agitation cycle had started. What was wrong with him? That invisible little creature that sat on his shoulder several times recently seemed to jump up and flick his ear. *I think it could be God's trying to get your attention, man.*

Grabbing up his magazine, he swatted his shoulder and said, "You are the worst pest in all the world! I told her I'd think about it!"

Glad that Ramon had come out as a distraction, Nancy went with the others to the car doors. Nancy slid onto the seat and Mel let out a contented sigh as he made himself comfortable on the cushioned backseat of Dillon's car. "Wow! I'll never complain about riding in the backseat of any car again."

"Don't make any promises you can't keep, Mel," Nancy said, beside him.

Mel sighed again and gave her a look. "Little miss sunshine. I'll sure be glad to leave you behind, too, believe me!"

"Just your conscience, Mel, just your conscience."

Dillon started up, but Nancy looked out the window. When she saw that Duncan was watching, she waved out her window at him, giving him a smile as she did. He didn't smile back or wave, but he gave her a salute. She chuckled to herself, the man was a hard nut to crack, but she had to believe that God had His plans in place for Duncan. They might not see each other again, but she'd laid the next layer on top of what Sandy had done, now it was in God's hands to do His part. She knew He would.

Dillon left the parking lot, turned and headed down the highway toward Blairsville. Nancy had to admit, she'd never been so glad to get off her feet and sit on something soft for a change. The sun was still shining as they went through town. As they passed the church, Nancy wondered if this was where Sandy and Ramon went or if they drove into Blairsville. If they came to Blairsville, they obviously didn't go to the one she went to, she was sure she'd have seen them. It was hard to miss someone who always sat in a wheelchair.

They were leaving the town behind, when Linda asked, "What are they doing there?"

Linda's question brought Nancy from her thoughts and she stared out the window. "It looks like they're planning to start a building, doesn't it?" Nancy asked.

"I'd say they got a bit washed up today," Mel observed.

"Yeah, it's probably a manmade pool about now."

Nancy sighed and closed her eyes, "We'll probably never know. What reason do any of us have to come back to this little town again?"

"Another hike with Duncan Roads, Nancy?" Dillon asked her.

Seriously, Nancy answered, "Dillon, when I was a kid I determined not to date or marry a non-believer. I've been on one hike with Duncan Roads. He does not share my beliefs, so there is no reason to come back for a hike with Duncan. If I need some other kind of distraction or entertainment, I'll find something besides going on a hike with DeLord's Hiking Service."

"You sure do limit yourself that way, don't you?" Linda asked.

"Yes, I do, but God has the right man out there for me. When the time's right, I'm sure I'll know who he is."

"If you say so," Linda sighed.

A bit stiff the next morning, Nancy swung her legs off the side of her daybed. She hurried to finish in her bathroom because she had napped until the very last minute she could spare and not be late for Sunday school. Since she didn't always get to go, she wanted to be sure and get there. She dressed nicely, but decided to take a change of clothes, in case she'd feel more comfortable spending dinner and the afternoon with Sandy out of her Sunday clothes. She rarely had a chance to dress up, even in church clothes.

After fixing a toasted bagel with cream cheese and brewing a small pot of coffee, she sat at her table to enjoy a hot breakfast. She decided there was no way to really enjoy little things more than to have to do without them for several days. The hot shower she'd enjoyed last night after stripping out of her wet clothes had made her feel like a million dollars and to sleep on the soft, lumpy mattress of her daybed last night had been a luxury she wouldn't forget for at least a week. The hot bagel and the brewed coffee topped the list of things that made this morning so much better than yesterday. Since she was dressed, she opened the drape to the sun shining. Of course that brought an instant smile to her face.

She left for church in her car and knew that her feet appreciated her consideration very much. Even the curls on her head had fallen into place very well, perhaps they liked it better being dry and clean than they had being wet, frizzy and caked in dirt. At any rate, she felt great and was so glad she'd asked off for this day, not just to recuperate from the hike, but also so she could go to church and spend time with other believers. She loved talking about her Lord and things from the Bible, but she was glad to spend time with others who believed as she did.

As she entered through the front door, planning to enter the sanctuary for the singing service before classes split up, an usher handed her a bulletin. She found a seat and looked at the picture on the front, then looked at the back at the tiny words that told where the picture was taken, because the scene looked very much like a scene where they'd spent their first lunch time on the hike. After that, she opened the bulletin. The first thing in bold print that she saw said,

Concert to be held at Blairsville Bible Church next Saturday. Nearby artist, Sandra DeLord to perform. Doors open at six pm concert at seven. All welcome.

Scowling, Nancy muttered, as she stared at the words, "There can only be one Sandra DeLord. Who ever heard of that last name except for Ramon and Sandy DeLord?" She guessed she could find out soon enough, since she was going to their house for dinner right from church. Sandy did more than be the hiking service receptionist?

However, during the announcements the pastor said, "Folks, you'll notice in your bulletin an announcement for a concert next Saturday evening. It's in a church across town, but if you're free you'll want to go. Mrs. DeLord can be classified as a concert pianist and is very talented. She's been asked to play with the Atlanta Symphony Orchestra. I understand she has accepted and will be playing with them some time this summer. Be sure to set aside that date. Your time will be well rewarded."

Six

Nancy scowled and looked at the piano at the front of the sanctuary where their own pianist sat on the bench. She, herself, had never played the piano, but she did know enough about playing a piano that to make the music sound like anything the person playing had to use their feet, at least one of them most of the time. Sandy sat in a wheelchair. From what Duncan said, she never left it, she'd never walked. How could she play a piano? Maybe Pastor was mistaken, perhaps she played an instrument like a violin or a trumpet where she could use her hands and someone accompanied her on the piano. She sighed, maybe she'd ask later on.

After church she shook hands with the pastor, but forgot to ask him her question about Sandy's playing. Several people greeted her and told her they were glad to see her. She said hello to several others, but then she hurried to her car. She didn't know if Sandy came to Blairsville to church or if she went to the little one in Vansville. If she went in Vansville, she could be holding the meal for quite a while until she arrived. She would plan to change clothes at DeLord's to save time now.

Behind the wheel, Nancy drove through town to the highway that went through Vansville. Once she turned on the highway, traffic was light. She expected as much, since it was Sunday. Remembering what yesterday had been like she looked out her side window and enjoyed the different shades of green she could see on the hillsides. With new leaves coming out, there were dozens of shades dotting the hillsides on both sides of the road. The blue sky overhead made for a perfect day. The sun had warmed the air, so Nancy rolled down the window a few inches and let the early spring air come in. She breathed in the fresh air and let it fill her lungs. She loved days like this! This early in the spring, the flowering trees were starting to bud and the early magnolias were sending out a delicate aroma. Even as she drove by she could smell the flowering trees.

As the miles went by, she smiled and said, "It's beautiful! Thank You, God, for giving me life. I want to enjoy it to the full." With a fresh breeze blowing in the window and the sun shining, she could almost feel God in the car with her. She also savored what she could remember of the sermon.

Duncan watched the clock over his small kitchen sink. Ramon had said that dinner would be at one o'clock. He knew he'd have to listen to Ramon or Sandy say a blessing over their meal, but he didn't have to go early to survive any of her probing questions. Last night, after getting all his clean clothes inside and put away, he'd stood in the shower for a long time enjoying the warmth and the cleanliness he felt as the water sprayed over his body and hair. When he'd left the shower, he'd wiped the mirror over the sink and felt the urge to cut the shag from his head, both across the top and in front.

When he'd finished with the scissors, his beard only curled under his chin and his mustache only met it at the sides of his mouth, not over top of his lips. The hair on top wasn't a professional job by any means, but it was much shorter and Duncan was pleased with what he saw. He decided he'd try to keep the look at least for the hiking season. During the winter he could do as he pleased.

He slept late at least it was late for him. He had no obligations until one o'clock at Ramon's for dinner, so he got up at eight and read his magazine before fixing a pot of coffee. At noon, he checked through his closet and found his newest pair of jeans and a polo shirt his sister had given him for Christmas. Instead of his usual hiking shoes, he found his tennis shoes that he'd bought over Christmas vacation and stuffed his feet into them. He combed his hair and ran the comb through his beard and felt as ready as ever to face Sandy...and Nancy, he sighed.

As he pulled the door closed behind him, he grumbled, "Why didn't I remember that Nancy was coming for dinner before I accepted Ramon's invitation? I'd have told him I'd come later on and gone to his office."

He made a face Sandy's cooking far surpassed any frozen dinner he had stacked in his freezer.

What are you chicken? That persistent little creature on his shoulder asked.

Flicking his ear, he muttered, "Am not!"

Heh, heh, actions speak louder than words!

As he stopped at the road to check for traffic, a car was too close to pull out. As he waited and the car passed, his heart did an uncharacteristic bump in his chest. The driver was none other than the woman who had driven him crazy on the trail! Nancy obviously recognized him, her smile could rival the sun and she waved as she went by.

"Drat it!" he exclaimed. "I'll have to walk her in."

Yup, you got it!

Of course, Duncan followed Nancy onto the DeLord's parking lot. She parked in the spot where Duncan usually parked. Trying not to look too annoyed, he parked right beside her then shut off his vehicle. Still with that smile on her face and just to annoy him, he was sure she stood at the front of her car and waited for him to leave his SUV.

"Hi!" she exclaimed. "I didn't know you were eating dinner here, too. She'll have a table full!" He could tell that she was looking him up and down that brought warmth to his cheeks that the sun wasn't putting there.

The sight that stood before him took his breath away. Yesterday, with frizzy wet hair and wet slicker clinging to her body, the hood nearly covering her face, soggy hiking boots and a soaking wet backpack weighing her down, Duncan was convinced he'd never seen a woman so beautiful as Nancy Southerland. However, today, her sandy hair lay in soft curls all over her head. She wore a fitted coat that accentuated a slender body and nicely showed off lovely legs encased in sheer hose. She was a bit taller today because of stylish, three inch heels. Of course, as he approached, she gave him her megawatt smile and her blue eyes twinkled.

"Yeah," he grumbled. "Ramon told me we have a new man we're to train starting tomorrow. We'll meet over dinner then the three of us are going over things in the office." He needed to make that perfectly clear, it was the three of them in the office. She was not invited.

Chuckling, Nancy knew exactly what he was saying, even though he wasn't saying it out loud, so she said, "But first of all, you must survive

Sandy and me browbeating you with how our church services went while we eat."

"That sounds about right," he groused. "So you went to church this morning?"

"Sure! Did you know Sandy's putting on a concert next Saturday evening in Blairsville?" she asked.

"No, I didn't know, but I do know she's quite an accomplished musician. I have heard her play a few times. She's played here and given a concert at that little church on the corner."

"Tell me something. Our pastor said she's a concert pianist. Didn't he misspeak? How can she be a pianist if she can't use her feet?"

"She is. You'll have to ask her how she does it."

Nodding emphatically, Nancy said, "I will! I looked at the pianist at church this morning and I know she uses her feet while she plays."

She gave the man at her side a measured look. "You cut your hair and beard! My goodness, isn't your head cold without all that?"

Still feeling the heat on his face, he said, "Yeah, as a matter of fact, it's a bit chilly out here. Let's head for the door."

Nancy's laughter rang out. "Oh, that's good!"

Instead of going to the door near the parking lot, Duncan walked Nancy to the front door that was at the end of a concrete walk. Before either of them could knock, the door opened and Ramon stood there, his hand out and a grin on his face. "Hi! Come on in! Didn't expect you two to come together."

Nancy had her mouth open, but Duncan beat her to it, by saying, "We sure didn't come together! I followed her down the street and turned in right behind her. Friend, why didn't you tell me she was coming to dinner too?"

"Duncan," Nancy said quietly, "I told you I was coming to dinner today."

"Yeah, but I forgot that, but if he'd told me I'd have come later. I mean, after all, as much as I eat, there's no reason for Sandy to have to cook for an army," he added quickly. All at once what he'd said and how he'd said it didn't sound too nice. He swallowed he didn't want to hurt anyone's feelings, of course. Not even Nancy's.

Ramon chuckled. "She loves to cook! The more there are, the happier she is. Come on in. We're getting the serving dishes on now. Neal should be along real soon. He's coming from Blairsville and said he had an errand to run before he could come."

Duncan stood back and like a perfect gentleman, ushered Nancy in before him. A cheery voice came to them from another room, "Hi, guys! Come on in!"

Nancy left the men and hurried to find the voice. At the kitchen door, she said, "Hi, Sandy. Can I help?"

"Hi, Nancy!" Sandy's voice held a smile, as she exclaimed and held out some bowls to Nancy. "Put these two dishes anywhere on the table, would you, please? Ramon was supposed to ask about drinks as you came in, but I didn't hear him ask. Duncan always takes coffee. Share a pot of tea with me?"

"Sure, I'd love a cup of tea. The sun's out and it's warmer than yesterday, but being March it's still a little chilly." Nancy took the two serving dishes to the dining room and sighed as she came back. "It's so beautiful today!"

Sandy turned to the stove and turned the knob for the burner under the large teakettle. "Great! I get tired of coffee all the time and Ramon despises anything but iced tea. I make good coffee, so I drink it, but it's not my favorite."

"Yeah, I make a lot of instant at my apartment."

Just after everything was on the table there was a knock on the front door and Ramon hurried to answer. As he opened the door, the others heard him say, "Neal, get yourself in here! We're about to sit down to dinner." Ramon led the young man into the dining room and said, "Folks, this is Neal LeGrande. Neal, that giant is Duncan Roads, my other associate and this is Nancy, a new friend who's come to get better acquainted with Sandy, my wife." He looked apologetically at Nancy and said, "I'm sorry, Nancy, I don't know your last name."

She smiled and said, "I'm Nancy Southerland. I'm pleased to meet you Neal. I went on a hike these past three days and enjoyed it very much."

Neal scowled. "In the rain and you enjoyed it?"

Without missing a beat, Nancy said, "Yes, the earth needs the rain to grow things. We can't be upset when we're out in it."

"I guess," Neal muttered, dubiously.

Sandy came in the dining room from the kitchen and rolled herself up to the place where there was no chair, and said, "Come on, everybody, find a place so we can say grace and get started. Food isn't good when it's cold."

Nancy found her place next to Sandy, since that was the only place with a cup of tea and the other three had a mug of coffee. Ramon sat next to Sandy on the other side and Duncan found himself sitting next Nancy. He looked at her then at Neal, who'd slipped into the seat next to Ramon. Nancy looked back and gave him her famous grin, but didn't say anything. What was there to say? Duncan had made his feelings abundantly clear.

Duncan muttered, only loud enough for Nancy to hear, "I should trade places with him. You could work on his soul."

"His time'll come, don't worry."

When everyone was seated, Sandy had her hands out. Ramon took hers right away, but Sandy said, "Come on, guys, hold hands while we say grace." Nancy held hers out and reluctantly, Duncan raised his.

Nancy noticed his reluctance, quietly, she murmured, "Come on, I don't bite."

"Depends how you mean that," he whispered back.

When all the hands were connected around the circle, Ramon said, "Father, God, we want to thank You for this food. Thank You for the privilege we have of going to church to worship You. We pray that You will bless our conversation around this table and bless this food to our bodies. In Your Son's Name, amen."

Neal looked around the table at the others. As Ramon, Sandy and Nancy raised their heads, he asked, "You always do that stuff before you eat? Didn't you say we usually eat breakfast here before a hike? You do it then, too?"

"Yes," Ramon said, "we know that without God's love and care for us we would be nothing. God supplies us with life, health and a beautiful place to live, called Earth. Everything around us has been supplied by God's loving care."

"Amen to that," Nancy murmured.

Swiping his hand through the air, Duncan said, "Can we cut this for now and just eat? We need to get busy on our itineraries for tomorrow."

Grinning at him, Sandy said, "I guess reading the book of John didn't do much for you?"

Nancy followed her by saying, "And all we talked about the flood and the fossils didn't help much either, it seems."

"Give it a rest!" he exclaimed and picked up the bowl of mashed potatoes. After taking a large helping, he asked, "So, have you heard the weather for the next couple of days? Is it going to rain again any time soon?"

Sandy laughed. "Duncan, you've had enough for a while? Where's your pioneer spirit?"

"After yesterday, I've had enough for a while."

After dessert and another cup of coffee or tea, Sandy said, "You guys go on and do your thing. Nancy and I'll clean up and get acquainted while we do it."

Ramon leaned over his wife and kissed her tenderly, before he said, "Thanks, Sweetheart. I'm glad you have somebody to pal around with. Maybe you'll play us a concert while we work out our plans. I think we'll have to get creative with three of us, at least for now."

"You know I must practice, Honey, so I probably will, if Nancy doesn't mind."

"Oh, no! I'd love to hear you play."

The men left the dining room and went down the hallway to the office. Duncan closed the door behind them and had to swallow a sigh. He was glad to be out of the presence of both Nancy and Sandy. What was it about those two women that wore him out completely? Perhaps it was that he was always on his guard.

Sandy pulled some things from the table and placed them on her lap, but Nancy stacked the dirty dishes from dessert and coffee and headed for the kitchen right behind Sandy. When the table was cleared, Nancy saw that Sandy had a hard time reaching the faucet to rinse the dishes, so Nancy took over that task, handing the dishes to Sandy to place in the dishwasher. They chatted as they worked together. Nancy never felt so comfortable in the presence of someone her own age before.

"You have a lovely home, Sandy," Nancy said.

"I know and I'm so happy here! Believe me I never thought I could have the love of a husband and a home of my own. But here I am and it's wonderful! I thank God every day for Ramon and the love he showers on me. We've only been married since the fall, but it's been the best months of my life."

Nancy scowled, as she handed Sandy the last plate. "Why didn't you think you could have a man's love? You're pretty, you have a wonderful personality and there isn't anything wrong with your mind."

"Actually, I never realized I did that, but I guess I let my mom's feelings cloud my thinking all my life. Now that I am away from home, I try not to think about it, but since I left home, I've realized that she's ashamed of my being in a wheelchair. Unfortunately, until Ramon told me otherwise, I guess I was, maybe not quite so much as her."

Horrified, Nancy exclaimed, "It's no fault of yours! You can't help that your legs don't function! Goodness!"

"I know, but she has been a powerful influence in my life. When Ramon told me he loved me and then asked me to marry him, I couldn't believe it. Until then, my chair loomed like a wall around me." She sighed and turned the dishwasher on. Then she said, "Enough of that, come on, Nancy, want to come with me while I practice for next week's concert? I don't know if you know, but I'm playing a concert in Blairsville at our church on Saturday."

Nancy grinned at her new friend and exclaimed, "Yes, it was announced in our bulletin today. I'm so impressed!"

"Thanks," Sandy said, simply.

Sandy led Nancy into the living room across the hall from the dining room. Nancy had noticed the picture over the mantel of the fireplace in the dining room, but hanging on the wall over the piano was a gorgeous scene that reminded Nancy of the places they'd hiked in. Sandy went to the piano, but Nancy moved beside it to look up at the picture. There was no signature, but in the bottom right corner was a G clef and two notes with tiny flags on five short lines.

Looking over the large picture again, Nancy asked, "Who was the artist? This is fantastic! It looks like where we hiked."

"Maybe it is. Ramon's taken lots of pictures and I've copied them onto canvas."

"Sandy, you did this?" Nancy gasped. "It's amazing! It looks like where we ate lunch our first day out."

With a smile, Sandy said, "I love to paint. When the guys finish in the office, we'll go in and you can have one of those paintings. This one and the one in the dining room I wouldn't dare give away, Ramon would have my head. Those are his favorites and they're from pictures he took last summer."

"But… but I didn't bring any money. I…"

"Nancy," Sandy chided, "didn't you hear me say you can *have* a painting?"

"Yes, but surely you didn't mean to *give* it to me!" she gasped.

"I most certainly did!" Sandy exclaimed. "You're the first girlfriend I've had since I moved here. I'm so happy to have someone like you and I want you to have one of my paintings. Will you accept it as that?"

Nancy threw her arms around Sandy and they hugged. "Oh, Sandy, of course! I'd be so honored! Does that mean when I have free time I could come and we'd spend time together?"

"You can't know how much I'd love that! Now that the hiking season's here Ramon'll be gone a lot and I'll be here. Raylyn Clemens comes when I give Heidi her lesson, but she's busy being a pastor's wife, plus she works, so she doesn't have much time. If you have some time on your hands, give me a buzz and we'll see what we can do. Don't think you'd always have to come here, I drive a van and I can come to Blairsville."

"You are obviously multi-talented! How could your mom be ashamed of you?"

Shaking her head sadly, Sandy said, "Not me so much as this chair. Anyway, I need to practice, want to listen?"

"Of course, go right ahead."

Sandy reached for the black pouch that lay on the music rack on the piano and as Nancy watched, she slipped it over the edge of her chair back. Sandy leaned against it and situated it until it was comfortable, then she raised her hands and with two fingers played a tune that children and adults everywhere recognize. Nancy said nothing, keeping her thoughts to herself.

After one completion of 'Twinkle, Twinkle Little Star,' Sandy launched into a much more complicated version of the same theme. Quite some time later, she raised her hands and Nancy felt the need to clap. "Sandy! That was awesome!"

Sandy turned to smile at Nancy. "Thanks. Since I teach so many children, I think that's become my theme song. Many of my students will come in and sit down on the bench and two finger 'Twinkle, Twinkle Little Star' and then they'll say, 'Come on, Ms. Sandy, you gotta play the rest.' Some times I do, some times I have them start their lesson. Actually, what I just played is a piece of music that was written that way by Mr. Mozart a very long time ago."

"Really? Wow! As you can tell, I'm not much of a music buff. Go on and play some more, will you?"

The afternoon flew by. The men stayed in the office all afternoon and Sandy practiced for her concert with a rapped audience of one. Finally, Sandy raised her hands as the chime clock started the strokes for five o'clock. Nancy clapped again, but Sandy looked at Nancy and asked, "Had you planned to go to church this evening? I've taken up your whole afternoon and here it is five o'clock already."

Nancy looked at the clock and shook her head. "No, I wasn't going to church and I've had the best time."

Conspiratorially, Sandy said, "Come on, let's go crash their party. Ramon and Duncan'll stay hold up in that office for hours working on that computer. I'll bet they need some iced tea."

The two women hurried to the kitchen and Sandy said, "In that cupboard is a tray, could you get it down for me?"

Nancy found the tray, then found the glasses and arranged them on it and realized Sandy had an ice maker. She filled the glasses while Sandy pulled the tea pitcher from the refrigerator. After all the glasses were filled, Nancy picked up the tray and followed Sandy down the long hall to the door at the end. Sandy gave one knock and opened the door.

"Okay, guys, it's time for a break. Besides, Nancy wants to look at the pictures so she can make her choice."

Nancy set the tray of glasses on the desk and turned slowly around, looking at the pictures. "Sandy! These are absolutely gorgeous!"

Duncan couldn't take his eyes from her. Maybe Sandy's pictures were beautiful, but Nancy was the one who was gorgeous.

Not long after Nancy left DeLord's office with her picture on Sunday, Duncan and Neal also left, planning on being back for breakfast early

Monday morning. Two groups were going out, Duncan leading one and Ramon taking Neal along as a guide-in-training. Along with going over the routes they would use, they had hunted up the weather on the internet and for these two hikes it was to be nice. Of course, Mother Nature could change her mind on that, she did much of the time. March was the month for changeable weather and April was the month for showers. However, mere humans must take what came along.

Monday came and Sandy made her usually excellent breakfast. The men talked while they ate, especially making sure that all of Neal's questions were answered. They would be gone until late Wednesday, but Sandy hadn't scheduled any hikes until the following Monday. Ramon, of course must be there to be the MC for Sandy's concert and Duncan wanted to go to hear Sandy play. Since no hikes had been scheduled, Neal said he'd like to come to the concert. As was her style, Sandy made no comment about the concert. Ramon knew it as humility, Duncan and Neal just wondered. Of course, the two single men had heard Sandy play all afternoon on Sunday as background for their hike discussion.

It wasn't long before car doors started slamming on the parking lot and all three men picked up papers from the printer and headed for the door. Sandy followed them to the door way, but Ramon lingered behind the other two and smiled at his wife. Handing the papers in his hand to Neal before he moved away, Ramon took Sandy in his arms and hugged her. As soon as Sandy put her arms around his neck, Ramon sealed his lips to hers and savored a tender kiss.

"I'll miss you, Love," he murmured.

Sandy's eyes were bright, but she whispered, "I'll be here praying, Honey."

"Thanks, Love," he whispered.

Nancy went to bed fairly early Sunday night, knowing she must be up and at the rehab center before eight. She had loved her job since she started three years ago, but lately, some of her patients had gotten her down. The boy she still had was the worst, he nearly always refused to do any of the exercises she had outlined for him and became belligerent when she insisted he must do them. She'd gathered from him but also the way his parents acted when they came to visit that he was a spoiled brat and got his own way every time he could. When she wouldn't give in to him, he made her life very hard while she was working with him. Many times she wished she could turn him over and give him a good swat on his rear, but he was not her child, only her patient and nurses couldn't do that to their patients, but oh, she could wish!

When she walked in the door to the time clock she was dreading her time in that young man's room. It was so close to eight o'clock that she had to stand in line to punch in. However, she momentarily forgot about him because there was a note on her card that said, "Nancy, come see me when you come in. Thanks, Dillon."

Scowling, Nancy pulled the note from her card and ran the card through the time clock. She looked at the time and hurried to the administration wing. Dillon's door was open a bit, so she knocked and walked in. "Hi, didn't you see enough of me the last few days? What's up?"

Dillon grinned. Waving to the chair across his desk, he said, "Have a seat for a minute. You weren't paying too much attention to me those three days, you know, but of course I wasn't paying much attention to you, either. That's not what I called you in about, anyway."

She settled in the chair and looked at him. "Lay it on me!"

"Remember when we were leaving Vansville on Saturday we commented on that big hole filled with water?"

"Yeah," she said, with a scowl. "I remember we commented about it and wondered what was going in there. Did you find out and really, what does it matter? It's in that podunky town."

"It's going to be a clinic there in Vansville. It won't open for several months, but I know you've dropped hints that you aren't as happy here as you once were. They're taking applications now for positions there and they need several nurses. The place won't be open on Sundays, so that'd be right up your alley. Want an application?"

Thoughtfully, Nancy answered, "Yes, I think I would. I'll pray about it first and see if it's something I should do. Thanks, Dillon for thinking about me, this time, unlike another time." She grinned at him mischievously.

Knocking himself in the head, he chuckled and said, "Give me a break, Nancy! Will you ever let me forget that I didn't ask you for that hike?"

"Maybe, some year I might." She laughed and held up the sheaf of papers. "Thanks for giving me a heads up about what's going in that hole in the ground. You have it right, I went on that hike so I don't get burned out, but with that kid I have now it's not too far away, believe me." She shook her head. "He is such a brat!"

"I hear that! Makes you want to tan his hide, doesn't it?" Dillon grinned, he saluted her and said, "See you again, Nancy. I'll keep you in mind if I organize another hike."

Nancy laughed. "Really, Dillon, don't do me any favors. I think I had enough hike for a while. Now if it had been sunny and warm like yesterday and today, I might have been more receptive. See you!"

"Yeah, break a leg out on the ward!"

"Mmm, thanks a lot, Dillon."

Nancy glanced at her watch and ran from the offices to her floor. She was in the building in plenty of time, but the charge nurse didn't care where you were if you were late coming on the ward or into the charge nurse office for report and it was now eight o'clock. Nancy breathed a sigh of relief as she ran behind the nurse's station desk the last person of her shift was reaching the door to the charge nurse office, so she stepped in behind her. Nancy was the one to close the door then she slipped quickly into the last chair. The day shift had the most personnel, so there were enough chairs for everyone to sit for report. Nancy pulled out her notebook, ready to listen for her patients. Even though she'd been gone for four days, she was sure who they'd be. It wasn't so much the patients as the room numbers. She'd had the same rooms for quite a while. She sat back to listen to the report on the other patients, hers were on the second hallway.

The night nurse started by saying, "You'll all be thrilled to know that we have doctor's orders to move Bill Kambro. He'll go as soon as papers arrive from the new facility."

"Bill!" Nancy gasped. "Why is he going somewhere? Surely he hasn't improved enough for discharge in the four days I've been gone!"

The night nurse chuckled. "No, that's for sure! We finally convinced his doctor that with his parents so close that they can visit so often isn't good for him. We're sending him to a rehab center in Atlanta. It's not that you haven't done your best, Nancy, but we've been fighting the parents constantly to do what we have been doing. I'm sure you know that! On Saturday it happened that the doctor came in while his mom was in the room and your sub was trying to do the exercises he'd ordered. He stood in back and saw first hand how Bill was acting when his mom was watching. It didn't take but five minutes for him to leave the room and come out to write the order. Needless to say, Mom and Dad are furious with us and the doctor."

Nancy clapped her hands softly and exclaimed, "Hurrah! I hope they can accomplish what we haven't been able to."

"That's what we've all been hoping for. That guy doesn't belong in a wheelchair the rest of his life, but with his parents interfering, that's where he'll be."

Nancy nodded. "That's the way I felt all along."

After report, the staff filed out of the charge nurse's office in time to see two EMT's going down the hall with a stretcher and turn into Bill's room. Only a few minutes later they came back out with a yelling Bill strapped to the stretcher, a woman, obviously his mom, weeping and trying to grab the man who was pushing the stretcher from behind. Another man, Bill's dad, was following closely behind his wife. He was also yelling and making loud threats and shaking his fists. Nancy ducked into the charge nurse's office she didn't want his parents to see her. They would know her, since she'd been his nurse most often and call down curses on her, as they had done so many times over the weeks that Bill had been her patient. Working with patients was challenging enough without dealing with family.

At the desk, Bill's dad stopped and pounded the desk in front of the charge nurse. "Listen, woman! You haven't heard the last from me! This'll be back to haunt you! You've no right to move my son to Atlanta where we can't come visit him daily!"

The woman was a bit older than the man, but she smiled sweetly at him, and said, "Mr. Kambro, it seems we can, now doesn't it? You and your wife have a good trip and get Bill settled down there, you hear?"

"Yeah!" He stomped from the desk the others hadn't waited for him. When he saw they had disappeared, he ran through the doors to catch up.

Nancy and her team hardly waited until the door closed behind the man before they danced and pumped their fists in the air, celebrating the discharge of the young man from their floor. He had been their patient ever since a few days after the new year, but had been one of their most obnoxious and uncooperative patients. His parents had never tried to encourage his cooperation, but taken his part, complaining constantly. They complained not only about the exercises and treatments, but also about the food and the care that he received, even though he was in a private room.

After leaving DeLord's house Sunday afternoon, Duncan had parked in his usual spot on Isabel's parking lot then walked beyond her last cabin to see the mess that had happened while he'd been gone. Because of all the rain on Friday and Saturday the place was a quagmire of mud but not much else. There were several pieces of heavy equipment sitting around, but it didn't look like they'd be used in the next day or two, since there were several inches of water in the deepest place. No one was there, of course, it was Sunday, so he couldn't learn too much about what was going on. He guessed, since it was so close to where he lived he'd learn soon enough.

However, before he left for DeLord's Monday morning, two pickup trucks pulled off the road right up to the edge of the mud. Duncan wasn't interested enough to investigate, but he wondered what they could do today. Granted, it had been sunny and fairly warm yesterday and it was sunny now, but it had been only twelve hours since he'd looked at the muddy mess. Surely they wouldn't try to move dirt today! He shook his head they'd probably expect their hourly wage just for standing around. He shrugged as he turned from the window and headed for his backpack. He supposed heavy equipment operators could do that and get away with it.

Duncan picked up his backpack from beside the door and before he opened the door, he reached over to the thermostat and turned the dial back to the lowest setting. He opened the door, pushed the lock in the door, and hurried to the SUV. After putting his backpack into the storage area, he got behind the wheel and headed out to the road. A car coming toward him was far enough back he turned in front of it. As he went down the street and the other car slowed coming into town, he noticed in the mirror that it was Neal. He waved and saw in the mirror that the other young man waved back. He liked the guy and was glad they'd be working together.

"At least it isn't some nurse from Blairsville," he grumbled under his breath.

As soon as the words crossed his lips he shook himself. He'd determined yesterday, as soon as Nancy left with her picture, that he'd put her out of his mind. He had, until he took a frozen dinner from his freezer and nuked it, then sat down to eat and almost bowed his head. He'd grabbed up his fork and stabbed the tasteless mashed potatoes. Later, he'd taken a shower and washed his hair. The unbidden picture of the soaked Nancy with her wet curls popped into his mind. He'd quickly banished that image. During the night, the siren of the hills had visited his dreams. He'd wakened in a sweat, wondering when he'd have to tell God he was a sinner. Just now he'd turned in front of a car and it had reminded him of her. Again.

He guessed Neal was about the same age as he and Ramon. From their talk yesterday, he figured he had a kindred spirit in the other man, he had no ties, although he lived with his parents, they had encouraged him to find his nitch in life. He loved to be outdoors and hiking seemed to be in his blood. Duncan was beginning to wonder if Ramon wasn't losing interest in the trail, now that he had Sandy. That thought renewed his own determination to stay unattached until the next millennium. Duncan wheeled onto DeLord's parking lot and pulled into his usual space, at least there was no curly-headed nurse ahead of him to take his spot.

Neal was right behind him and pulled in beside him. The two men took their backpack's from their vehicles and took them up to the office door. Ramon opened the door immediately and grinned at them. "So, you're both here ready for breakfast!"

Nodding, Duncan said, "You could say that."

"Sure am!" Neal exclaimed.

Stepping back, Ramon said, "Get in here! Sandy has coffee ready and she turned the eggs into the bowl. The last of the toast came out of the toaster and her mom sent a care package the other day with some of her homemade jelly. Believe me you have a treat in store! That woman can make jams and jellies to curl your hair!"

"Sounds like something I could go for!" Neal exclaimed.

Duncan entered the house and said, "That coffee always makes my stomach growl whenever I smell it. Lead on, boss man!"

Ramon grinned at his friend and slapped him on the back. "Sure! Just 'cause I'm the original and it's my house we leave from doesn't make me any more the boss."

Looking harshly at Ramon, Duncan said, "You didn't pull a fast one on me and have that sandy, curly headed vixen here, did you?"

Scowling, Ramon asked, "Who are you talking about?"

"The little vixen who was here for lunch yesterday!"

Ramon threw his head back and laughed. "No, she left before you yesterday, remember? Sandy says she must work all this week, but she's coming to the concert on Saturday."

"Great." Duncan grumbled. "Maybe I should stay away, I mean, I heard lots of what she'll play on Sunday. Nothing good can come from seeing that woman again. I swear! She's like Sandy, pushing somebody's buttons about God!"

"I heard that!" Sandy announced from the kitchen doorway. "You'd better not chicken out and not go since you know already that she'll be there!" Sandy grinned up at the giant. "You aren't afraid of her are you?"

Sticking his thumb into his chest, Duncan said, "Me? You talking about me being a chicken about some little nurse?" He brought his other hand up to smooth back his hair.

Sandy laughed and poked Duncan on the arm. "Yes, I would be talking about one big man who says he's not afraid of anything on the hiking trails. I do believe that one lady named Nancy has put fear and trepidation into your life."

Shaking his head, he said, "Surely not! I've put her out of my mind."

"Watch it, your nose may start growing, Pinocchio." As everyone pulled out chairs at the table and Sandy rolled to her place, she added, "Actually, Duncan, it couldn't happen to a nicer guy." Thoughtfully, she continued, "Although she probably wouldn't give you the time of day."

Scowling, Duncan asked, "Why?"

"Because you aren't a Believer!"

Being a blond, his cheeks turned red, but he still exclaimed, "Sandy! I'm not interested in that woman! She hounded my steps during the whole hike! She believes like you do, in all that creation stuff and a world-wide flood and… and insisting you must believe you're a sinner and God loves you! Come on! We're from two different camps completely. You know I don't believe all that!"

Sandy's face showed how serious she was, as she said, "You will, Duncan, I am convinced that the day isn't far away." Duncan had his mouth open to protest, but Sandy held out her hands and said, "It's time for Ramon to ask the blessing." She grinned at Duncan and said, "If we don't pray now and then eat, you'll be late getting on the trail, you know. Just like you were the other day and Nancy put a stop to your forward motion."

Ramon grabbed both Duncan's hand and Sandy's, then dropped his head, so Duncan and Neal finished out the circle and Ramon said, "Thanks, Lord, for this food. Take control of our hikes today and in the coming days. Keep us safe and bless every hiker who goes out from here today. In Jesus' Name, amen."

As the food went around the table, Neal asked, "Do you do that at every meal on the hikes?" He moved his hand around and added, "You know, pray?"

"No, I pray silently. Some of the groups we take are church groups and usually they'll say grace before the meals. Some of those groups even have evening devotions after supper."

Gulping past a sudden lump in his throat, Neal asked, "You have groups like that? People like that go on hikes?"

"Sure! Anybody who contacts us and wants what we offer, we take them. A group like that's what got me thinking last year. Between those groups and Sandy's persistence, I finally gave in to the Lord's prompting. I was injured on a hike I led of just such a group."

"You take all those, right?"

Ramon grinned and his eyes twinkled. "Not all the time, not this year."

The young man threw his head back and sighed, "Ah, man!"

Looking at Sandy and seeing her smile, Ramon said, "Both groups today are church groups. One I've had before, so I'm letting Duncan have them. We'll take the other group."

Duncan had taken a large gulp of coffee as Ramon spoke. He set his coffee mug down on the table with such a whack that several drops sloshed onto the table. He tried to swallow it quickly and said vehemently, "Thanks, buddy!" Looking at Sandy, he said, "Look, couldn't you have encouraged them to pick another time when I wouldn't have had to take them?"

Shaking her head, Sandy smiled and said, "No, this was the time they wanted. Ramon says they're a good bunch and won't give you any problems."

After another mouthful, Duncan glared at Sandy and said, "It'll be a problem if they have devotions every night!"

"You mean you'll be a chicken and run away? You're a big man, you're not afraid of anybody, are you? Why, I don't believe you'd run away!"

"Sandy, I swear, you're like that little conscience critter that sits on my shoulder and whispers in my ear all the time."

Laughing, Sandy clapped her hands. "I love it! I'm more convinced than ever that it won't be long for you."

"Sandy, cut it out!" Duncan warned.

Ramon grabbed the carafe from the coffee maker in the kitchen and brought it back to the dining room table. After pouring everyone's mug full, he said, "Come on, guys, we need to print out our maps. The groups'll be here soon."

Duncan stuffed the last mouthful into his mouth, grabbed his napkin and swiped it across his mouth, then pushed the chair back from the table. "I hope you're happy, Ms. Sandy. I hope I don't get indigestion from having to rush through my breakfast. By the way, tell your mom that jam is the best I've ever tasted!"

Sandy laughed and the sound followed him. "One day soon, Duncan, one day soon!"

The printer still ran when Sandy came to the office door on the last chime of the clock. A car drove onto the parking lot as the first stroke out of eight sounded from the clock in the living room. Duncan stood in front of the printer watching the papers spit out. As the last one finished, he grabbed them up and took them back to the desk, sorting out his from the few in his hand.

Ramon strode over to his wife in the doorway, so Duncan handed the other papers to Neal and said, "You may as well take these, he'll be occupied for the next couple of minutes. Aren't you glad we aren't tied up like that?"

Neal shrugged. "I don't know a pretty face could turn my head."

Duncan shook his head. "Not me! I'm a free agent and I intend to stay that way for a good long time!"

"So that Nancy who was here yesterday isn't a special person to you?"

Duncan glared at the young man. "How could you think that! Of course she's not! She spouts that religion stuff, besides, she's a woman."

"So?"

"I'm not about to get tangled up with a woman and **especially** not with a religious woman! No way, Jose!"

After a long, tender kiss and a loving hug for his wife, Ramon straightened and said, "You never know. That's what I said before August last year. That's when my assistant came and took over my office. It wasn't too long after that when she took over my heart and I couldn't seem to live without her." Looking at Duncan, he said, "You know, I couldn't be happier."

"I'm glad for you, but it's not for me!" Duncan said, dogmatically. "Deliver me from the wiles of a woman!"

"We'll see!" Sandy said, airily. "We'll see, Duncan!"

Seven

Soon, more cars pulled on the parking lot and the men went out the door. Sandy followed them and sat in the doorway watching the activity. Most of those on the parking lot were young people, but there was one man who seemed a bit older. He came over to Sandy and said, "Mrs. DeLord, I'm happy to see you again!"

"It's good to see you! So you're back with your group again this year?"

"Yes," he sighed. "They convinced me to take them, but I told them not so long a hike as last year, that's why we're going now."

Remembering that he'd been the leader who'd had to stay with the injured hiker last year, she said, "Have a fun time and no injuries this time."

"Believe me, I will keep that front and center all the time we're gone! We don't need a repeat of last year. My wife and I looked at the weather report and it's supposed to be nice for this whole time and I'm praying the weatherman's right."

"I agree with you there!"

Duncan stood nearby and heard the man's statement. He groaned this must be his group. How did he rate? The group he was to lead had a leader who prayed about the weather. "I'm lost," he grumbled under his breath.

Sandy watched them go and waved them off, then closed the door and went to the desk for the morning routine. She decided that word had gotten out quickly that now they had not two but three guides the slots were filling up fast for the rest of the spring and summer. The house was quiet and although the parking lot was full of cars, nothing moved on the lot. As far as she could tell right now, that's how it would be for the next three days. She smiled, though, because she'd have her husband home for several days after that.

After she ate a little lunch, she put the phone on immediate voice mail, went to the living room and put the little black pouch on the back of her chair. She had given two concerts in the little church in Vansville, but she was a bit nervous, because this concert was being given in a much bigger auditorium and many people she didn't know would be coming. However, she knew it would be good experience for the concert she had agreed to give later on in the summer in Atlanta. Derek Casbah had been persuasive after her last concert in Vansville and she had finally agreed to be put on the schedule for the Atlanta Symphony as a guest pianist.

Derek had promised to get her the music that she was expected to play for that concert. So far, she hadn't seen it. She practiced, but then she pulled out her easel, paints and the picture she had decided to reproduce. While the men were gone and when the house was quiet was a good time to paint. The gallery in Philadelphia was all sold out again and she needed one more canvas before she could send them another group. She also had a commission that she needed to start, but that would wait until after the concert.

The weather was nice for the three days of the hike and the men were glad, March could be so unpredictable. Of course, Duncan worried for nothing, the youth leader didn't expect him to attend the devotions he had each night with his group. Each night they camped in a large field so Duncan could escape quite easily, giving the excuse of looking for wood for the morning's fire. Every time he made that excuse he remembered when he'd taken Nancy's group.

Saturday finally came. As was her custom, Sandy went about her usual day, but didn't touch the piano. After lunch, she went in their den and spent time in prayer alone. Ramon never joined her for the first hour, then he knocked and Sandy invited him in, then they prayed together for another half hour. When that time was over, Ramon lifted her from her chair and held her on his lap. They talked quietly in between their kisses. As the hour drew closer, Ramon lifted her back to her chair and Sandy went to the piano to gather her music and put it into her briefcase. Ramon usually brought his notes and laid them on top.

After a light supper, which Ramon fixed, Sandy dressed in the new gown Ramon had bought for her especially for this concert. It covered her legs quite well for which she was glad. Unless she had on slacks she was very conscious of her legs, because they were quite thin and spindly, nothing like the rest of her body above her waist. The gown looked lovely, it matched her blue eyes and was made of shimmering satin. She had fallen in love with it as soon as Ramon had brought it from the box he'd had the saleswoman fold it into. Even so, Sandy didn't feel like she was anything special to look at, but she slaved over her hair, hoping to make the curls behave. She finished her preparations with a light touch of makeup.

Of course, Ramon took Sandy's breath away in his tux. He was so physically perfect from his hiking that his broad shoulders flowed perfectly into a narrow waist. The black tux, with its shiny lapels and stripes showed his well built physique and was complimented perfectly by his dark good looks. Of course, his jet black hair completed his person. Sandy never stopped wondering what he had ever seen in her when he told her he loved her. Of course she loved him with all her heart.

During Sandy's time of prayer, Ramon had taken the front passenger seat in the van and secured it behind the wheel. Sandy had insisted that she was too nervous to drive, so Ramon would take them, along with Isabel, Ruth and Duncan to the church. Many others, including the Casbah's and the Clemens were planning to come from Vansville to give moral support as well as to enjoy the beautiful music.

Sandy's briefcase, with all of her music, sat open on the chair beside the piano. Of course she had every piece memorized as she always did for a concert, but she planned to look everything over before the program and run through a few bars of each piece before she was to be on the platform at seven o'clock. Of course, she made sure her black pouch was in the briefcase along with the music. Ramon had also put his notes in as well. Even though he had done this several times before, he always kept notes with him. He had all the names of the pieces on his notes and a joke or two to fall back on.

At five thirty, Ramon raised the big garage door with the remote, then started the van and let down the lift. He held the briefcase that held the music while Sandy wheeled herself on the lift, then he put it up, but when it was half way up he stopped the mechanism and kissed his lovely wife. She smiled at him as he brought the lift level with the van floor. She wheeled herself off and he closed the door. Sandy went to the passenger spot and fastened her chair in place while Ramon went to the driver's side and climbed in, pushing the briefcase ahead of him.

Ramon closed the door, then looked at his lovely wife and smiled at her. Sandy held out her hand and Ramon quickly put the briefcase down in front of the console and took her hand. He knew from the other concerts and from looking at her face that she was a bit nervous. He also knew she had nothing to worry about, but he felt the slight tremor in her hand and squeezed it, then Sandy said, "Honey, will you pray? I really need that extra help from the Lord tonight."

Ramon found it hard to deny his wife anything, so he said, "Of course, Sweetheart. Father, God, be with my darling tonight as she gives this concert. You know she's a bit nervous right now, calm her and give her fingers the touch they need to play each note as it should be played." He took another breath and added, "And, Father, help me do a good job with being the MC, You know I'm never really comfortable with the role. In Christ's name, amen."

They raised their heads, Sandy squeezed his fingers and with a smile on her face, said, "Thanks, Honey. I love you."

"Darling, you know I love you. You'll do fine, I know."

Sandy sighed, but didn't respond, as Ramon knew she wouldn't, so Ramon pulled the stick down into drive and headed out of the garage. They went the few blocks through town and pulled on Isabel's parking lot, to see Isabel and Duncan standing together in front of Isabel's house. They were quite a pair, Duncan was a giant of a man, very well built and also quite handsome, now that one could see his face without so much hair on it. His hair was blond, no other color would describe it, both that on his head and his beard. He was dressed in what was probably his best clothes, black pressed jeans, a snow white T-shirt, a leather vest and black leather boots. Even for the end of March it was a bit chilly, but he wore no coat.

On the other hand, Isabel was a rather frail eighty year old lady, with many wrinkles and salt and pepper hair that she always wore in a loose bun at the base of her neck. She didn't even come up to Duncan's shoulder, but she had a commanding presence about her. She was dressed in her best Sunday coat and had obviously been to the hair dresser for a new do to honor the occasion. For an old lady, she was dressed very stylishly. Ruth was the image of her mother.

Ramon pulled up in front of them then from the driver's seat put the controls in motion to open the back door and lower the lift. When it was on the ground, Duncan helped Isabel on and Ruth stepped on, but he continued to stand on the ground until Isabel sighed and said, "Sonny, will you get on here! It'll hold all of us."

He gave her a grin that split the hair on his face and as he put his foot on the lift beside her, he said, "Yes, Ma'am!" Then Ramon brought them up.

When the lift was level with the van floor, Isabel and Ruth only had to duck their heads to get inside, but Duncan had to bend over because he was so much taller. They stepped off and the lift whined its way up to the closed position. The door made its slow trek across the opening and clicked shut. Duncan watched, this van always fascinated him.

As they walked the few steps to the back seat, Sandy exclaimed, "Duncan! I've never seen you so dressed up and handsome!" Her eyes twinkling, she switched her gaze to Isabel and said, "I bet it's because he knows Nancy's going to be there! What do you think, Isabel? They struck up quite a friendship on that hike."

Letting out a 'humph', Duncan sprawled onto half of the seat and exclaimed, "Sandy, don't even go there! I have not thought of that woman…" He remembered what Sandy said about Pinocchio's nose growing and let his words die on his lips. Quickly, he turned and looked out the window.

Shortly, into the silence she said, "Uh huh."

Ramon left the parking lot and Isabel, not knowing Nancy's name, said, "Sandy, have you heard from your friend? Will she be coming to the concert?"

"Yes, Nancy said she'd be there right on the front row to clap and cheer. She's already sure this is the best concert she's ever been to." Sandy sighed, "I told her she better hold judgment on that until after it was over."

"Girl!" Isabel exclaimed, since she was one of the very first to hear Sandy play, "I think she's right! I've heard you play both of the other times and when you lived in my cabin. I know you're the very best there is. Don't go putting yourself down. You know God gave you the talent and I'm glad you use it."

It wasn't hard for the others in the van to hear a loud sigh from Duncan. Under his breath, he muttered, "I shouldn't have come."

Isabel glared at him. "Sonny, don't even think like that! Of course you should. Not only should we support our own, but Sandy's the best and you know it!"

Duncan decided not to comment. He knew that both Sandy and Ramon knew why he'd said what he had, even if Isabel didn't.

"I'm glad we'll get there early, we can get those front row seats," Isabel said.

In a half hour Ramon pulled onto the church parking lot. He pulled up to the tiny ramp to the sidewalk and started the mechanism to open the door for the lift where he usually let Sandy off. From there a ramp went beside the walk all the way to the door at the side of the building. When the lift was in place, Duncan, Isabel and Ruth stepped on first. After they were off, Sandy had the briefcase on her lap and was ready when Ramon took the lift back up for Sandy's chair.

Many times the ushers had told Ramon to leave the van by the ramp, but Sandy didn't want to be treated any differently, so after she was off, he parked the van in a regular handicapped spot, then pocketed the keys as he walked back to the sidewalk where Sandy waited for him. He lifted the briefcase from her lap and they went up the ramp together.

The other three had already gone inside through the side door. Even though they had arrived well before time, there were already several cars on the parking lot, but the front doors hadn't been opened yet. Ramon and Sandy went to the side door where they usually went in and disappeared. They went to the children's meeting room. There was a tuned piano there and they had been assured that no one would bother them before the concert. Sandy took her music from the briefcase and Ramon found his notes.

Nancy had another Saturday off. She was surprised to have two Saturdays in a row, but she wasn't complaining, especially, since she wouldn't have gotten off until six thirty or so if she'd had to work. She was scheduled for Sunday, but her new patient that had replaced Bill Kambro was a Christian lady, she knew they'd share some time together in the morning that she would enjoy. She always carried a little white testament in her uniform pocket and she had seen the lady's worn Bible in a prominent place on her nightstand. She was glad the lady had replaced the spoiled boy.

She dressed carefully for the concert, planning to look her best. She didn't own a slinky black number that many women wore to concerts and such, but she put on her best Sunday dress. She would wear the coat her parents had given her for Christmas and matching heels and purse. As she did her hair, her mind flew to the man she'd met on the hike. She knew Duncan would be at the concert, but she assured herself that it was not for him she was taking so much care to look her best. Unless he sat on the front row, she would not sit beside him. Besides, she'd been so busy she hadn't thought of him but maybe every half hour while she was at work.

Her days off were another story.

It was after six when Nancy pulled on the street where the much larger church on the other side of town from where she lived was located. She came to an abrupt stop even before reaching the turn-in for the parking lot because there were quite a few cars ahead of her, all with their turn signals on to make the turn she wanted to make. There were many coming from the other direction planning to make the turn as well. When she finally reached the turn-in, there were many cars already on the parking lot and several men who were busily directing traffic. She was shocked, not realizing that Sandy was so well known. The man closest to the road smiled at her and motioned her on.

Nancy found herself several rows from the church. She quickly locked her car and headed for the church. She wondered if she could fulfill her promise to Sandy to sit on the front row, with this many cars in the lot, it might not happen. Just as she reached the walk and turned toward the front door, the side door opened and a giant of a man stood taking up the entire opening. Against her wishes, Nancy's heart did a flutter in her chest. The man's eyes were directed squarely at her. With as little motion as possible he signaled her to come up the walk to the side entrance, so she backtracked a bit and went toward him.

"Hi!" she said, a bit breathlessly, when she reached him. "I didn't realize there would be so many people who would get here this early."

"Hi, yourself," the giant said. "My mission today was to watch for you. I was emphatically instructed to make sure to bring you in this door and position you on the front seat." He sighed, "I guess I fulfilled my mission." He turned and motioned to a rather large empty place on the front pew. The person sitting at the edge of the space was an old lady with a grin that went from ear to ear.

Nancy was tempted to say, *But I'm not that big, I don't need that much space.* However, all she could make come from her mouth was the sound, "Oh."

Duncan followed her to the first bench and said, "Nancy, this is my landlady, Isabel Isaacson. Sandy instructed her to save you the seat and me to watch out the door for you. So I guess we've fulfilled her instructions now."

Isabel reached for Nancy's hand and said, "Deary, you're a lovely young lady. Sit by me so we can talk. That big oaf can sit here, but I intend to get to know you a bit this evening. Maybe you don't know that Sandy used to live in my first cabin when she came to Vansville." Looking at the big man taking the next step to sit in the space next to the aisle, she continued, "You know, she was my all time favorite renter. We struck up a special friendship right off."

Nancy left her hand in Isabel's and sat down beside her, as she said, "So you own those cabins right there as you're going into town?"

"Yes, those would be mine. You live here in Blairsville?"

"Yes, for now. I work at the rehab center here."

Scowling, Isabel asked, "What do you mean for now?"

"I understand there's a clinic going in there in Vansville and I've applied to fill one of the nurse positions."

Up to this point, Duncan had pretended to be engrossed in his surroundings, looking around watching the people come in, but when Nancy spoke about taking a position at the clinic, he leaned forward and exclaimed, "What?"

As he bent forward to stare into Nancy's face, Isabel waved her hand to shew him away and said, "Sonny, Nancy and I are having this conversation, you go on and mind the people around you who are coming in. We don't need any male contributions here."

Without acknowledging Isabel, Duncan said, "You've applied for a job at that clinic?"

"That's what I said, Duncan. Do you have a problem with that?"

Duncan cleared his throat, ran his fingers through his hair and swallowed. "But... but that place'll be right next to Isabel's land!"

Nancy turned back to look at Isabel and said, "Really?"

"Yes, that's so and since there isn't much choice of where to live in town and it's quite a ways from here in Blairsville to Vansville, I know it would be most convenient for you to rent one of my cabins. I do give a good rate by the month, you know."

"Why, that's very kind of you, Isabel, I haven't been accepted yet, but I'll keep your offer in mind and let you know if I do get the job."

Duncan nearly choked on his own saliva. Maybe he'd better start thinking about pitching a tent once that building was built! He couldn't seem to get away from Christian women! Isabel was his landlady, Sandy was his partner's wife and now Nancy had made application to work in the clinic coming in next door! If the beautiful woman sitting beside him moved in as one of his neighbors, in a cabin, he was a doomed man. He jumped up, as he said, "Excuse me I seem to have a catch in my throat. Isabel, where's the closest fountain?"

Giving him a scowl, she said, "Sonny, if you came to church once in a while you'd know it's in the Sunday school wing. But there's no time to hunt it up. You'd better sit down and clear your throat. Sandy and Ramon'll be on stage in a minute or two and you don't want to miss that first chord, even if it is 'Twinkle, Twinkle Little Star.' So sit yourself down now."

Obliging, he slouched back onto the pew with a long sigh. "Yes, Ma'am."

It wasn't but a few minutes later that Ramon walked onto the stage with his arm lovingly around the shoulders of his lovely wife as she wheeled herself to the piano. Neither of them had said or done a thing when the standing room only auditorium resounded with a standing ovation. People clapped and clapped. Finally, with his free hand, Ramon waved at the audience, but his smile stretched from ear to ear.

As Ramon and Sandy came onto the platform, Nancy heard clapping behind her, so she looked around to see that the entire audience had jumped up and were clapping. Her eyes turned to saucers as she jumped up. "Wow!" she murmured. "She hasn't even played anything yet!"

"Just wait," Isabel whispered back, "she's well worth every bit of what these people give her. She's played here at church sometimes and these people all know she's the very best."

"I heard her last Sunday while she practiced. She really didn't need to practice, but it was wonderful to hear her."

Duncan looked down at Nancy and scowled. "Hush, will you! You know you're being very disruptive."

Nancy sighed, "Duncan, she hasn't even started, nobody can hear me with the clapping."

Finally Ramon stepped to the mike, smiled and said, "Come on, folks, have a seat, you ain't heard nothin' yet!"

Good-naturedly, there was a soft chuckle throughout the auditorium as the people found their seats again. Ramon sat down behind Sandy and without any introduction, she began the two fingered introduction to Mozart's beautiful piece that most people know as <u>Twinkle, Twinkle Little Star</u>. The children started clapping as soon as they heard the first few bars of the piece, but the large room grew quiet as Sandy moved into the rest of the beautiful piece of music. Of course, that piece was Sandy's signature. Ramon introduced the next piece after the applause and the concert was underway.

The music filled the room and Nancy sat spell-bound as the music flowed from Sandy's fingers. She and the audience, were overwhelmed, there was no other word for it. When she'd been to Vansville and heard her on Sunday, Sandy hadn't played any piece completely, only the parts she felt the most uncomfortable with, but as she moved from one piece to the next, Nancy was convinced she had never been to a better concert. Sandy was indeed a master. It never crossed her mind that Sandy couldn't use her feet. When Sandy played a concert, Ramon always made sure the piano was situated so Sandy's little black pouch didn't show to the audience.

When Ramon introduced the intermission, he motioned Nancy to come backstage and she followed the two from the platform out of sight. The three of them hurried to the room where Ramon and Sandy had left their things. Nancy came to Sandy and hugged her. "You are awesome, Sandy! Your fingers fly over those keys!"

As Nancy stepped back from Sandy so they could look at each other, Sandy smiled at her friend. "Thanks, Nancy. I really love to play, so it's not a problem, but I'm glad people enjoy hearing what I enjoy so much. I'm glad you came." She grinned and added, "That big oaf isn't giving you a hassle, is he?"

Nancy laughed. "No, I don't even notice he's there while you're playing. He did try to escape when Isabel offered me a cabin to live in if and when I get the job at the new clinic. Isabel wouldn't let him go, though, she said you'd be starting soon and he'd better sit back down. He gave one of those defeated sighs and sat."

Both Ramon and Sandy laughed, but Ramon said, "He's something else!"

"So you're moving to Vansville?"

Nancy shrugged and said, "I don't know yet. Dillon gave me papers to fill out, so I put in an application the Monday after the hike to the new clinic that's going in. I haven't heard yet if I'm getting a job there. I won't mind, the clinic's not open on Sunday, which'll be good and the hours it's open aren't as long as I do at the rehab center. It's to open for July Fourth weekend, so I'll know fairly soon, I hope."

"How neat! That'll be great if you're that close. We can spend lots of time together," Sandy said, happily and grabbed Nancy's hand.

"Yes, that's true."

Those words barely left Nancy's mouth when there was a timid knock on the door, but the knob turned at the same time. A little head with auburn curls moved to the opening and a little voice said, "Ms Sandy! You played my favoritest piece! You played awesome tisday!"

Heidi ran into the room and as Sandy held out her arms, the little girl didn't hesitate she ran to the lady, put one foot on her footrest and clambered into her arms. She wrapped her hands around Sandy's neck and hugged her, but then leaned back and said, "Mommy said I can't gib you a kiss 'cause it'd hurt your makeup."

After Sandy kissed Heidi's cheek, she laughed and pulled the little girl away from her chest a bit. "Heidi, the only makeup I have on is a bit of lipgloss to cover these pale lips. Besides, you always rub your kisses in."

Her grin broadening, Heidi said, "So I can kiss you?"

"Of course!"

Heidi didn't waste any time she took Sandy's cheeks between her hands and gave her a big, slobbery kiss on her cheek, then rubbed it in with her hand. "Good, I not kiss you in a long time, Ms Sandy." Heidi slid from Sandy's lap and looked at Nancy. "Who be her, Ms Sandy?"

"That's my new friend, Nancy. Nancy meet my friend and special student, Heidi. Her last name pretty soon will be Clemens, but right now, it's Keys."

Nancy held out her hand and said, "I'm glad to meet you, Heidi. So you're one of Sandy's pupils, are you?"

"Oh, yes! I be really good. I play <u>Twinkle, Twinkle Little Star</u> right first time. I gots to play lots more since I learned that, though."

"Yes, you have," Sandy agreed. "Soon, we're going to have a concert that all my students will put on. We'll have that in Vansville, though."

"Oh, my!" Nancy said, "I bet that'll be great!"

"Uh huh, it be long, too. Ms Sandy gots lots of students."

The door opened again and Raylyn poked her head in and said, "Come on, Heidi, you need to let Ms Sandy and Mr. Ramon rest up a bit. There's more to the concert and it's going to happen in a few minutes."

"'K, Mommy. I comed now."

After the door closed behind mother and daughter, Nancy said, "She's precious!"

"Yes, she's Isabel's great-granddaughter. Raylyn, her mom and Vansville's pastor fell in love over Thanksgiving and got married after New Year's. Her daddy was killed in Iraq, so Roger's adopting her. They're a sweet family."

Only moments later an usher poked his head in and said, "Sandy, Ramon, the lights went down. I guess you're on in a couple of minutes."

"I'd better run!" Nancy jumped up and raced for the door. "I can't wait to hear the rest."

"Thanks for coming back," Sandy called after her.

When she found her seat between Isabel and Duncan, he looked at her and scowled. "So where'd you run off to?"

Nancy slouched into the seat between Duncan and Isabel. "Didn't you see Ramon motion for me to go backstage?"

Scowling, he looked at her and asked, in a voice that clearly showed he felt put-upon, "Would I ask if I'd known that's where you went?"

Nancy sighed, "No, probably not. I went with them to their dressing room."

"Great," he grumbled, "us peons gotta sit out here on these hard benches."

Her eyes twinkling, Nancy said, "I'm real sorry for you, Duncan. We were only in a big Sunday school room. There weren't any soft seats there, either, just straight backed chairs."

Lifting her program, Nancy said, "It looks like this is the last piece, so you'll surely survive until the end. Besides, this padded bench has to be softer than those hills and hollows you hike in and make camp in. I never knew ground, gravel and roots to be very soft to sit on."

"Listen," he groused, then lowered his voice and said, "she saves the longest piece until after the intermission, then there's always an encore. If we're not sitting here for another hour or so, it'll be a first, believe me."

"And you're complaining? She plays so beautifully it makes the time fly by. I haven't been to a more awesome time in my life!"

"Yeah, well…"

Ramon was at the mike and Sandy at the piano, so Isabel looked at the pair and put her finger to her lips. "Shhhh, you two, it's about to begin again."

"Yes, Ma'am," Duncan sighed.

As they clapped for the close of the number and continued clapping so that Sandy would play an encore, Nancy leaned over to Duncan and said, "So, Duncan, have you read any more in your Bible?"

"Woman, it's not *my* Bible. Isabel sticks one in every one of her cabins."

Nancy shrugged. "Okay, but the question still stands. You read any more in it?"

Scowling at her, not happy that she wouldn't drop the subject, he sighed a long sigh and said, "Yeah, I asked Isabel where that flood story was. She informed me it wasn't a story, it was part of history and that I needed to start at the front of the Book. She didn't tell me exactly where it talked about the flood, so I did start at the beginning. That's some book, that Genesis, if it's all true, that is," of course, he had to add that, because he felt ornery.

"Duncan, you know it's true! God was the author, but He used Moses to write it all down and God was the only one there in the beginning."

"If you say so." He turned his face forward Sandy was hooked to the piano ready to play an encore.

Isabel leaned around Nancy and glared at Duncan again. "Listen, you need to be quiet! She's about to play again."

He sighed again, "Yes, Ma'am." Then he looked at Nancy and aimed his thumb at her, then grunted, "She started it, though."

"No matter, Sonny, you talk louder."

Duncan sighed again and shook his head as Sandy began to play. Nancy had to chuckle, Duncan looked so put-upon.

Sandy and Ramon had joined the foursome when Derek Casbah came up, briefcase in his hand. "Ms Sandy!" he exclaimed, grinning. "You continue to out-shine yourself every time I hear you! Tonight was truly awesome! I'm glad you consented to play with the Symphony later on. They gave me the piano pieces they'd like you to play, so I brought them along tonight."

"I'm glad you brought them, Mr. Casbah, I was beginning to wonder."

He chuckled and laid his briefcase on the bench. "Wonder no more. By the way, Ramon calls me Derek, surely you can call me that, too."

Sandy gave him her lovely smile. "Thanks, I'll do that from now on." Still smiling, she said, "Mom taught me to call someone by their last name until they gave permission."

Opening his briefcase, while Ramon opened theirs, Derek pulled out a stack of music and said, "Here's all this. Have a fun time practicing."

Sandy laughed. "Thanks, I'll have to work really hard for my fingers not to tremble while I'm practicing, knowing what an audience there'll be."

"Listen, you have nothing to fear on that score!" Derek said, fiercely.

After the really heavy rains Vansville had in March right after the heavy equipment had dug the hole for the clinic, work began as soon as the ground dried. Most people in the town didn't know there were movers and shakers who lived in the small community, but these folks were determined to get a medical facility up and operating as soon as possible. Vansville was the largest town for many miles around. Soon, the hole was covered over and walls went up and Duncan had a front row seat to watch the progress. Each time when he came home from a hike he could see that something new had been done.

One day he had time on his hands, he'd gotten home in the late afternoon on a Tuesday and wasn't scheduled to be back on the trail until Thursday morning, so on Wednesday, he looked out during the day to see if someone was around so he could learn about the place. About eleven he saw a man standing beside the building with his hands in his pockets looking at the outside of the building, so he hurried out.

"Hi," he said, as he took long strides up the walk from his cabin. "So, did I hear it right, is a clinic going in here?"

"Yes, that's what it'll be. We're under a deadline, so we're working long hours. We aren't disturbing you are we?"

Duncan shook the man's hand, as he answered, "No, no! Not in the least. I'm gone most of the time. I was just curious. I saw the place when it was a flooded hole in the ground."

"Yeah, not a very auspicious time to get started."

Duncan smiled. "I saw two guys come the next day or so and I wondered what they could do in all that mud and water, but when I came back a few days later, I saw the slab, so it must have dried out pretty good."

"It did. Now the bosses have us on a deadline, so we're working our tails off to get done. They even got us a penalty if it's not done on time."

"That's the pits! Well, good luck, I hope you meet your deadline."

"I'm pretty sure we will. Sometimes I have to light a fire under some of those subcontractors, but we'll get her done. Say, you wouldn't want a job, would you?"

"No, I'm a hiking guide and I've been pretty busy this spring so far. I only have today off and I'm back on the trail tomorrow. But thanks anyway."

The man shrugged. "Can't blame a guy for trying."

"Absolutely!"

Life was good hikes went out the weather improved, even in April, the month known for rain. Once it became the middle of April, the hikes started lengthening and now Ramon, Duncan and Neal couldn't eat breakfast together before they left on their hikes, because some hikes were longer than others. Word must have gotten out that DeLord's Hiking Services had expanded, because none of the three men had much free time. Sandy's phone rang daily with people wanting to schedule hikes. She was glad for the computer program she'd learned, because it was much easier to keep the schedules straight for the three men. However, she'd had a secret wish that with Neal joining them that Ramon would get more time off, but obviously it was not to be, at least not this soon in the hiking year.

On a rare morning off, Ramon lay in bed beside his wife, holding her and savoring the moments together. After their good morning kiss, he said, "You know, with three of us doing the hikes equally, we need some sort of pay schedule. I don't think I should keep so much of the money, when the other guys do just as much. It's not like I take harder hikes or anything. Love, is there something on that program you have on the computer that we could work up for the finances for this business?"

"I think there is." She looked at him fiercely and said, "But I'm not even looking today! You're off only today and we're going somewhere where the phone doesn't ring, the computer doesn't boot up and there aren't any hikers so we can be just the two of us."

Ramon chuckled. "I know, Love. We promised ourselves this day to spend together just as we wanted. We'll let the answering machine pick up starting now and you can listen to the messages tomorrow after I'm gone."

Laying her hand on his chest, she said, "I will and I'll figure out something for the finances. Do you want to divide everything by thirds?"

Looking at her fiercely, he said, "Sweetheart! Of course not! You're in the equation, too. Besides, both men are single and they surely don't need what we need to run the business. I tell you what, since it's our house that's the base of operations and you're the executive secretary, we should divide all that comes in by four and a half. The fourth is yours and the half will pay the new mortgage and expenses. That should work out about right." He pulled her close and gave her another kiss. Loving the feel of his wife in his arms, he said, "Mmm, did I tell you yet this morning that I love you?"

She giggled. "No, Honey, you've been too busy talking about money."

"That stops now! I love you."

"Oh, Honey! I love you too, so much!"

"Good, let's savor that for a while."

"Yes, Honey, I'm all for that."

As spring came in full force, Sandy was glad for Nancy. Whenever she had a free day, she came out to Vansville. Usually, she glanced at the progress on the new clinic, but then she'd drive on to Sandy's place and spend either the day or the afternoon. Several times when she came for the day, Sandy had her van loaded with a picnic lunch and all her painting supplies. The two women would take off for parts they hadn't seen before and they'd enjoy the day in the hills and mountains close to Vansville.

Duncan tried his best to not be around when Nancy came. After the concert and for several weeks in April he'd been on a trail when she came, but one Saturday a car slowed coming into town and Duncan wasn't aware how slowly it was coming until he was ready to turn onto the street and realized he'd waited for Nancy. He nearly hit the steering wheel in frustration when he had to follow her to DeLord's. That was definitely not the way to avoid her!

Nancy had been to DeLord's enough times that she knew what spot Duncan usually took, so when she saw who was behind her and when she reached the parking lot and saw the empty space, she pulled on the lot, but took another spot. However she was on the lot when Duncan came around to the back of his van to pull out his backpack. She walked up and smiled, as he opened his back door to retrieve his pack.

"Hi," Nancy said, "I haven't seen you since the concert."

"True," Duncan said, not willing to let on that he'd tried very hard not to see her.

Giving him a smile that covered her face, she exclaimed, "I got some good news! You're the first person I can share it with!"

"Oh?"

"Yeah! Dillon called me in his office yesterday and said I got the job at the clinic when it opens here in Vansville. I think I'll stop by Mrs. Isaacson's this afternoon and see about renting one of her cabins."

Duncan's eyes turned glassy and he muttered, "Oh, great!"

"Yeah, I think it is!" she exclaimed. "I've had some really obnoxious patients in the last couple of weeks at the rehab center and I can't wait to be out of there."

"So when does the clinic open? It's not ready yet, is it?" *Maybe it'll be after October and I can be gone,* he thought.

She walked over so she wouldn't have to speak so loudly. "They want it open for the Fourth of July holiday. Lots of statistics claim that's a busy time for tourists and people to get hurt. The staff must be there the week before the Fourth for orientation and stuff. The guys that are funding the project are offering the builder an incentive to have it finished by then."

"Huh, how about that." *Talk as little as possible to the woman, Roads, she can't affect you much that way.*

Looking at the huge pack Duncan pulled from his SUV, she said, "You're leading a hike today, I see."

"Yeah, and you?"

Nancy chuckled. "I'm not leading a hike, but weather today is super for one. I have the day off, so I'm here to help Sandy with stuff. She and I'll go for a drive this afternoon. She hasn't mentioned anything spectacular happening, so I guess the hikes are business as usual?"

"Yeah, you could say that, I guess. Of course, we never take anything for granted. You put amateurs on a trail in woods and mountains and the leader has to be on his toes. Especially if it rains." He set the pack on the edge of the storage area and opened a side pocket. He pulled out a cellphone and said, "I've invested in one of these, one never knows when some mishap will befall and I don't want to be left on the trail with no way of getting in contact with someone as soon as possible."

Nancy nodded. "I can understand why that'd be an essential part of your gear. Nobody ever wants something bad to happen on a hike, but things do happen and many times they happen against all odds. Sandy hasn't told me of anything bad happening this year so far, but since you got a cellphone, have you had a mishap?"

Stuffing the phone back in the pocket, he said, "No, not so far, but it's better to be prepared. Ramon had an accident last year when one of his hikers fell and broke a leg. Another hiker had her cellphone, it saved the day. So tell me, if we do have something bad happen on a hike, would I call your clinic after you open or the person that Ramon contacts and I have programmed into my phone in case of emergencies."

"You'd better call that number. We'll be for local people and we won't have any type of rescue equipment. The helicopter will have to come from Blairsville like it has been."

Duncan nodded, turning toward the office. "It appears charged up, ready to go." Duncan shrugged. "I wondered, can't hurt to ask, especially when it's someone who'll work there."

As they turned toward the office and started across the lot, Nancy said, "No, that's true. Probably it'll be some time before this clinic'll be equipped for receiving helicopter patients. Of course we'll have an emergency area. That's what most clinics handle most often." Just before they reached the door to the office, she grinned, her eyes twinkling and asked, "Been with any church groups lately, Duncan?"

"You would have to bring that up, wouldn't you?" he groused and stood the pack up against the wall beside the door into the office.

"Well, have you?"

He made a face and grumbled, "As a matter of fact, the one that's coming today is some youth group that got their feet wet on Ramon's hike last year and really had a good time. I told Sandy to save them for him again, but they didn't want his slot, they wanted this time." He sighed, "So I get the chore."

She grinned at him. "So are you gonna chicken out, as Sandy says, when they bring out their Bibles for devotions after supper?" Putting her finger on her cheek, she said, "Don't I remember you ran away on our hike when I was the only one who pulled out my Bible?"

He sighed, as he grabbed the handle on the stormdoor of the office. "Listen, I've had about enough religion shoved down my throat this spring by both you and Sandy to last me a good long time. I enjoy the great out-of-doors, I'll think of something to take up my time while they have devotions."

She turned to open the door into the office, but she smiled and said, "Like I thought, a great big chicken. You know, the saying goes something like this: 'The bigger they are, the harder they fall.'"

Duncan made no comment, just stood back while Nancy walked in. He closed the door and went immediately to the desk and booted up the computer, while Nancy went on into the house. When she'd shut the door behind her, Duncan grumbled, "I knew there was a good reason I'd worked so hard to avoid her!" *Really? So you are that great big chicken that nice girl, Nancy just called you!* That little voice from his shoulder sounded like Isabel.

When Sandy saw Nancy in the hallway, she exclaimed, "Ah, my friend Nancy! You're here! That's great. I thought it was Duncan and I have a mug of coffee for him. Could you run it down to him? He'll be so appreciative, I know." she finished, tongue in cheek.

Nancy took the large mug of rich smelling, brown liquid and turned back the way she'd come. She opened the door to the office while Duncan was still grumbling. "So now you talk to yourself?" Nancy asked, cheerily.

Not looking at her, because he was busily striking the keys on the computer, he said, "I'm told it's not a bad thing unless you answer."

"Yes, I've heard that, too. Sandy sent me back with a mug of coffee for you. It smells really good, you know."

Eight

Holding out his hand, but not looking at her, he continued to press computer keys, but Nancy stood just out of reach and didn't stretch out her hand. After several minutes when nothing connected with his hand, Duncan sighed and turned toward her. "What is this? You'd better not want me to sing for my coffee!"

"Nope, just eye contact."

On another sigh, he looked at her and said, "You got it, woman. Give me the coffee! I ate breakfast at the cabin, but I always have another cup after I get here. She makes the best coffee in north Georgia."

"I've heard that before. If the smell's anything like the taste, it's great!" She handed the cup over and said, "Duncan, God forbid that you do, but if you were to die on that trail, where you'd go for all eternity wouldn't be a place of happiness, or even as beautiful as the scenes along the trail, only torment, forever!"

Turning his back on her, he continued to hit keys, perhaps even faster than before and said, "Woman! I'll take my chances!"

Knowing she'd said enough, Nancy turned and headed back into the hallway, closed the door leaving Duncan alone. He was so angry, he put the mug to his lips and took a mouthful, then nearly spat it back into the mug it was so hot. He took his other hand from the keys and fanned his open mouth. "That woman!" He fanned his mouth again. "She makes me so mad! I will never get her out of my hair! She'll be living next door!!"

He set the mug down on the desk, disgusted and typed in more information. He clicked the mouse to start the printer and heard car doors slamming on the parking lot. He gingerly put his lips to the rim of his mug, but the steam didn't burn his nose, so he drank several swallows. The leader knocked on the door and Duncan took the mug with him as he went to answer. He took a deep breath before he answered the door; there was no need for him to take his frustration out on his innocent group leader.

The man looked up at Duncan and said, "Sandy said that Duncan Roads would be leading our group. Would that be you?"

"Yes, I'm Duncan. I need to collect my papers from the printer and I'll be right out. Tell your crew to get their packs on we'll leave in a few minutes."

Nodding, the man said, "I'll get them on the move."

Before Duncan got the door shut, his eyes fell on the car parked next to his on the lot. Nancy's words came back to haunt him, *God forbid that you do, but if you were to die on that hike, the place where you'd go for all eternity wouldn't be a place of happiness but of torment forever.* He closed the door behind the group leader and mumbled, "I will not die on this hike!"

Sandy and Nancy had heard all the doors slam, so as Duncan was collecting his papers from the printer, the office door opened and Sandy wheeled herself through with Nancy right behind her. Duncan wouldn't look at either one of them, as he set his empty mug down on the blotter on the desk and turned toward the door. He had a group to lead, a backpack to hoist onto his back, why look at two women inside?

"Duncan," Sandy said, "we'll be praying for you to have a safe hike. It's supposed to be nice weather while you're gone, but who knows?"

"Yup, April showers bring May flowers. My gramma told me that little bit of wisdom when I was barely out of diapers. We'll be careful, don't worry. I'm sure we'll be fine and enjoy the flowers along the trails. You know you're sending me with this church group, I'm sure they'll have lots of prayers to spare."

Nancy shook her head. "There's never too many, Duncan."

He had his hand on the doorknob, but he turned back and said, "Why do you women pick on me for your prayers? You know, I was fine last year and the year before without all this religion and prayer stuff."

"Because, we know you need them, Duncan. Be safe." Sandy said, as the door closed behind the big man.

Looking at the door, Nancy said, "Maybe I was too hard on him."

Before she could respond, the phone rang and Sandy had to answer. When she finished with the call and entering the information into the computer, Sandy said, "You know, I don't think you can ever be too hard on a non-believer about his soul, Nancy."

Nancy was at the window, watching as the hikers and Duncan shouldered their packs. None of them knew she was watching and she didn't call attention to herself by waving or opening the door. However, she did see the group gather around Duncan and everyone bow his head. She had to smile, he'd get some more exposure to Christians whether he wanted to or not.

Sandy turned from the computer and smiled at her friend, as she switched the phone to the answering machine. "I have some errands to run, but then we can have our picnic and spend the afternoon going around the countryside. With such beautiful weather today it'll be great! I love spending time with you."

"I saw that big box, is that going to the post office?"

"Yes, actually, I have two boxes for the post office. One's going to the Philly library and the other is going to one of my aunts who lives outside Philly. A friend of hers saw the picture I painted for them for Christmas and she wanted something I painted from the scenery around here, so I have that ready to go, too."

"Great! Have you looked into displaying your paintings around here?"

Sandy sighed, "Nancy, I'm so busy supplying the library in Philly and doing commissions I can't imagine taking on another gallery! Soon after I left Philly, I did think of looking for a local place, but that one up there sells out even before I can get more to them and they told me when they found out I'd moved that that was no excuse, they wanted my pictures in their gallery." Shaking her head, she continued, "If Ramon were here more he'd probably be bored with all the time he had, because I'm so busy. Besides my painting, I have all my piano students and they keep me hopping, too. Actually, I do have all these pictures here and I sell quite a few from here in the office."

As they left the office, Sandy said, "The last time I was to Isabel's I saw that the building next to her place was finished outside. Have you heard about that new job?"

With a grin, Nancy said, "Yes! I'm so thrilled! Dillon called me in yesterday and told me I got the job! If all goes as planned, we're to be at the clinic for orientation the week before July fourth. I need to see Mrs. Isaacson to get a cabin. I don't want to commute from Blairsville and besides, it sounds like the cabins are bigger than the little efficiency I live in now. Duncan described his, it sounded bigger than what I've lived in for so long."

Sandy clapped her hands and exclaimed, "Cool! I need to get those packages mailed, but as soon as we do, we'll come back by and stop so you can talk with her. It's this time of year her cabins get booked, so you'll need to get your needs in now. Nancy, I'm excited for you!"

"Yes, so am I! Dillon told me what the pay is and it's more than I make at the rehab center and the hours have to be better, because the place isn't open twenty-four-seven and it's closed on Sunday. I'll get every Sunday off, at least."

Glad to make his escape from Sandy and Nancy, Duncan closed the door and snagged his backpack from beside the door. It was huge, but he hoisted it up and slid his arm behind the strap, then worked his other arm behind the other strap. The young people in the group were huddled together, all with their packs on their backs. The leader also had his pack in place and was looking at Duncan.

"So," he said, "A couple of things before we set out. Everyone has a place to sleep under cover and you all have rain slickers and hiking boots, just like our literature says. Since your leader led a group last year, I'm sure you know."

"Yes," Tom, the leader answered. "Those were the requirements along with hiking boots. I was on that shale last year; tennis shoes don't cut it on that stuff."

"That's true. We won't go across shale this trip, but hiking boots are the best footwear, of course." He looked at the eight young people and said, "Lets get a move on and enjoy this beautiful day!" He grinned at the group and added, "You know, it's April, so we can't expect that this beautiful weather'll hold. It could rain before we get back, one never knows."

"Umm," one young man said, "Could Tom pray before we leave?"

Duncan swallowed a sigh and said, "Sure, be my guest."

Not knowing if all the hikers would bow their heads, Duncan did, but didn't close his eyes, as Tom said, "Father, God, we pray for our hike. We desire that You take us safely from this place and go with us each step of the way until we return in a few days. Be with Duncan as he leads. Keep each of us in the palm of Your hand. We pray this in Jesus' Name, amen."

Duncan did sigh as he turned toward the trail. The man had prayed for him. Surely he was all prayed up for years to come!

One of the boys was smaller than the other four boys on the hike and Duncan noticed that Tom fell in with him as they started out. He wondered why the special treatment until he heard the boy call the man 'Dad', then he knew. The boy was probably barely old enough to qualify for the group and dad was excited to have him go. Duncan sighed again. He hoped the boy wouldn't be a whiner but would keep up with the rest of the group. For some reason, that brought to mind Nancy's group and the man who was a real whiner. He hadn't been younger or smaller, but he'd been a pampered guy who wasn't used to much physical activity. He'd often wondered why the guy had gone on the hike in the first place. He set off at a brisk walk and the others fell in behind him. After all, it was a beautiful day and in the hills it was cool.

The girls piled into Sandy's van and she hit the remote to open the garage door. No one had ever parked in front of the garage door, but Ramon had posted a big sign on the door that there was positively no parking in front of it. Sandy didn't start up until the door was all the way up, then she drove out and closed the door. It was April, the sun shone and Sandy smiled.

She drove to the post office. Sandy let Nancy take the large package, while she took the smaller one on her lap and they went in. The postmaster wasn't busy, so he saw them coming and exclaimed, "Ms Sandy! Have you got more pictures to go out today? I do believe you're one of the busiest women I've ever met!"

"Yes, Granger, I have two packages. One's to go to the gallery and the other goes to my aunt. A friend of hers commissioned me to send her a painting I'd done of a scene from here in Vansville. She's not satisfied with stuff there in Philly." She grinned. "Her words were, 'Things around here are a dime a dozen.'"

"I'm with her, nothing around Philadelphia could possibly compare with the views we have around here." The man took the big box from Nancy and put it on his scales. "Say, did you hear that the clinic'll open over Fourth of July weekend?"

"You know, Granger, my friend here told me this morning because she's going to be one of the nurses there."

"What do you know! Well, miss, I'd say you'd better get yourself over there to see Isabel if you're wanting a place to live. She'll be booked up real soon."

Nancy nodded. "We're going over there from here. I'm excited to move here to Vansville. I've met Mrs. Isaacson and I'm hoping she still has a place I can rent."

The man smiled at Nancy. "If anybody can get a favorable response from Isabel it's that lady right beside you. Believe me, she's our town's darling."

"Granger, will you get on with putting the postage on that package! We have places to go and people to see!" Sandy scolded.

Chuckling, Granger put the postage sticker on the box and said, "Yes, Ma'am!"

Soon, they were back in Sandy's van and she drove to Isabel's office. She parked as close to the walk as she could, but then she said, "I can't go in her house, as you can see, because of her steps. She'll probably come out when she sees me here."

Only moments later Isabel came onto her porch and Sandy called, "Isabel, I got a potential renter for you. Have you got a long term opening?"

Nodding, Isabel held up one finger then disappeared into her house. Soon she was back with a wad of keys in her hand and came down the steps. Nancy opened the passenger door as Isabel came toward the van on her sidewalk. "I sure do! Is it our friend from the concert?"

"It sure is, Isabel! She got word yesterday that she got the job at the new clinic, so now she needs a place to live."

Nancy came around to Sandy's open window and asked, "You'll be okay while I go with Mrs. Isaacson?"

"Of course! Go on! My chair doesn't fit in most of them anyway."

Isabel looped her arm with Nancy's and said, "Come on, Deary, let's get you hooked up with a cabin. By the way, nobody knows me as Mrs. Isaacson, you must call me Isabel, like everybody else."

"Thank you! I'd love to call you that."

"So when do you want this place, Deary?"

"I was told I needed to be ready to start at the clinic the week before the Fourth, so I plan to resign where I am on June fifteenth. I'm not sure how much packing up I'll get done before then, but I'll move within the week."

Nodding at one of the cabins, Isabel said, "That one's the one Duncan rents from me. How close do you want to be to the clinic?"

"It really doesn't matter, Isabel, it's just over there."

She skipped the one next to Duncan's and took Nancy up the walk to the next one. "Okay, let me show you this one and see if you like it. Actually, except for that very first one, all my cabins are the same size and the insides look alike. Of course, they're all furnished, since most of the time I rent to overnight guests."

Looking at the rustic cabin with the porch across the front, with two wicker chairs and a tiny wicker table between them, Nancy said, "Isabel, this has to be a dream place! Just from looking at it I know it's lots bigger than what I'm living in now." They walked up the steps and Isabel opened the door then motioned for Nancy to go in.

Smiling at the young woman, Isabel asked, "So, what do you think?"

Nancy clapped her hands together then covered her mouth with them. Her eyes shining, she exclaimed, "Isabel! This is beautiful! I love it! It'll be perfect for me. Everything is in such good shape, not anything like where I live now."

Without saying anything else, Nancy looked around at the large living area. There was a couch and two upholstered chairs grouped around a fireplace. An entertainment center sat beside the fireplace with a TV on top. Over to one side was a small table with chairs and a small kitchen behind it. The kitchen was in a corner and had a window facing the beautiful mountains in the distance. Another window looked down on the table. Across the back were three doors, so Nancy went to explore.

The door beside the kitchen led into a nice sized bathroom and in one corner was a washer and dryer stacked on each other. Nancy exclaimed, "Isabel, how super! I'll be able to wash my uniforms right here!"

"Yes, Missy, as I get ahead a little, I'm getting a set for each cabin. The next set goes in Duncan's cabin. That poor boy comes back from his hikes and has to take his stuff to the Laundromat down the street. So, you haven't seen it all, keep on."

Nancy clapped her hands again. "Isabel, I'm so excited! Maybe I'll quit earlier so I can come live here sooner."

Isabel laughed. "Now Missy, no sense in doing that. Working is important when you're young and single."

Nancy moved to the next door. She opened it, anxious to see every square inch of the lovely cabin. Behind it was a huge closet. There were rods for hanging clothes and a large dresser at the far end. There was also another door that led into the last room which was in the opposite corner of the building. Nancy walked into that room from the closet and looked around at the large, cheery room.

"Isabel, I've never had such a huge bedroom! This is the best place I can't wait to start living here. Do you have a contract I can sign or what?"

Smiling, Isabel chuckled at Nancy's enthusiasm. "Missy, I only rent these by the month, but of course you can keep renting them as long as you want, just so you let me know a day or two early. Let's go back to the office where we can sit down and have a glass of tea. We'll get you all signed up in no time."

It wasn't long before Nancy came bouncing out of Isabel's home with a huge grin on her face. She circled Sandy's van and hopped into the passenger seat. As she clicked the seatbelt in place, she exclaimed, "Sandy! I've never lived in something so huge before and the rent isn't any more than I'm paying for the little room they call an efficiency apartment back in Blairsville. She's got my name in the slot for that cabin starting June twentieth and I can't wait."

"I'm so happy for you, Nancy! When you walked down the sidewalk, she pointed to another one. Why was that?"

Nancy giggled. "That's Duncan's cabin. I'm not next door, but two doors away. Think he'll stay or move out?"

Sandy chuckled. "If he doesn't want to pitch a tent someplace else, he'll have to stick it out. The clinic's the only building project in town that I know about."

Nodding, Nancy said, "I'll try to curb my assault on him when he's home."

Sandy grinned at her friend conspiratorially. "Don't do him any favors!"

The sun was definitely slanting in the west, sending long rays across the path as Duncan led his hikers up onto a small plateau. This was a high spot in the area and you could see for miles, but there was also a small pond that had to be either rain fed, or a spring, he and Ramon hadn't had time to research it. It had to be one of those two, since water doesn't flow up hill. He hadn't said much to the group all day; just to tell them when to stop for lunch and breaks. He'd found from past experience that teens didn't mingle too much with strangers and Tom was occupied with his son a lot. Duncan didn't feel much like talking with them, his dealings with Sandy and Nancy this morning wouldn't leave his mind. He shook his head; he couldn't be preoccupied like this. He would not admit it was the words they'd said that were truly haunting him. He'd been dealing with that little critter on his shoulder most of the day.

They came from the trees onto the little meadow and Duncan said, "We have arrived at our destination for tonight. You guys need to start pitching the tents and girls, fixing supper falls on you. I'll get the fire going."

There were four groans, two from girls and two from the guys. Duncan turned toward the two male groaners and grinned. "Putting up tents can't be that bad."

"Yeah, if you never done it before," one boy admitted.

Duncan grinned at the boy, "Pair up with someone who knows, you'll be on it soon. I'll let you in on a little secret, guys are supposed to know that kind of stuff. Girls really go for guys that are in the know." He winked at them.

"Maybe," one of the guys said, dubiously.

One of the girls dropped her backpack and went back into the woods. She was gone for several minutes, but when she came back, she asked Duncan, "Is that little pond what we use for water tonight?"

"Yup, that would be our water source tonight. Take your filtering device and your pan over there with you. It's good clean water, but one can never be too careful, since we don't know what's in it."

"Could we swim in it?" another guy asked.

"Sure, if you're a member of the polar bear club. Remember we're in the mountains of north Georgia and it's only April. And…" he added, "it's all rain water or maybe even a spring. Either way it'll be cold and as cool as it's been this spring, I'm sure there's not a drop of warm water in it."

"Yeah, I guess that's right."

Tom chuckled as he looked at his group. "Sorry, folks, no hot showers tonight. You'll have to be satisfied with warming water over the fire. In the morning it'll only be cold water to splash on your faces to wake up." He gave the group a big smile. "But then, that's what camping's all about, isn't it?"

One girl visibly shivered. "I'll pass."

Tom looked at his kids and saw their backpacks on the ground, but no one was moving. He clapped his hands and said, "You heard Duncan, let's get to our chores, time's wasting!"

Without a word, the boys unfastened the tents from the backpacks and the girls rifled through the packs for the packets to make the stew they were to have. Duncan, of course, wasted no time, as soon as he had his backpack off he left the group to scour up bushes and limbs for his fire. The girls had barely opened the stew packets when Duncan had a roaring fire going.

The girls were obviously not as adept at fixing the meal as the guys were at putting up the tents. The tents were long up and there was no good smell coming from the pans by the fire, even though they'd started their chores at the same time. Tom came to help the girls and the guys set off to do some exploring without their packs. Duncan was trying to keep an eye on everyone, but it was hard when the guys slipped into the woods

About fifteen minutes later those in camp heard a scream and Duncan was on his feet, with Tom right behind him, racing toward the sound. Duncan's eyes zeroed in on the pond and "What the… What's going on?" his voice boomed across to the other side where the boys were all gathered around a large rock overlooking the pond.

Tom never broke stride. He raced on around the pond toward the group of boys. "Alex!" he called, at the top of his lungs. "What's happened?"

Duncan had figured out during the day that Alex was Tom's son. He kept moving but looked at the faces of those standing on or beside the rock, but Alex's face was not among them and he knew the boy was not at the fire. His heart gave a lurch; Alex was the smallest of the hikers and also the one with the least amount of meat on his bones. If he was in the water, he could be chilled to the bone in no time. That could prove very dire consequences for the boy.

Because his legs were longer and he was more in condition than Tom, the men arrived at the same time. "Where's Alex?" Tom asked, breathless, looking at the boys. "I don't see him!"

One of the teenagers pointed to the water. "He, umm, fell in." Another boy looked very guilty, but didn't add anything to the statement.

"He doesn't swim very well surely he wouldn't get that near the water!" Tom persisted, tears clogging his throat. "He **fell** in, you say?"

Duncan didn't stand around to talk. He felt his adrenalin spike instantly. The minute he heard that Alex had fallen in he pushed two boys out of his way and took another step closer to the water. The water was so clear it was easy to see Alex was thrashing toward the top, but he wasn't getting far very fast. His lips, even through the water, were blue and his eyes were open, his stark fear reflected in them. Duncan sprawled on his stomach and moved as far out from the bank as he could, then plunged his hand into the fridged water. He connected with Alex's small hand and pulled.

As the boy moved toward the bank and Duncan backed up, he yelled. "Somebody get a couple of sleeping bags and get them over here NOW!!"

The group of gawkers fled at the sound of Duncan's voice. Tom was the only one to stay and he grabbed his son the second Duncan hauled him from the water. The boy was shaking from head to toe, his lips were blue, his eyes glassy and fixed. Even dripping wet, Tom wrapped his arms around him and held on tightly.

Duncan shook the water from his arm, then after several attempts to get his attention, Duncan finally shook Tom's shoulder and said, "Put him down on the ground, the boys are almost back here with some bags. We'll have to wrap him up, but we'd better make sure he's breathing and nothing's clogging his airway first, Tom."

Tears rolled down Tom's cheeks, as he finally relinquished his son to Duncan who carefully laid him on the ground. He turned Alex's head to the side, ran his finger around in his mouth, then pressed on his chest.

Instantly, a gush of water projected from his mouth and one of the boys, who was coming with a bag was in the way and his pantleg was soaked in seconds.

"Oh," the boy squealed and jumped sideways to get out of the way of any more.

Duncan still pressed on the boy's chest, but he said, "Open up two of those all the way and lay them one on top of the other. Open another and have it ready. At least one of you'll have a wet sleeping bag tonight or else you'll sleep without one. Tell me the truth, boys, did Alex fall or get pushed. I'm not sure you are all completely aware what a serious situation we have, but Alex could have drowned. Still he can be so chilled that he'll get pneumonia If he develops any symptoms, we'll have to send him out and the rest of you'll have to return home."

There was a long silence. The girls had come back with the guys and were standing behind all the boys. Even they were quiet, looking over their shoulders toward Duncan. "I'm waiting for an answer," Duncan said.

"Umm," one boy said, "We were sort of horsing around and ummm, we got sort of close to the water. It's like he got too close and…."

"Did he fall or get pushed?" Duncan persisted.

Into the silence a shaky voice whispered, "He got pushed."

"I see," Duncan said, loudly enough that everyone heard him. "Do you remember what I said about this water?" He looked up from pressing on Alex's chest and glanced around.

"Yeah," a scared voice said, "You said only polar bears would swim in it."

"That's right. Not only was Alex in the freezing water, but he had all his clothes on, so now he's wet, his hiking boots are soaked and he's filled his lungs with that freezing water. Is there anything anyone wants to say to your leader?"

"Umm, Tom, umm, we're awful sorry," the biggest, oldest boy muttered.

"Yes, I am, too. Thanks to Duncan's fast work, things may turn out okay. Alex has another set of clothes, but no dry boots. We'll have to set them by the fire tonight and hope they dry out enough before morning." He glanced over his shoulder and saw that no one was watching the pans, he said, "Girls, is supper ready? It'll be getting dark soon, you know."

"Umm, almost, Pastor," one girl said.

The girls broke away from the group and raced back to the fire. Someone instantly grabbed a spoon and it clattered on the side of the pan as she stirred. Duncan was satisfied that Alex's lungs were clear, no more water came out of his mouth and he seemed to be breathing normally. He still hadn't opened his eyes, but his body was shaking all over. Duncan picked the boy up and took him to the center of the two bags and laid him down.

As he pulled first one side, then the other across him, he said, "Pull his boots off and take them to the fire. We'll try to get them as dry as possible before the fire goes out. Tom, you take them over, I think I need a word with every one of these boys."

Tom still had tears in his eyes. He swallowed and tried to speak, but nothing came out, so he nodded and knelt at Alex's feet. He untied Alex's boots and struggled to get them off. When they were both off, he stood up and moved back so Duncan could cover Alex's feet with the bottom of the bags. Tears still in his eyes, Tom took the boots and left for the fire.

Duncan finished covering Alex, then rocked back on his heels and looked at the silent boys gathered around. Letting his eyes rest on each boy for several seconds, he finally said, "Listen up, guys. This is the first day of a five day hike. Depending on how Alex is in the morning will determine whether your group goes on or goes back. If Alex suffers any ill effects from this plunge in the water we will be going back, no question." He looked at each boy, but especially the boy he'd seen look guilty. "Do I make myself clear?"

All heads nodded and one boy, the obvious leader answered, "Yeah, real clear."

Putting his feet under him and standing up, Duncan said, "Good, we'll make a human stretcher for him and take him back to the fire. While we eat, two of you'll watch him. We'll turn him from side to side every fifteen minutes so that he can warm up all around. I hope this was a very solemn lesson to all of you. It's okay to go exploring but not near any water source. All of you knew that Alex was the smallest of the group and I'm sure some of you knew he was not a good swimmer. It really upsets me that you boys let something like this happen." He pointed into the group. "You and you on this side, you others over there so we can carry him."

The boys quickly and silently arranged themselves around the still shaking bundle on the ground. Duncan took the part of the sleeping bags that held Alex's head. When they had the bundle in their arms, they slowly began to move around the pond, across the field toward the fire. Tom came back and grabbed the part that held Alex's feet.

"Supper's ready," Tom said, into the silence.

Duncan led the way, going backwards and glancing over his shoulder. The girls had moved everything from the closest side of the fire, so he walked beside the fire and motioned for the boys with their backs to the warmth to move out of the way. They carefully laid Alex down only inches from the edge of the firepit. They could all feel the warmth radiating out to them.

Looking at the western sky that only had beautifully colored clouds in it now, Duncan said, "Everyone better get your bowls for supper right away and get started, it'll be dark soon and you won't be able to see to clean up. Remember it's imperative to clean up after each meal, we don't see any right now, but there is wildlife all around us and they like to find a free meal any time they can."

All the hikers scrambled to their backpacks. Tom ladled out the stew the girls had finally gotten to cook. When the last bowl was filled, he said, "I think we need to pray before we eat." He looked around as everyone, including Duncan, bowed his head. "Father, God, thank You for this food. May it nourish us and thank You for Duncan's quick actions in getting Alex from the water. We pray he'll be back with us shortly with no ill effects. In Jesus' Name, amen."

Only a few minutes later, the bundle stopped shaking. Duncan noticed and said, "Boys, we need to turn Alex around so the other side of him can warm up. Come on."

Tom moved to Alex's head and saw eyes looking at him. Tears welled in the father's eyes and he choked out, "Son, you're awake?" The teeth were still chattering, but the head went up and down. "*Thank You, God!*" he breathed. "*Thank You for bringing him around so soon.*"

Duncan noticed that several of the tents were two man tents. He said to Tom, "Was Alex sleeping with you in one of those?"

"Yes, that's our tent over there."

"Since he's awake, after supper, since he's not shaking so violently, take him inside and get him into dry clothes, then get him into a dry bag. If he feels like eating, take him a bowl and let him eat. The warmth from the stew should help to warm him up. We'll have to see how he is in the morning. I hope he wasn't in that cold water too long."

"I'm sure we all feel the same way, Duncan." Tom looked around at the solemn group there hadn't been any joking around during the meal. He certainly hadn't felt like joking. He looked at the kids and said, "While Alex and I do that, everyone help with cleanup and get your Bibles. Those of you that have flashlights bring them, too. I'm sure we'll need them before we're finished with devotions."

One of the boys came over to Duncan and said, "Umm, my sleeping bag is the one Alex's wrapped in. When Pastor Tom takes him into his tent can I get my bag and get it close to the fire to dry out?"

"Sure!" Duncan said, "No problem with that! Get all of them as dry as you can before you go in your tents for the night."

"Thanks." The boy gave Duncan a half smile.

Tom finished his stew quickly and put his bowl beside the pot they'd used to cook in. There was water heating over the fire for washing the dishes. He went to the bundle that still held his son and moved the bags from around him. Quickly, he lifted Alex into his arms and hurried to his tent, acutely aware of the soggy clothes plastered to the boy's body. He disappeared inside and the rest of the group heard the zipper rasping shut. All eyes followed the pair into the tent and the girls shivered. The three boys whose sleeping bags Duncan had used to wrap Alex in jumped up to separate the bags and get them into a better position to dry out by the fire, but out of the way for their cleanup. It was a solemn group who did their chores and found their Bibles and flashlights.

Duncan watched the group as the light faded from the sky. He had no Bible, of course, but he wondered what Tom would preach on. Would he find some passage that would give the guys 'what for' or would he leave the topic alone. He was inclined to lean towards leaving it alone, the group seemed subdued enough and probably what he'd said was enough to give the guys their heavy thoughts. He knew there was no wind inside the tent and that should help Alex to warm up. The breeze wasn't much, but it was enough to keep the boy chilled

Inside the tent Tom rolled out Alex's sleeping bag, but didn't put the boy on it. Instead, he kept him away from the bags and began pealing the wet clothes from Alex's body. The boy had started shivering again, now that he was away from the heat from the fire. Tom had a hard job, between the wet cloth and Alex's shivering to get him undressed. As soon as the last wet cloth was gone, he slid him inside his dry bag.

"Dad," the boy said, embarrassed, "I w-wanna p-put s-s-some clothes on!"

As he pulled the bag up around Alex's shoulders, he asked, "Are you hungry?"

"Oh, D-dad, I-I'm s-starved."

Tom immediately called from the tent, "Can someone bring me a bowl of stew for Alex, please?" While he spoke, he rummaged in Alex's backpack and found the boy's warmest sweatshirt, some sweats and sox. "Here you go, Son. Put these on before your food comes. With the food, you should be as good as new real soon."

The boy's arm flew out and grabbed the clothes, then pulled them inside the bag. Alex wasted no time, but pulled the shirt over his head, then pulled the sweats down beside him. He soon had the clothes on and said, "These feel great!" Tom could tell the boy immediately put his hands in his armpits right away.

One of the girls was on her feet as soon as she heard Tom's request. She filled a bowl, picked up a spoon and hurried to the tent close by. Tom unzipped the tent flap part way and reached out for the bowl. "Thanks, Marylyn, Alex says he's famished. Tell everyone I'll be out in a second, as soon as I find my Bible."

"Yes, Pastor Tom."

Duncan was a little chilled from putting his arm up to his armpit into the cold water to pull Alex out. It made him wonder if perhaps it was spring fed, since it was so very cold. Rain water, even on a cool day wouldn't be that cold and since the pool was quite deep, and on top of the hill, a spring seemed to be a logical answer.

The stew was good and warmed him, but he wished he'd thought to bring some coffee. He realized that he and Tom were the only adults and probably the kids didn't drink coffee, but it would taste and smell good right now. Beside his phone, he'd start carrying some packs of instant coffee. He wrapped his arms around his knees and scooted closer to the fire. The breeze had picked up since they'd set up camp, so he tossed another large branch on the fire, glad he'd found so much dry wood. For some reason, he remembered how little he'd found that night on Nancy's hike. If this group was having devotions, keeping the fire going was important.

After Tom called for the stew, Duncan wondered how Tom was he'd held his dripping wet son for several minutes right from the pond. He knew Alex's clothes hadn't dried out much inside the sleeping bags, they'd only absorbed so much of the water and Tom had carried Alex against him from beside the fire to the other side to his tent. Most of the time a cool breeze was blowing on him. He hoped the man found dry clothes for himself before he left his tent.

Before Tom reappeared, the teens had finished cleanup and had everything put away. They gathered back around the fire with Bibles and flashlights. As he sat down, one guy said, "Umm, Duncan, you got a Bible?"

"No, I left it at my cabin." *Well, that's sorta true, I left a Bible back in my cabin. Just because it's not mine....*

"You wanna share, I got a flashlight."

Duncan nodded. "I'll look over your shoulder." *What? Aren't you gonna run away?* that pesky voice from his shoulder asked.

It was nearly dark when Tom zipped the flap open on his tent and climbed out, then carefully zipped it closed, bringing the empty bowl and spoon along with his Bible and a powerful flashlight. Duncan nearly sighed out loud he was glad to see that Tom had some dry clothes on, which included a sweatshirt.

When he reached the group, one of the girls immediately asked, "How's Alex, is he getting warmed up, Pastor Tom?"

"Yes, he feels much better now that he's had that stew. He said it warmed him inside. By the way, girls, that stew was excellent! Try for the same taste tomorrow and I'll be happy. After Alex put on dry clothes and ate that stew, he snuggled down in his bag and fell asleep, so I think he'll be as good as new in the morning."

The girl sighed, "I'm so glad! He didn't look so good when Duncan first pulled him out of the water."

Duncan didn't say anything, but he was, too.

"Okay," Tom said, looking around at the teens. These were his kids each one had a special place in his heart. "On this first night of our hike I think it'd be a good idea to have some discussion, so let's open our Bibles to the gospel of John and read the first few verses." He waited until everyone stopped rustling pages and then he read:

"'In the beginning was the Word and the Word was with God, and the Word was God. He was with God in the beginning.

"Through him all things were made; without him nothing was made that has been made. In him was life, and that life was the light of men. The light shines in the darkness, but the darkness has not understood it.'"

Everyone looked at Tom expectantly, but Tom took his time looking around at the teens. "Okay, who will tell me Who *The Word* is?"

"It's Jesus," one girl said, immediately.

"How do we know that?"

Looking at her Bible, she pointed to the page, then looked at Tom and said, "It says that He was with God in the beginning and only God was in the beginning. It says that Jesus made everything there is."

"Great, Ashley! You are absolutely right!" Putting his Bible on his lap and shutting off his flashlight, Tom said, "Look around us. What do you think of what Jesus, God's Son made? Look at everything!"

The other flashlights clicked off and soon the only light was the burning campfire and the millions of stars over their heads. Another girl gasped, "Pastor Tom, it's awesome! It's so vast, Wow! Look at the sky! Up here we can see billions of stars and Jesus made them all!" Before Tom could say anything else, she added, "You know, I never thought about it before you read that tonight. I thought of Jesus as the Baby in the manger and the Man who walked on earth and died, but that verse you read says He's the Creator, too. That's truly awesome!"

"Yes, it is, Cheryl. Okay, let's think about some of the things we see all around us, but we take for granted that God made." Into the silence, Tom added, "Remember, He spoke and the things came into existence. Man can make things, sometimes things that have never been before, but he makes them out of something. God made everything, things we see and things too small to see out of.... nothing."

"God made the trees and plants," one boy said.

"He made all the animals," another said.

Another boy said, "He made the water and the air we breathe. He made the fish so they can live in the water and birds so they can fly."

"That's so," Tom said. "Did you ever think about the fact that God made light on the first day, but didn't make the sun, moon, and stars until the fourth day?"

Duncan was getting interested, but before he could say anything, another boy spoke up and said, "How can that be? Those are the sources of light, aren't they?"

"They are now, but God is light, remember that verse we read that said God is light? God chose to have the light that shines on the earth come from the sun, moon, and stars, but if He'd chosen not to make those things, there could still have been light, because He made light first."

"Wow! So just because the earth revolves around the sun; God still created the sun as part of the universe. I hadn't thought of that before."

"Yes, that's right."

Duncan pulled in a deep breath; he rarely took part in the hikers' after dinner discussion, whatever it was. "So you believe that God did all this creating in six days?" Duncan asked, trying to keep the skepticism from his voice.

"Of course, I believe that! God spoke and it happened. God was the only one here at that time, so He's the only One who'd know. God inspired Moses to write all His words down and that's how we have the record. It's not quite so easy when you read the account in English, but in the original language, it's clear that God made everything in six twenty-four hour days."

"So when it says '*the Word*' there in what you read, that means Jesus?"

"Yes, Duncan, that's Who it means. All three parts of the Godhead were present at creation. Here in John it says that the Word, or Jesus was there and in the first chapter of Genesis it says that God's Spirit moved about, so They were all there."

"Wow!" one of the boys said, "That's awesome! You've taught us that God was the Creator, but I'm like her, I never thought about Jesus being the Creator or that the Holy Spirit was there, too."

"Look! There's a shooting star!" Ashley exclaimed. She fell back so she could stare up at the sky and watch as the light moved across the sky.

"Just think," Cheryl mused, "The universe is so vast we can't even see all the stars that God made by looking up into the night sky."

"You're right, Cheryl. Let's pray, then I need to go check on Alex," Tom said. "Our God and Father, we thank You for all the signs You have given us to know for sure that You are God. Being here in Your creation brings us to our knees before You. Thank You for being so loving toward us, since we are born with a sin nature and are so prone to sin, that You sent Your Son, who was there with You at creation, to die on the cross to be our Savior. May we never forget what Jesus willingly did for us. Thank You, in His Name, amen."

There was a chorus of, "Amen's" from all the teens.

Nine

Tom raised his head and asked, "Duncan, we need to be on the trail by seven thirty?"

"Yes, that's it. My alarm's set for six o'clock. That'll be about enough time to get camp dismantled and breakfast fixed and eaten."

"I'm gone!" Ashley exclaimed, jumped up and ran for the woods, Cheryl ran, too.

The boys also jumped up and ran for a different part of the woods, leaving Duncan sitting by the fire. Tom stood, holding his Bible and flashlight in one hand. He looked first at his tent, then down at Duncan. "Duncan, I want to check on my son, but do you have more questions you need answered? I'll be glad to come back and talk."

"Nah, go ahead. Alex's more important right now."

"Duncan, if you have questions about where you'll spend eternity, that's the most important topic of all. I'll check on Alex then come back."

Duncan jumped to his feet and motioned Tom toward his tent. Tamping down his anger, he said, "I gotta think awhile. I'll catch you tomorrow."

Duncan immediately left the fire as if the demons of Hell were after him, not wanting to hear what Tom had to say. He strode away, into the woods where he could be alone. He stopped by the pool where Alex had fallen in. The moon was a bright orange ball on the horizon. Duncan slouched onto the rock and watched the moon climb higher and turn to cold silver. Soon the camp was quiet, the teens were in their tents and Tom was in his, but had his flashlight on.

Duncan sat, contemplating what he'd heard around the campfire. He'd read the gospel of John, twice, after Sandy had told him to, he'd read the first few chapters in Genesis, after the hike with Nancy and talking with Isabel about the flood, but tonight, listening to Tom and the teens talk about Jesus the Creator who also came to die for the sin of the world, he couldn't put it from his mind. God, the Creator, came to earth to die for his sin! How awesome was that?

"*God*!" he cried out, "*I'm a sinner! I can't run anymore, I repent! Save me!*" There was no earthquake; he hadn't expected one, but his heart felt different... he felt different. Could it be that God had really heard him and would hear him if he prayed? "God, You would hear me? You would want me to be Your child? How awesome is that? Wow! It's more awesome than that shooting star we saw earlier!" A tear slid unnoticed down Duncan's cheek and then another. God had heard him, He'd listened to his cry and Duncan knew he was God's child.

By this time, everything was quiet. Birds were in their nests asleep. Because he was sitting by the pond, none of the tree toads were making noise. Far off in the trees a whippoorwill started calling. Off in another part of the woods an owl began hooting and only seconds later another answered from across the field. Because it was so quiet, Duncan heard trickling water close by. It was too dark, the moon didn't give enough light, but he was sure now that there was a spring underneath the rock he sat on that fed the pool and made it ice cold. The moon was well up in the sky when he finally left the rock and headed for his tent. When he was on the trail he never stayed up this late, but his decision and the awesome night kept him up. As he crawled into his bag he was sure he'd never forget this night.

Nancy and Sandy spent the afternoon together. It hadn't taken them long, but they were best of friends. They picnicked in a wide place on a side road. Sandy was a good cook, she always brought a lovely lunch and Nancy enjoyed being with her. Right after lunch, after putting away the picnic leftovers, Nancy took her camera and moved down a trail close by while Sandy pulled her easel from the back of the van and set it up. She always brought a photo to paint from but often she looked around and in the quiet, deserted spot where they'd stopped for lunch she found a vista with a view she had to paint. When Nancy came back with several new pictures on her digital camera, Sandy sat painting. Nancy took one look at the picture then looked up from it to see the scene that Sandy was painting and her breath caught.

"Wow! Here I walked so far away and didn't find a picture near as pretty as you've got right here. You've captured the colors perfectly."

Sandy smiled. "You know, I've been wanting to start that commission for that lady in town and I didn't know what to paint, but today when I turned from the van and saw this, I decided this was the picture I needed and now it's nearly done."

Nancy shook her head. "If she doesn't like it, I'll buy it. The walls in Isabel's cabin only have windows, no pictures. I have my picture that you gave me, but I'll need some more."

Sandy chuckled. "You tell me what you want and I'll let you have a picture or two at a good price."

"Sandy, you would not! I know you too well. Any 'price' you'd quote me would only be pennies on the dollar for what it's worth. How much will you charge the lady for this one?"

"We agreed on a certain size and a certain price, but you and I are friends, I wouldn't charge you what I'm charging her."

Nancy nodded. "We'll see."

When Sandy finished the painting, Nancy helped her load her supplies into the van, then took the painting and laid it on the back seat inside. Sandy took herself up the lift and locked her chair behind the wheel. The shadows were long as the girls headed back to Vansville.

After Sandy had the van going and turned around, she asked, "Will you stay and eat supper with me, Nancy?"

"If you don't mind, I'd love to. You know how much fun it is to heat a frozen dinner and sit in front of the TV on your sofa-sleeper to eat it?"

"I've never done that, but I imagine it's pretty boring."

"Believe me, it's bad! I am excited to move into Isabel's cabin, I can hardly wait. Then, if I want, I can sit on my porch to eat dinner. How perfect is that? When will Ramon be home?"

"His hike's over tomorrow afternoon. He's hoping to get home early enough that he can clean up and we can go to Roger's church for evening worship."

"I was going to ask you about that church. He does have morning and evening worship? Sometimes little churches don't have anything in the evening."

"Yes, once he got his head screwed on straight and Raylyn came into his life, he's become an excellent pastor. We go in the evenings a lot and it's great."

"Good, maybe when I move here I'll start going there instead of driving all the way back to Blairsville to attend the church where I go now."

"You'll like it, I'm sure. He has become a very good preacher and he has a pastor's heart. He and Raylyn love these townspeople."

Over a delicious supper that Sandy whipped up in no time at all, Nancy asked, "Why did you move here from Philadelphia? I'd think that place…"

"The major reason was I saw an ad for a receptionist that Ramon had placed in a magazine. The ad was a full page with pictures from the area all around his ad. I felt stifled with always painting the few scenes around the park I went to at home and those pictures drew me. The other reason was that my mom had tried for twenty-five years to hide me away from life."

"She wanted to hide you?"

"Yes. Actually, hide my chair from people. I knew if I didn't get away from home, far enough that she couldn't come for me I'd be stifled for the rest of my life. Don't get me wrong, I love my family, but not my mom's stifling. The people at the gallery in Philly have told me that my painting has gotten better since I moved here and I think it's because I feel a new freedom in my life that I couldn't find in Philly."

Nancy nodded. "I think I can understand, since I work in the rehab center. Of course, I never saw your work before or heard you play before, but both of those things that you do are awesome. I love to hear you play and your paintings are masterful. If this is what happened because you moved to Vansville, I'm so glad you moved!"

Sandy smiled at her friend, took her hand and squeezed it. "Thanks, Nancy. I'm very glad I moved here, too. Everything has worked out so well. I really love having you come spend time with me. I never really had a friend my own age before. Having you for a friend is awesome and the way we do things together makes me feel so normal."

"That's great! I love having you as my friend, too." She shook her head and grinned at her friend. "Believe me, I never think of you as any other way but normal!" The clock in the living room began the Westminster chime and Nancy said, "I'd better get a move on! I'm to be to work by eight and I still have to drive back to Blairsville. I'll call you when I can come out again. We've had a great time today!"

The two girls went to the front door and Sandy said, "Yes, we have. Thanks for staying for supper with me. Drive back safely."

"I'll do my best!"

Nancy left the house and hurried to her car. She saw the big SUV beside her car and wondered how Duncan was. He had been in a really bad mood when he'd left the office that morning. She was sure it was because God was trying to get his attention. As she drove off DeLord's parking lot, she prayed, "Lord, make Duncan see his need for You. He needs You as his Savior. Maybe something on this hike will turn him toward You and he'll come to You for forgiveness of his sins. Thank You for being the God who is there, who is everywhere, here in this little town, in the city or on the trail. Thank You for being my Savior, amen."

Even though she had to be on duty at eight, Nancy was reluctant to return to the tiny efficiency that was her home for now. She came to the turn off where Sandy had first turned off last year. She pulled into a parking spot, turned off the car lights, then the ignition and climbed out. The night was quiet and since the darkness had fallen there were no birds still twittering in the trees, instead the tree toads told her there was water not far away. She climbed up on the warm hood of her car and leaned back to gaze at the sky. It was dark, the moon hadn't come up yet, but the stars were brilliant. Only moments later a shooting star streaked across the sky. All she could do was exclaim, "Oh!" She watched the shining body streak across the sky. "Oh, my Father! How awesome are Your works!"

Finally, she climbed behind the wheel and drove the rest of the way to Blairsville. She parked in her slot at the apartment building and made her way into the lobby. The elevator came as she reached it and a couple stepped off. She stepped on and pushed the button for her floor. She went to her door, opened it and went inside, then closed the door and turned the deadbolt. Only a few minutes later she pulled down the covers and lay down on her bed.

However, she was too keyed up to fall asleep right away. In the darkness she looked around and thought about the lovely cabin she'd been in this morning and that she'd soon live in. It was April, she had nearly two months to work at the rehab facility before she could quit and move to Vansville to take her new position and live in the cabin she'd rented from Isabel.

"Make the days go by really fast!" she breathed and fell asleep.

About two weeks later, Nancy dressed in her scrub outfit, then ate and left for the rehab center. She wasn't looking forward to work, not after spending such a great day with Sandy. Just because they'd gotten rid of the spoiled teen who'd fallen off the horse back in January, didn't mean she never got another bad patient. Now one of her patients was a man who had been in an auto accident. He was the complete opposite from that boy. The man was impatient to get out of the center and he was obnoxious because he'd become frustrated with himself and took that frustration out on all the staff who worked with him.

Nancy walked on the ward for eight o'clock report and could hear that man, still in his room, yelling at the aid who had brought his breakfast. She needed to get report, so she walked into the head nurse's office and said to the night nurse, "I hear Rodney down the hall. I guess his attitude hasn't improved over my days off."

Shaking her head, the nurse said, "He thinks his last name is Dangerfield and that we give him no respect! I'm glad you're back he seems to be better when you're on. What do you do to him, anyway?"

"What do I do? I don't take any of his swearing or any of his lip. I tell him that God's watching and I don't want to hear anything from his mouth that he couldn't say to God if He walked in. It usually works, at least when I'm there."

"Keep it up! I'm not much on this God stuff, but if that's what keeps him from yelling at my crew, then go for it! Say whatever you have to. Maybe you can tell him God's watching him twenty-four seven."

Soon after report, Nancy walked into Rodney's room. For the moment the man was alone, so he raised his head off the pillow and looked to the door to see who'd come in. "Oh, it's you!" he snarled.

"Yup, it's me, Rodney. I heard you yelling at the aid who brought you breakfast, weren't you being a little hard on her?"

"D...!" he swallowed, "You can't know how frustrating it is for someone to wait on me!"

Nodding, Nancy said, "I've worked here long enough to know about all the things that frustrate those who are here, Rodney. The thing of it is, the sooner you let those frustrations drain away and work with your body, the sooner you'll be on the road to getting out of here and moving on your own. The doctors all feel you'll make a complete recovery. That'll happen if you work with your body and stop fighting it. Letting that frustration drain away is part of it."

Rodney took a deep breath and much less belligerently said, "I hear you, Ms Nancy. It's a lot easier said than done."

Nancy chuckled. "I know that for a fact."

"Do I get to walk in the parallel bars today?"

"I think so. You're ready, I think and your stitches have healed well. I'll get a wheelchair and we'll get right after that."

"Fine! Be about it!"

A few minutes later, she took the chair up close to the bars and locked the wheels. After Rodney stood up, she moved behind him and stayed at one end of the bars as Rodney walked toward the other end. His first few steps were very shaky, but then they straightened out quite well. He turned around and walked back to her, still holding tightly to the bars, but then stood there holding on and looked at her. After all that exertion his legs were a bit shaky but not so he couldn't hold his own weight. "Ms. Nancy, what is it about you that makes you so different from the other nurses and aids that work here?"

She smiled at him. "I'm glad you can notice the difference, Rodney. I'm a Christian. I believe that God, through His Son, Jesus Christ, has forgiven me of all my sin, past, present and future and that when I die I'll go to live in Heaven with God my Father and Jesus, His Son, my elder Brother," she said, confidently.

Rodney stood silently, just looking at Nancy for several seconds, before he said, "Wow! That's quite a mouthful, Ms. Nancy! I'll have to think about that."

"When we get back to your room, I'll pull out the Bible that's in your bedside stand and show you all about it."

"Thanks. That'll give me something to do."

It was lunchtime and one of the aids came up to Nancy, as she washed her hands following a treatment and asked, "Were you going to lunch soon, Nancy?"

Shaking the water from her hands, then reaching for a paper towel, Nancy said, "I sure was, Sally. Actually, I was on my way to tell Linda I was heading downstairs. Did you want to come with me?"

"If you don't mind?"

Nancy looked at the young woman earnestly and said, "Sally, I never have a problem eating with a friend."

The girl's eyes lit up. "Thanks, that's great!"

After speaking to Linda, they took the elevator to ground floor and got in line behind another nurse, picked out their preference for lunch and looked for a table. They found a small table in the crowded cafeteria and put their trays down, then sat across from each other. Before Nancy could even say her blessing for her food, Sally said, earnestly, "Nancy, I heard you tell Rodney stuff from the Bible this morning after he'd been in the parallel bars. Could you tell me about that, too?"

"Of course, Sally! Just a minute, let me say grace." Nancy bowed her head and silently thanked God for the food, but also for the opportunity to talk about Him to Sally. "What would you like to know?" she asked, after she raised her head. She smiled at the young woman. "Not that I have all the answers."

Sally scowled and leaned toward Nancy. "You told him he needed to let Jesus into his heart. What did you mean by that? Why is that important?"

Without wasting any time, Nancy said, "What I meant is that each one of us does things that are wrong. Don't you agree?"

The girl nodded. "Oh, yes, too often, it seems." The girl sat holding her unwrapped sandwich, but it was forgotten.

"God, the Creator, who is all powerful, all knowing and everywhere, is interested and loves each one of us and wants us for His children, but because we sin, by doing what we know is wrong, He cannot."

"I didn't know that."

Nancy nodded emphatically. "Yes, it's true, Sally. But, you see, God loves us so much that He Himself has made a way for us to become His children and when we die we can go to live where He does, in heaven." Nancy pulled out her little nurse testament and opened it and said, "There is a verse I love very much that says it so well. It says, "'For God so loved the world that he gave his one and only Son, that whoever believes in him shall not perish but have eternal life.'" (John 3:16) The Way that He made was for His Son, Jesus, who was also sinless, to become sin and die on a cruel cross. When He died, God heaped all the sin on Him, even yours and mine so many years later. Because of that, we can come to God, ask His forgiveness and He'll cover our sins with Jesus' blood. When you ask for His forgiveness, it's like He uses white-out and blots our sin record from His book and makes you clean in His sight. He also makes a place for you in heaven."

Nancy smiled at the girl and said, "The reason it's important to do this is because, if you don't, when you die you'll go to a place of torment called Hell. Our bodies may go in the ground when we die, but our souls live forever and go either to heaven, if we have been forgiven or to hell if we have not."

"Wow! Nancy, I never heard this before! You told him you'd show him in the Bible. Will you show me?"

Nancy glanced at the wall clock, wiped her mouth and said, "I'll be glad to." She put her little testament in her pocket and said, "It's time to get back to work, but during our afternoon break I'll be glad to sit down with you and show you everything I mean. Is that okay, Sally?"

"Yes! I really want to know!"

Nancy chuckled. "Great! It's a date."

Later that afternoon, Nancy's supervisor came to the ward. She held some papers and sat down at the nurse's desk, then after only a minute, because of so much going on around her, she scooped up her papers and went to the head nurse's office, but didn't close the door, still it was much more quiet and she needed to concentrate on what she was reading. She turned on the desk light, then spread out the papers and studied them for a few minutes, then went to the door and asked one of those who was there if Nancy was working.

An aide stood up and said, "Yes, she's in with Rodney right now, you want her? I'll go get her if you want."

"Rodney, would be Dangerfield?" the woman asked, after listening for a minute.

The girl snickered, "Yeah, that Rodney. She had him up walking in the parallel bars this morning. She seemed to think he was doing better. Anyway, he hasn't been yelling since she went in after report this morning." The girl grinned. "I think she puts a spell over him when she's on duty, anyway, he's not in a bad mood today."

The older nurse cocked her head and grinned. "Wow! How about that! He's not yelling! I guess I didn't notice the silence. When she comes out, have her come see me. I'll be in here for a while." The lady went back to the head nurse's desk again, but still left the door open. After another minute she turned to another page.

Soon, Nancy walked into the desk area and someone said, "Miss Osborne wants to see you in there."

Nancy nodded and moved to the door, but still stood in the doorway and asked, "Hi, Miss Osborne, what is it you need?"

The older woman pulled in a deep breath, shuffled her papers again and said, "Nancy, come on in, close the door and have a seat." After Nancy did as she was asked, the woman said, "Okay, just so you know up front, I'm not here to chew you out." She smiled a little and added, "So you can relax."

Nancy nodded, she couldn't think of any reason the woman would have to chew her out anyway. "Okay," she said, tentatively.

The woman took another deep breath, then let it out slowly and said, "Do you recall a patient we had named Bill Kambro?"

Nancy sighed, shaking her head, "How could anyone on this floor forget Bill? He and his parents were always giving the girls a hard time. They were never satisfied with anything. I don't think anyone was sad to see him leave."

Smiling and nodding in agreement, Mary said, "Actually, Nancy, I think you're being kind about those people. I think we all cheered after his dear doctor got a dose first hand of his actions." Mary Osborne lifted several papers that sat directly in front of her and said, "However, this is a letter from a law firm stating that the Kambro's are bringing a suit against the center and this ward and you in particular."

Nancy's hand flew to her throat and she pulled in a sharp breath, it seemed she couldn't get enough air in her lungs at that moment. After she swallowed and cleared her throat, she asked, "What is it about me? Miss

Osborne, me? Why me? I did his care as the doctor prescribed as best I could!"

Still looking at the top page, Mary Osborne asked, "You were his major care giver?"

Nancy thought a moment and nodded. "Pretty much, his room has been one of my rooms for a long time and I'm full time. I've had that bunch of rooms forever. Anyone who comes in those rooms becomes my patient. It's the same with all us fulltimers."

Mary shook her head. "This says that the Kambro's suggested that you singled him out to make his life miserable. They claim that because you talk about the Bible that you did that in his room and therefore harassing their son."

Shaking her head, as she looked at the older nurse, she said, "Miss Osborne, there is no way that can hold up! I may have mentioned a Bible story or something like that in passing, but I never quoted scripture to him or forced him to listen to any Bible reading. I don't do that, not unless a patient asks me to show them something or asks me to read or pray with them. Bill never asked me anything about the Bible or asked me to pray with him. Yes, I'd have loved to quote something like 'Your sin will find you out' or 'God'll get you for that.' but I never did."

Mary chuckled. "I know we all wished we could have zapped him with something to shut him up and make him more cooperative or locked the doors to keep his parents away. What you've told me is what I thought, but I'm afraid that this attorney's office is calling you on the carpet and being pretty specific about it. The trial will be in three weeks and unless something else happens, you'll be expected to testify. Do you have an attorney of your own? I'm sure that will be something you'll need."

Giving the older nurse a weak smile, Nancy said, "Miss Osborne, that's laughable! I certainly don't have an attorney. I own nothing, only the clothes in my closet and my ten year old car. I live in a one room efficiency apartment down the street. I have a tiny savings account that I've started within the last year to buy another car when the time comes, but nothing that makes me feel the need for legal protection. I'm on my own my parents cannot help me in any way. They live hundreds of miles away, but they still have my little brother at home to support."

Writing on the edge of the paper in front of her, Mary, said, "That's what I thought and perhaps one of the attorney's for the center can give you some advice on how to get out of appearing or what to say when you must appear."

With a sigh, Nancy said, "I'd appreciate help from anywhere. Hopefully it'll be free. The pay here's good, but nobody gets rich."

The older woman smiled at Nancy and said, "How about your pastor, could he give you any insights do you think?"

Nancy was surprised, she didn't know Mary Osborne was in any way interested in spiritual things, but she nodded. "That's a good idea, I'll ask him. Thanks for that advice, Miss Osborne. Was I the only nurse named?"

"Unfortunately, yes, I was named because I'm the supervisor for this ward."

Nancy shook her head again. "What a bummer!"

Mary Osborne smiled at Nancy. "Don't get discouraged about this. I'll talk to the attorney I'm to meet with soon and I'll ask if he'll help you out. We'll go from there. Very often a ward nurse can give a written statement to the attorney and it'll be enough. I'll see you, so keep up your good work, Nancy, if what Rodney sounded like when I came on the ward is any indication of your work, you have my vote."

Smiling back, Nancy said, "Thanks so much, Miss Osborne. You know I'll be leaving here the middle of June, don't you?"

The older lady sighed, "Are you on your way to Vansville, too? That critter from administration seems to want to empty out our center of good nurses!"

"Yes, I found out just the other day they've accepted my application." A thought came to her and she scowled. "This law suit won't make anyone change their mind, will it?"

"I should think not! I'll make sure of that!"

Miss Osborne opened the door and said, "See you, Nancy, don't let this get you down."

"Yes, Miss Osborne." *How can it not?* she wondered.

After the supervisor left, Nancy sat for a minute in the little room, collected her thoughts and said, "Lord God, You know about this. Help me be Your witness however this works out."

After another minute Nancy left the head nurse's office and slouched onto a chair behind the nurse's desk. "What was that about?" her friend asked.

"I'm sure you don't remember Bill Kambro…" a touch of irony in her voice.

"What! Of course, what's with him? He's still in that center in Atlanta, isn't he?"

"I don't know about that, but his parents are suing this center, our ward and me."

Looking up, directly into Nancy's eyes, she asked, "What! What ever for? What in the world do they have to sue about?"

"They say I harassed their son by preaching to him."

The woman's mouth dropped open. When she finally found her voice she smacked the desk top and exclaimed, "That is laughable!"

Nancy shrugged, "Maybe so, but Miss Osborne advised me to seek legal council. She said she'd find me someone to talk to"

"You do that! That's ridiculous! You shouldn't even have to testify, we should file a counter suit for all the verbal abuse he gave us." Nodding, the other nurse said, "But isn't that like that crowd! Bringing a suit against you; what a crock!"

Nancy nodded and went down the hall to another patient's room to do a treatment that was due. "Yeah, it is," she called over her shoulder.

Nancy rarely went to Bible study on Wednesday evening at her church because it started only a few minutes after she was off work and she had to drive several blocks to get there, however, she changed into different clothes at her locker at six thirty and drove to the church where she attended. She didn't have her Bible and she'd never gotten a study guide, but she'd gladly sit through the class if she could talk to the pastor afterward. What the supervisor had talked with her about had bothered her for the rest of the afternoon and she felt she needed some council and support. Her pastor was the man to do that and to pray with her.

She hung back after the class was over until she and the pastor were the last ones in the room. The man saw the last couple out the door, then turned to her and asked, "Nancy, I rarely see you here on a Wednesday evening. If I remember right you usually work on Wednesdays until six or so, don't you? I noticed you didn't have your Bible or a study guide, either one, so there must be something major that's troubling you or you wouldn't be here."

Nancy sighed. "You have that right, Pastor. Can you spare a few minutes? I really need some council and support in this."

"Of course, Nancy! Come to my office and we'll hear what's on your mind right now." The older man smiled at the pretty young woman, patted her on the arm and led the way down the hall to his office.

"Thanks, Pastor."

After they were seated, the pastor automatically pulled out a pad and pen, Sandy sighed, looked down at her hands, twined together in her lap and finally said, "Pastor, my supervisor called me in for a talk this afternoon. She showed me some very legal looking papers then told me it seems the parents of one of our former patients who was transferred from our center to one in Atlanta, much against his parents wishes, are suing the center, our ward and me in particular."

Alarm written on his face, the pastor asked, "Whatever for? Why in the world would they single you out for something so harsh?"

Stretching out her fingers and pressing her palms onto her thighs, she said, "They say I harassed him by preaching to him."

The man slapped his hand down on the desk and exclaimed vehemently, "You wouldn't do that! That's absolutely ridiculous!"

"No, I certainly didn't. Like I told Miss Osborne, I'd very much have liked to say, 'Be sure your sin will find you out.' or 'God'll get you for that,' but I never did and I never quoted Scripture to the guy or prayed with him. I may have said I'd pray for him, but I never quoted Scripture or prayed with him."

"Do you have a lawyer?"

Shaking her head, Nancy said, "No, Miss Osborne said she'd have one from the firm the center retains get in touch with me."

"Good, that's the worst I've ever heard. If you ask me, that's harassment against you if I ever heard of any! Did your supervisor think you'd have to appear in court?"

"She wasn't really sure." Nancy sighed again, "I truly hope I don't have to. It's not something I've ever done. I can't remember ever being in a courtroom!" Wiping her hands on her thighs again, she said, "I'm trying not to be scared, Pastor."

"If you must appear, I'll be there, Nancy. I'll support you all the way." He stood up and came around his desk and said, "Come on, let's pray. Father, God, take this situation Nancy's told me about and work it for Your glory. Give Nancy peace."

"Thanks, Pastor, I appreciate that."

"Of course, Nancy! I'm glad you came to me about this."

Only a few days later a woman in a navy blue power suit, with matching heels, shoulder purse and black briefcase came through the door onto the ward from the visitor's lounge. Her hair was perfect everything about her was in place. She looked around at the busy ward, some would call it organized chaos. She stopped at the nurse's desk and asked, "Is there a Nancy Southerland working here today?"

Nancy looked up from writing in a patient's chart and was instantly aware of how disheveled she looked for having been at work for nearly eight hours, but she said, "Yes, I'm Nancy. Is there something I can do for you?"

The woman gave her a ghost of a smile and said, "I think it's me to do something for you. Are you free enough you can get away? I'm Ann Blakestein, from the law firm representing the Blairsville Rehabilitation Center in the lawsuit brought by Mr. and Mrs. Ernest Kambro."

The three other nurses at the desk looked at Nancy immediately. Nancy closed the chart she was writing in right away, put it back in the chart rack and walked out from behind the desk. Feeling self-conscious in front of her fellow nurses, she smoothed down her pant legs, leaving little patches of sweat from her palms behind. "I'm as free as I can be while on duty, Ms Blakestein. Where would you like to meet?"

"There's no one in this waiting room, why don't we sit back in the corner and see what we can come up with."

Nancy joined the woman in front of the nurse's desk and said, "I'd offer you some coffee, but I happen to know when it was made and I don't think it's fit to drink."

Ann laughed and turned toward the exit into the waiting room. "Sounds kind of like the coffee in our break room."

Nancy followed the woman into the waiting room to a corner away from the TV. As soon as she sat down, Ann set her briefcase on the low table, then opened it and pulled out some papers, a notepad and a pen. Looking up, she asked, "Okay, do you know what's going on?"

Nancy shrugged. "Only a bit. Miss Osborne, the supervisor for this ward came up the other day and told me I was named in the Kambro's suit. She never read me the exact words."

Holding the papers in one hand, Ann pulled first one, then the next paper away and laid them on the table. Looking at the third paper, she said, "Here's what it says, 'We wish to include Nancy Southerland, a nurse on this floor, in this action because in her over-zealous treatment of our son, she constantly and methodically harassed our son with her Bible quoting and her loud prayers. The facility we placed our son, William in is not a religious institution and we do not want our son deluged with such treatment.' It goes on to other things from there."

Nancy sat there staring at the other woman with her mouth hanging open. Finally, she whispered, "You can't be serious!"

Ann held up her hand and said, "Wait! Wait a minute, I'd better record this. Let me get my machine out then we'll start over." She pulled a small recorder from her briefcase, checked to see it had a tape in it and batteries then turned it on. Then she said, "This is Ann Blakestein and I'm talking with Nancy Southerland, a nurse at the Blairsville Rehab Center." After saying that, she carefully reread the statement word for word from the lawsuit, then prompted Nancy to say what she had already said.

As soon as Nancy spoke, Ann nodded and said, "Yes, I'm very serious, Ms Southerland. In fact, I didn't paraphrase what is in the lawsuit I read it to you word for word. What they have stated would be considered harassment. As this document states, Blairsville Rehab is not a religious institution, nothing like they state should happen here."

Shaking her head, Nancy said, "Ms Blakestein, those are lies, total lies! I never, ever quoted any Bible to that young man and I certainly didn't pray, loudly, or quietly in his room. You can ask anyone I work with I do not do that in any patient's room and certainly not in his room. I knew he was very antagonistic to anything we said or did for him from the first time I entered the room. I did my job according to the orders the doctors had written in his chart and that was all. I told him frequently that I didn't appreciate his attitude or his fowl language and that he was being obnoxious, not only to me but to everyone on the ward, but that was all! Ms Blakestein, we all decided he was a thirteen year old spoiled brat."

"So, let me say this again, for the record. You never quoted any Bible to him or forced him to listen to you pray."

"That's correct! The closest to either of those things would be to tell him I didn't appreciate his foul mouth or his yelling at me. Those two things he did as much and as loudly as he could. Not only myself, but the other nurses and aids who were assigned to his room liked his foul language. His room was nearly to the end of the hall and whenever we came on the ward from the back elevator we could hear him yelling. I can't imagine why his parents would single me out. Not only that, if his tray didn't suit him, he'd sweep his hand across his table so that everything went on the floor, then someone assigned to that room had to clean up the mess, including broken dishes. That happened at nearly every meal!"

"Were you his primary care giver?"

"I work four tens a week, which means on my shift I would be giving his exercises three times. Obviously, he would have someone else do them one other time in a twenty-four hour period. We do exercises seven days a week, since this is a residential facility, so yes, I would be the one to do his exercises most often. Of course, there were aids who brought his meals, assisted him in his personal hygiene, things like that."

"Miss Southerland, would you be willing to come to the courtroom when the trial starts and say what you have told me?"

Realizing the tape player was still operating, Nancy said, "Ms. Blakestein, if you feel I must come, I will, but if there's any way that I can give a written statement and don't have to appear, I would prefer that."

Nodding, she said, "I'll let my colleague listen to this tape and see what he says. I'll have to get back with you about this."

Ann shut off her recorder and gathered her papers, but Nancy stood up and said, "If there's nothing else, I need to get back to work."

"That's fine, Miss Southerland. Thank you so much for your time." She held out her hand and Nancy shook it. Nancy turned and went back through the door to the ward and Ann went to the elevators and left the center.

Nancy was pleasantly surprised when she'd seen her schedule for the period to see that she had another weekend off, it was a rare thing to have so many off in so short a time. When she arrived at her apartment that evening, she called Sandy and said, "Sandy, I'm off tomorrow, I have some heavy news, are you free? Could I come?"

The cheery voice on the other end said, "Of course, Nancy! Come on out! Ramon's hike gets over in the late afternoon. You can come for all day and then stay for supper with us."

"Are you sure that's okay? I hate to take some of the time you have with Ramon, you have so little together."

"Of course it is! You know it only takes a few minutes to whip up supper and their hikes don't usually get back until four or so. I'd be bored to death if you didn't come. You'll be here in the morning?"

"Yes, I'll see you after breakfast, Sandy."

"Great! I'll be watching for you."

"Thanks, I'm looking forward to it."

What Sandy didn't tell Nancy was that Duncan had been back and Saturday morning would be there preparing to leave on another hike. Sandy knew, of course, that Nancy wouldn't show any attraction toward Duncan since he claimed to be an atheist, but she could see the attraction, the chemistry between them, even though the two involved wouldn't acknowledge it. She knew Duncan would fight the attraction to the end.

Nancy left her apartment early and headed for Vansville. She was interested to see how much more was finished on the clinic. As she drove by, she had to admit that most of the work had to be inside now, the outside looked nearly complete. She felt an excitement she hadn't felt for her work in a long time. Even more now, since she'd found out about the lawsuit. Surely, walk-ins didn't bring lawsuits against nurses in a clinic.

Several minutes later, she pulled onto the parking lot at DeLord's and saw Duncan's SUV in its usual spot. She didn't think too much about it, because it usually was there when he was on a hike and since the hike she'd been on, she hadn't kept track of his hikes. However, even before she reached the house, Duncan came from the office to go to his vehicle.

"Duncan! Hi!" Nancy exclaimed, as she stepped from her car. "You were leaving with a group the last time I was here. You're on your way now again? Actually, I can tell you're leading a hike you're dressed like you were when you took us. You guys must be doing a land office business these days."

Duncan stuffed his hands in his back pockets as he talked with her. "Yeah, came back on Thursday, back out on Saturday. It's the way it is in the spring, summer and fall. It's the same for all of us, but we rarely see each other, because now the hikes are all different lengths. You must have a day off again."

"Yes, and I got some disturbing news while I was at work, this week"

"Oh?"

"I've been named in a lawsuit along with the center."

Duncan's face showed his incredulity. "You? What for?"

"The people say I was harassing their son because I quoted the Bible and prayed loud prayers in his room."

Scowling, Duncan stopped right in front of her. "You wouldn't do that!" After another second, he leaned back, his eyes twinkled and his mouth twitched, as he said, "Now on the trail, when you only had an audience of one, maybe, but not at your work." He shook his head. "I've never seen you at work, but I'd swear you wouldn't."

Nancy's eyes sparkled and a smile came to her lips, as she said, "Now Duncan, you know you asked most of the questions and I answered the questions you asked. That's not harassing and you know it!"

Chuckling, he said, "If you say so, Ms Nancy." He stepped aside and added, "Can't stay to chat, I forgot something back at the cabin I must get before my hikers arrive. You know they'll be here right at eight o'clock. You have a fun day with Sandy, she's waiting for you." He waved to her jauntily and walked on to his vehicle.

"Thanks, Duncan." She turned to watch him and said, "Say, what's different about you?"

Duncan stopped, turned a bit and stroked his chin with his short beard and flattened his hair, scowling, he shook his head, baffled as he looked at her. "Nothing, Miss Nancy. Why?"

"Duncan, there is something different about you. It's not your clothes or how you look, it has nothing to do with your hair or anything…" She was silent as they continued to look at each other. She took a step toward him and asked, "Duncan, have you made peace with God? Asked forgiveness for your sins?"

Soberly, he looked at her. Shaking his head incredulously, he said, "How can you tell, Nancy! I've told no one, but you can tell?"

Ten

Without thinking, she ran the few steps to him and threw her arms around him. "You have! You've asked Christ to be your Savior! God has taken away your sin burden! It's there, it's on your face you don't have that haunted look anymore! Oh, Duncan! I'm thrilled! How did it happen?" Realizing where she was, that Duncan only stood in front of her, he hadn't returned her embrace, but she had her arms around him, she pulled back, dropped her arms, her face turned red and she whispered, "Oh, I'm sorry!"

Nodding, he said, "On that youth group trip I rescued a boy who almost drowned. Things they said in their devotions that night and the next night got to me." He shrugged. "I sorta didn't have a choice, you know?"

"I'm so glad!" Turning away, she said, "I'm keeping you from getting whatever and Sandy's waiting for me. Have a good hike."

"Yeah, I'll do that."

Nancy turned her back on Duncan and hurried toward the front door. *What got into you, woman? The man's sworn off women, he plans to be a bachelor the rest of his life and you threw yourself at him! You have to be nuts! He showed me too, he didn't even touch me!* She felt the red on her neck her face felt like it was on fire as she went up the walk to the front door.

Duncan was rooted to the spot. Nancy had hugged him! He watched as she nearly fled from him up the walk to Sandy's front door. Sandy was in the office when he'd walked out, Nancy would be more embarrassed when she realized she'd have to come back and go in the office door. Before she reached the front door, Duncan pulled in a deep breath, spun on his heel and nearly ran to his SUV. He determined not to be in view when she came back, so he was behind the vehicle, about to open the door, when Nancy realized Sandy wasn't in the house, but in the office. He slid behind the wheel when she turned around, with her head down, and hurried to the office door. She didn't look his way as he started up, but he saw the color on her cheeks.

Duncan chuckled, as he left the parking lot. The woman was embarrassed! He drove the few blocks to Isabel's parking lot, pulled into his space, left the SUV running and ran to his cabin. He hoped Isabel wasn't in her favorite chair, because she'd see when he came back that he'd have the Bible from his cabin in his hand. He ran in the cabin, picked up the Bible from the night stand and ran out, the door slammed behind him. Minutes later he was back in his vehicle, squealing his tires back on the highway. He had to hurry to get his spot on Ramon's parking lot before the hikers came. At DeLord's he jumped from the driver's seat and hit the remote for his door to his storage area where his backpack was. He opened one side and laid his Bible down beside his pack. He looked around, but only saw Nancy's car, but he heard traffic on the road.

He had barely put the Bible down when two cars pulled in behind him. They had come from the other direction and soon they were parked and the people were milling around on the lot. Duncan walked up to one of the men and said, "Hi, I'm Duncan…"

The man was looking at DeLord's house, but as Duncan spoke, he whirled around and said, "You must be our guide then."

He chuckled. "If you're part of the hike that leaves in a few minutes, I suspect I am."

The man smiled. "I guess you are. You seem the outdoors type, very competent in the wilds, for sure. I'm Trevor Dallas, glad to meet you, Duncan." Gesturing at those pulling their backpacks from the trunks, he said, "These are my accomplices… Not in crime, mind you."

Duncan grinned. "Glad to meet you. If you're ready, we'll leave in a few minutes."

Just to see if he could torment Nancy, Duncan went to the door to the office and opened it. Both women were there and Sandy was on the phone, but Nancy sat in a chair looking at the paintings waiting for her to finish.

Duncan cleared his throat and when Nancy glanced at him, he grinned at her and saluted. In a whisper, he said, "I saw that blush back there on the lot, Nancy, it was sorta pretty on you, you know."

The red crept up her neck, but she slapped her hands on her neck to cover it and said, "Duncan! You know how to embarrass me, for crying out loud! I thought you'd left."

With a chuckle, he started to close the door. "We're out of here, but I had to say that, didn't want you wondering all weekend, Nancy, see you!"

The door closed, but Nancy could still hear him chuckling. "That man!" she muttered and deliberately looked back at the picture she'd been looking at.

Sandy finished her call and her recording on the computer then looked out at the parking lot to see that all was quiet, the hikers had left. She looked at her friend and said, "Nancy, what was it that bothered you yesterday when you called?"

Nancy turned from the pictures and looked at Sandy, as she blurted out, "Sandy, I've been named in a lawsuit!"

"What! Whatever for?"

Nancy started immediately to tell her, so when she finished, Sandy came from behind the desk and held out both hands and said, "We're going to pray about this right now!"

Nancy took her hands and said, "Yes, please!"

Sandy said, "Father, this is the work of Satan against my friend, Nancy. Please put a hedge around her and protect her from all the fiery darts of the Devil and I know he has many. If she must go to court, give her the words to say, but if she doesn't, may nothing be used against her or keep her from getting this new job here in Vansville. You know exactly why this has happened and we pray that You'll get all the glory in Nancy's life, amen."

They raised their heads and Nancy said, "Thanks, so much Sandy. I can't tell you how much you're always such a help to me."

Not acknowledging that, Sandy grinned and said, "Now then, what were you doing with your arms around Duncan out on the parking lot?" She chuckled, her eyes twinkling. "'Fess up, now, girl, I saw you."

Covering her face with her hands, Nancy whispered, "Nobody was supposed to see that! I...I can't tell you. It's...it's not my place..."

Shaking her head, Sandy waved her hand, as if erasing what Nancy said and said, "What could that man have said to make you hug him like that? I mean, really hug him!" She scratched her cheek and said, "The man's claimed he's sworn off women, but he sure looked like he was enjoying himself."

Still with her hands in front of her face, Nancy's voice was distorted, as she said, "He'll have to tell you. Besides, he wasn't enjoying himself he stood there like a statue and nodded when I said I was sorry."

Sandy scowled. "**He**'ll have to tell me why **you** had **your** arms around **him**?"

"Uh huh. Are we going somewhere?"

Sandy threw her head back and laughed. "That sure was a fast change of subject, but I guess. Actually, Roger has an all day meeting in Blairsville and Raylyn called to see if I wanted to come out to the farm. I told her you were coming and she said to bring you, we four ladies can have a great time together. How about it?"

"She's the pastor's wife?"

"Yes."

"Great! I'm ready! Let's go!" Nancy nearly sighed out loud, she was so glad for the change of subject.

"Well, let me get my purse and the keys and we're out of here!"

"Oh, yes! A day in the country."

Duncan still chuckled as he walked back to his SUV and pulled his backpack closer. He unzipped a pocket and put the Bible in, then shouldered his pack. After a few preliminaries with the hikers, he started on the trail. As he walked, the group fell in behind him, but no one walked with him, even though the trail was wide at first. He shrugged he had things to think about.

He truly was perplexed how Nancy could tell he'd given his life to Christ. He hadn't told anyone, not Sandy or Isabel, so Sandy wouldn't have told Nancy when she called about coming out today. Surely he didn't look *that* different, did he? What had she said? *You don't have that haunted look anymore.* Haunted look? What was a haunted look and how could she tell he didn't have it now? He shrugged, who could tell the mind of a woman?

Since nobody came to walk with him, he decided to enjoy the day. It was warm for the first part of May and as the sun filtered down through the leaves of the trees, some of the bright spots held new ground cover. The May apples were starting to leaf out and the tiny wild flowers were beginning to show some color. He'd enjoyed the out-of-doors most of his life, but now it seemed more vibrant. Just then, he heard a bird singing at the top of its lungs. Was this all happening because he didn't have what seemed like the weight of the world pressing down on him any more? His step seemed lighter, he looked back and realized he needed to slow down the hikers were not keeping up with him. He stopped and waited for them, slouched against a tree and looked around him. It was a beautiful spring day. The sun was bright in a clear blue sky and the breeze was light and warm.

Sandy was about to turn the phone onto automatic pickup for the answering machine when it rang. She sighed and picked up the receiver, "Good morning, DeLord's Hiking Service, this is Sandy!"

"Sandy!"

"Yes, Isabel, what's on your mind?"

"I was sittin' here looking out when that big lug who left about twenty minutes ago came back squealing around the corner, left his machine running, ran to his cabin and only minutes later came back out with that **red** Bible I'd put in his place. He jumped back in his car and barreled out of here. He never looked toward my place it was like he didn't want me to see him! Sandy, the **Bible,** did you hear? Why, the man buried it back in his closet when he first came!"

"Isabel, are you sure? The **Bible** from his cabin?"

"Yes, I'm sure! It's red, how can you miss it if it's red?"

"You have a point, but the **Bible**? The man's an atheist! He's told us over and over! Amazing! You're sure!"

Nancy stood by the door, but she didn't realize she was shaking her head. Sandy looked up and saw her and said to Isabel, "Nancy's shaking her head." Sandy looked at her friend and said, "What, he's not an atheist?"

Nancy stopped shaking her head, but looked up at a picture, she wouldn't answer her friend. Sandy spoke into the phone again, "Isabel, something's going on that I don't know, but I'll find out real soon."

Sandy put the phone back in the cradle and looked at Nancy. "Okay, you're acting really strange. First you throw your arms around Duncan..." Her eyes sparkled and she said, "He told you he'd become a Christian? Is that what you're not telling me? Listen here, young lady, you gotta tell me something like that!"

Nancy started shaking her head again. "No, I guessed. There was something about him, he acted different or something. I asked him and he was surprised that I could tell. He said it was something that happened on a hike."

Sandy flipped the switch on the phone and wheeled herself from behind the desk. "Nancy! You weren't going to tell me, were you?"

"No, it should be him, don't you think?"

"I suppose, but really! Oh, praise God!" Sandy came up behind her friend chuckling. "Now you can chase him!"

Red crept up Nancy's neck again she looked at her friend horrified. Waving her hand in front of her, she exclaimed, "Sandy! I will not!"

"You can so! In only a little while you'll be neighbors." Sandy laughed. "Oh, wow! Isn't this something?"

The phone rang again and the answering machine automatically picked up. As soon as it beeped Isabel said impatiently, "You didn't run off yet! I know you didn't move that fast! You said you'd find out! Come on, what about Duncan!"

Sandy snatched up the receiver. "Isabel, the best news! Nancy found out that Duncan gave his life to Christ on one of the hikes he led!"

"Praise God. Why that old coot! He never told us!"

"No, Nancy guessed. We're out of here, Isabel. Have a great day!"

"You do the same, girl!"

"Oh, we will! We're going to the farm!"

Duncan moved along ahead of the group he was leading. He was enjoying the May weather, the bright sunshine and the soft breeze. It wasn't until after lunch when one of the men moved up beside him and the two led the others away from the little stream that they had used for water to eat some dry rations. "Do you like this kind of work?" the man asked, still working on getting comfortable with his backpack on his back. Duncan decided that he was a year or two older than he was, but still in his prime and quite good looking.

"Sure! I love the out-of-doors, I have since I was a teenager. I've hiked in several places across the country. Are these folks all friends of yours?"

The man shrugged. "I suppose, I only met them about a week ago, but I decided I needed to learn about the area before I really started my new job."

"Oh?"

"Yeah, well, you see,... well, you know that new clinic that's being build here?" Duncan nodded. "I'm to be the doctor there. I've hiked before in the Rockies and when I learned from Dillon Marshall that there was a hiking service here I decided to take a look around in the area. It's a small town, do you have many hikes?"

Duncan nodded. "There are three of us guides and we have been covered up since March leading hikes. Most of the people are from places within seventy-five miles of here. I can't think of anyone who's from another state. So you'll be the resident doctor here at the clinic when it opens? Will you live here?"

The young man finally stood straight and said, "Yes and no. I'll be here at the clinic three days a week at first. We aren't sure if the place can pay for itself until it's open, so those of us making policy decided we'd go with a doctor on the premises three days a week to see how it works out. The rest of the time will be staffed by full time people a nurse will be in charge when I'm not here. Actually, I'll be in the ER at the Blairsville Hospital, or on call there, so I'll live in Blairsville, at least until we see how it's going here. Besides, I was told there aren't any places to rent or for sale in this little burg."

Duncan turned with his hand out. He grinned and said, "I'm glad to meet you, I'm Duncan Roads. Did you tell me your name?"

Sheepishly, the man took Duncan's hand and said, "No, I guess I didn't tell you my name, Duncan. I'm Stan Miles. I finished my residency in Atlanta in ER medicine a few weeks ago. I kind of wanted a small place to get my feet wet, you know? Blairsville hospital's good size, but I'm excited to be in charge of this clinic."

Duncan chuckled. "I'd say Vansville's about as small as they come. Whoever told you there's no place to rent didn't have it quite right. I'll grant there isn't much and I don't know of any places for sale. That clinic was the first place built in a good many years. However, I rent a cabin from a lady whose place is right next to your clinic. She owns six cabins one's a handicapped equipped cabin, then five others. I rent one and now one of the nurses who'll be working at the clinic has rented another."

"So she rents them long term?"

"By the month, but she's glad to have you stay for as many months as you'd like. Especially in the winter she's happy for the long term renters. She's really good to me she keeps my cabin clean and knows my schedule. When I leave on a hike I turn down my heat, but when I get back, she's turned it up so it's comfortable and now it's the air conditioning. One time I forgot to pick up my clothes and she'd washed and folded them. Man, she's eighty years old! I determined she'd never do that again."

"That is something! Like I say, for now my job here's only for three days a week, but there is the possibility the practice'll grow, so I'll keep that in mind. You know some of the staff who's going to be there?"

"That Dillon you mentioned went on one of the first hikes I led in the spring and also on that hike was a nurse from his establishment and now she's leaving there and coming here full time." He made a face. "She's rented one of Isabel's cabins, too."

Stan chuckled. "She'll be able to roll out of bed and still be on time."

"Yeah, I guess she will. You have a wife and kids?"

"No, I'm single, no kids. If you're a hiking guide and rent a small cabin I'd hazard a guess you're single, too."

"Mmm, and I intend to stay that way for a very long time."

"Don't like women?"

Duncan shrugged. "You might say that. Oh, I like women well enough, but I like my freedom lots better, if you know what I mean. You, why aren't you attached? You must be older than me."

"I'm from a small town in Kansas. When I came to Georgia the girl I was going with, that I hoped to spend my life with, decided that Georgia was too far away and family was much too important to leave for a guy who had another four or five years of schooling. She said goodbye the night before I was to leave for Atlanta and I've never heard from her since. My mom has told me she married my good friend who came back to our home town after four years of college." He shrugged. "I guess that's how it happens some times."

"Rough. Precisely why I'm unattached."

Only a few days after Roger and Raylyn picked up Heidi after returning from their wedding trip, Roger asked the man who had helped build the ramp at the church if he'd help him build another at his home. Both his front and back doors had steps leading up to the doors and he wanted to be able to have Ramon and Sandy come visit sometimes. Of course that couldn't happen with stairs, because Sandy's chair was too heavy to lift. During a warm spell in January, they had removed the steps and built the ramp from the back porch to the driveway. In the last several months the DeLord's had visited several times and Sandy had been happy for the ramp. She had brought them another picture to show her appreciation.

Sandy and Nancy hurried out the door before the phone rang again. When Sandy drove up to Clemens' house, Heidi ran down the ramp, her face wreathed in smiles and her little arm waving wildly. She was first at the van when Sandy put the stick in park. "Miss Sandy! Miss Sandy!" They could hear through the glass.

"Isn't that child adorable?" Nancy exclaimed, before she opened the door.

"She is. I love her to pieces!" Sandy exclaimed. "She and her mommy came from Michigan to spend Thanksgiving with her grandma Isabel. I had invited Isabel and her company for dinner, along with Roger." Sandy laughed and started the mechanism to open her lift door. "That child nearly got them married before the weekend was over!"

Nancy laughed. "Oh, how super!"

Jumping up and down from the foot of the ramp, the little girl clapped her hands and shouted, "Mommy, Mommy, come quick! Miss Sandy be here!"

The old dog joined Heidi and stood wagging his tail, as if he was greeting old friends. Nancy was already out of the van and Sandy had the passenger door open when Raylyn hurried down the ramp to stand beside Heidi. Out of breath, Raylyn, said to Sandy, "Why is it the phone always rings when people drive up to the house? Usually, it's a telemarketer, just like now."

Nancy agreed, "Absolutely! I'm hardly ever home and I rarely get company, but when I hear my door buzzer it's usually at the same time as the phone. Either that or it's supper time!"

Raylyn smiled at Nancy and said, "Hey, it's great to see you again! I'm so glad you could come with Sandy today. I hear you're moving to Vansville soon."

"Yes! I'm excited about moving, especially after what's happened at work this week. You wouldn't believe, but I've been accused of harassment by a former patient's parents. They're suing both the center and me."

Shocked, Raylyn asked, "Whatever for?"

Shaking her head, Nancy answered, "They say I preached and prayed loud prayers in their son's room."

"Ridiculous! I mean…"

"Isn't that the truth?" Sandy said, coming to the foot of the ramp. "Of course, she wouldn't do that! I can't imagine…"

Heidi didn't understand what the ladies were talking about, but she was anxious to get the day going, so she put her hand on Sandy's chair arm and said, "Come on! Mommy made some yummy buns for you guys. You gotta come eat 'em!"

Nancy scowled, but Sandy asked, "Yummy buns? What are they?"

"They be big like this…" she held her fingers in a circle and continued, "and they comed outta the oven. Mommy puts white stuff on top and they be **good**!" Rubbing her tummy with her other hand, she said, "Come on, Miss Sandy! Push the button on your chair and let's go! They aren't so good when they get cold!"

"You mean your mommy made cinnamon buns like Isabel makes?"

"Uh huh and they be inside!"

Sandy pushed the control on her armrest and said, "Jump on here, girl! What are we waiting for? Isabel's cinnamon buns are to die for! Your mommy's are probably just as good."

"Uh huh!" Heidi's little face was beaming, as she stood on Sandy's footrest and the chair started to move up the ramp.

As they entered the house, the aroma of fresh brewed coffee welcomed them. Sandy raised her face and sniffed. "Wow! Fresh coffee and cinnamon buns, you can't get any aroma any better than that!"

Following behind Sandy and Nancy, Raylyn closed the door and said, "Come on and sit down at the table. I have hot milk for Heidi's hot chocolate and fresh coffee for us. Thank goodness Linus is outside, he loves these buns and he won't take any scolding when he's inside and I make them."

Sandy nodded. "Cat knows what's good! Nancy, sit right down, you haven't tasted anything like Isabel's buns and I'm sure Raylyn has the same recipe, so you are in for a treat!"

Nancy slipped into a chair and sighed, licking her lips. "If they taste like they smell, I can't wait to have one. Home made cinnamon buns, mmm mmm, good!" She looked up at Raylyn and smiled. "Since I'm a nurse, I take my coffee black. Night duty in nursing school sorta trains you for needing that black caffeine fix."

Heidi climbed up onto her chair and kneeled on it with hot chocolate and her own bun, she took a big mouthful and barely had it swallowed before she grinned at Nancy. "You know what? We got some new chickies out in the barn you wanna see 'em?"

Nancy grinned. "How many, Heidi?"

"Oh, lots! Daddy say they be growed up pretty soon."

"I want to see them when they're still little!"

"Ya gotta hurry, then!" she said, taking another bite.

"Heidi," Raylyn said, wiping her hands from the sticky confection before she picked up her mug, "You need to slow down or you'll get an upset tummy. They won't be grown up before we finish our snack!"

Seriously, Heidi said, "You never know, Mommy, maybe. Daddy feed 'em lotsa grain."

Nancy put the last bite in her mouth, wiped her mouth and fingers and picked up her mug. Just before putting the mug to her lips, she said, "Heidi, I'll come as soon as my coffee's gone. You think that'll be soon enough?"

Heidi nodded. "Yeah, they be probly only half growed now."

"Can I come see, Heidi?'

Heidi shook her head solemnly. "Miss Sandy, there be a step up into our chicken room, you cudunt get your chair up there. Asides, their mommy be in the last box, you can't even see 'em from the walk outside."

"But couldn't you bring a chick to the door and show me?"

"I duno, Miss Sandy, Daddy din't say I could touch 'em. Asides, if they be half growed, they be too big for me!"

Chuckling, Raylyn said, "Come on, let's go see. They only hatched out two days ago. I can probably pick one up to show Miss Sandy."

Heidi breathed a sigh of relief. "Good, Mommy, I sure don' want Miss Sandy to be dist-a-pointed, you know."

Nancy cleared the table and put the dishes in the sink, then Heidi hopped on Sandy's foot rest, but Raylyn pulled Heidi's sweater from a hook by the door and held it for her. Heidi huffed and slid her arms in it, then Raylyn opened the back door and held it open for Sandy, then she and Nancy followed the chair down the ramp. Sandy went carefully across the uneven gravel driveway and waited as Heidi jumped off to open the door to the small barn. Heidi didn't wait for her she ran down the wide aisle to the far end and jumped up on the step to reach the block that kept the door closed to the chicken coop.

"I not scared no more, Daddy let the rooster and the lazy chickens outside, now. Only the mommies stay inside wif the chickies."

"That's good, I won't be scared either, then," Nancy said.

Heidi grinned at the young woman and said, "Miss Nancy, you not scared, you a big lady. Big ladies not get scared!"

"But I never lived on a farm like you do." She stopped beside Sandy and looked at the little girl. "I never got this close to chickens."

"Yes, but you lot bigger than chickens."

"I don't know, Heidi, chickens can make an awful lot of noise."

Heidi jumped from the step, then reached for Nancy's hand and said, "Come on, Miss Nancy, we go in together. If I not scared, you not be scared either."

Heidi pulled the door open and all was quiet in the coop. There were three hens sitting on nests, but they could hear soft cheeping sounds coming from the far nest. Heidi looked up at Nancy and whispered, "See, Miss Nancy, it be real quiet in here, you don't gotta be afraid. The chickies be real small and their mommy only sit on the nest."

"Okay, so I can see the babies?"

Heidi nodded and tiptoeing took a step toward the last nest. She put a finger across her mouth and whispered, "Shhhh, you gots to be real quiet not to scare the chickies." She pointed to the last nest. "See, there be free chickies by that mommy. They comed out from under their mommy two days ago."

"Wow!" Nancy said, as she saw the tiny yellow puffs.

Raylyn stood with them, but closer to the door, so Heidi said, "Mommy, can we show Miss Sandy a chickie?"

She pushed up some of the feathers from the hen's side and said, "Of course, but I think I'd better take the one to show her, don't you?"

"Yes, Mommy. Daddy showed me tis morning. They got sharp toenails. He say I not get scratched if I not touch 'em."

Picking up the tiny chick, Raylyn said, "Yes, I guess that's true. You show Miss Nancy the other two while I show Miss Sandy this one."

"'K, Mommy, we be real careful and look at the chickies."

Heidi looked up at Nancy and said, "They be real cute, huh?"

"They are! They make a lot of noise for being so small."

"Yeah, Daddy say they be hungry when they make so much noise." She looked down the short walk and said, "Mommy, can Miss Nancy and me feed the chickies? Daddy lef' some stuff in the pail here."

"Heidi," Raylyn said, from the doorway, "take only one handful and put it around the hen. We don't want them eating too much. It's not good for them."

Heidi nodded. "'K, Mommy." She looked up at Nancy and said. "I gotta do it 'cause your hand be too big, Miss Nancy. I 'member now, Daddy tell me tis morning I not give the chickies too much."

"I want to watch you, Heidi!" Nancy exclaimed. "I'm sure the chicks know you better than me and you won't scare them like I would." Nancy was having more fun watching and listening to Heidi than she was seeing the chicks.

Heidi nodded solemnly. "Yeah, maybe so."

A few minutes later, Raylyn brought the third chick back and put it in the nest beside the others. Heidi was busily picking a few cornels of grain from one hand and putting it in front of a chick. Nancy stood watching with an indulgent smile. The chick that Raylyn brought back tried to snatch some grain from in front of another chick, but Heidi scowled and said, "Chickie, I gots yours. Leave hers alone! I told you tis morning you gots to share. Go on! Here be yours."

Sandy was out of sight, but she could hear Heidi clearly. She chuckled softly and murmured, "That precious child! I love her to pieces."

After feeding the chicks, until her hands were empty and watching them for a while, Heidi was out the door, even before Raylyn and Nancy came out. While Raylyn closed the door and fastened the block of wood, she hopped onto Sandy's footrest again, but this time she put her hands around her mouth and whispered, "Miss Sandy, Mommy gots a secret, her and Daddy. They not tell nobody else but me."

Giving her a horrified look, Sandy said, "You aren't going to tell me Mommy and Daddy's secret, are you?"

"You be special, Miss Sandy, you my teacher." Just to be sure, Heidi looked at Raylyn as she came from the coop. "Mommy, it be okay to tell Miss Sandy 'bout your secret?" She turned back to Sandy, before Raylyn could answer and said, "Asides, it be only part their secret."

"Oh?"

"Uh huh, 'cause I get a sister or brother 'cause of their secret."

"I see," Sandy said, chuckling. "Are you excited about that?"

A grin spread to cover Heidi's whole face. "Oh, yes! I be big sister! Mommy say I be big 'nuff, I can help change him!"

Raylyn sighed. "Heidi, you didn't let me say it was okay to tell Miss Sandy our secret."

Looking at her mommy, exasperated, she said, "Mommy, you know I not tell her your part, just my part."

"I know, but since you told your part, now she knows our part."

"Uh oh, I guess I flubbed up," she said, looking at Sandy and covered her mouth.

"I guess you did, Heidi!" Sandy looked at Raylyn with a grin and said, "Congratulations are in order! When will this big event take place?"

Heidi clapped her hands. "Mommy say it be near Tanksgibbin!"

"How about that!"

"Yeah, Daddy say we can make a pumpkin pie wif a face for him."

Raylyn and Nancy had come up beside Sandy's chair and Nancy was chuckling. "Is that so? You won't scare the baby, will you?"

"Oh, no! I make a happy face. It make baby smile."

"That's good." Sandy held out her arms to Raylyn. With a smile, she said, "Raylyn, I'm so happy for you! Congratulations!"

Raylyn hugged her back. "Thanks, we're so excited!"

Nancy came and put her arms around the other two. "I'm happy for you, too."

After they let go of each other, Raylyn stood up and said, "You know, there was a time, not too long ago, when I was totally crushed and devastated, but now I'm extremely happy. Roger has been everything I've ever hoped for and more."

Sandy nodded. "I'm so glad!"

"Believe me, so am I!"

There was a "Moooo" outside the window and Heidi scowled and said, "Mommy, how come Cow's so close?"

"Maybe she wanted to get some of the scratch grain the chickens have."

Heidi let out an exasperated sigh. "Mommy, she be bad cow! Her not to get into chickens' food! You go spank her!"

Both Sandy and Nancy laughed, and Sandy asked, "Heidi, why don't you go spank her?"

"Oh, no! Her too big for me to spank!"

"And I'm not?" Raylyn asked, skeptically.

"Mommy, you told Daddy you be big as a house when you had me, you be big 'nuff. Asides, you not scared of Cow."

Heidi jumped on Sandy's foot rest and said, "Come on, Miss Sandy, we go aside and watch Mommy spank Cow."

"Okay," Sandy said and turned her control on, then headed down the walkway. Nancy followed her and soon they were outside in the sunshine.

Raylyn didn't come with them, but turned back into the chicken coop, closing the door behind her. When Sandy's chair reached the side of the barn, Heidi said, "See, Mommy gots her little switch." After a huge sigh, Heidi said, "I don' know how Cow get in wif chickens. Daddy make a big fence and the gate have a big lock on it, but she like to eat their stuff, so she gets that gate open. You know she don't ask chickens if she can have some! She Mooo and they run away 'cause she so big."

"I should think so!" Nancy said. "She is big! She could step on one of those chickens and squash it."

"Yeah, but she don't."

From the other end of the barn they heard Raylyn say, "Cow! You did it again! Roger will be so mad!" She swatted the cow's rear and headed for the gate between the chicken yard and the open field. She swung the gate open and smacked the cow again. "Come on; get out into your own grassy field! That's where you belong! Look at all that green grass and you aren't eating it! Now go on!" The other three at the fence could see the look on the cow's face, and her tail swished.

Raylyn slammed the gate shut right behind the cow, because the rooster was at her feet trying to sneak out and that was not to be. From outside the gate, the cow turned her head and looked at Raylyn over her shoulder. "Moooooo!" she said, then kicked up her back feet and started galloping across the field.

From the safety of Sandy's footrest, Heidi said, "Mommy, Cow be mad at you. Daddy say she be mad when she kick like that."

"Yes, I know, but she can get over it!"

Just then the rooster crowed and Heidi said, "Uh oh, he not like Mommy, either. He want to get out, too." As Raylyn hurried toward the door into the chicken coop, Heidi yelled, "Hurry, Mommy! Rooster be comin' real fast afer you!"

Raylyn went back into the barn and only moments later joined the others. "He'll get over it, Heidi. He can strut around for the other hens now."

"Yes, he like to do that."

Raylyn grinned. "Come on, after all that excitement let's go back inside."

Sandy started her chair and headed for the ramp. "Great! We're almost there!"

After a very happy time spent with Raylyn and Heidi, Nancy and Sandy left in the van for Sandy's home in town. Instead of stopping at their house, Sandy said, "I need some groceries. You won't mind going to Alex's with me, will you?"

"Oh, no! Alex is a nice guy and I'll need to get to know places and people in town real soon. You know, I'm excited about moving here!"

"I'm glad. We'll get to spend more time together, I'm sure. What kind of schedule do you think you'll have?"

"From what I've heard the clinic'll be open from eight in the morning until five or six in the evening, Monday through Saturday. I don't know who else'll be on staff, but surely there'll be other nurses beside me. I'm sure we'll split the time between us."

"Will there be a doctor here?"

"I think I heard there'll be one part time, but I don't know how part time he'll be here. It probably depends on the demand."

"Even so, our guys'll have to call for a helicopter from Blairsville, won't they? Your clinic can't do something like that."

"Yes, there wouldn't be any possibility of a clinic here being equipped for something like that, even for a long time in the future. For an airlift they'll have to call Blairsville Hospital. They're the only place that has a helicopter."

Sandy drove into town and parked in front of the grocery store. Not long after Sandy moved to town, Alex had painted a handicapped parking space right in front of his store. Since it was such a small town and everyone knew Sandy, no one parked in that spot unless it was Sandy, so she pulled into her spot, let down her lift and went in the grocery store with Nancy.

"Hi, Alex! How are you today?"

Coming from behind the counter, Alex gave her a grin. "Hi, yourself, Ms Sandy! I'm fine, how's yourself?"

"I'm great Alex, especially since Ramon's coming home today and his next hike cancelled last evening. He doesn't know it yet, but I'll get to keep him for a whole week! I think that's super!"

"Wow! What'll you do with all that time?"

"We'll go to church tomorrow, but we'll wing it then. Anyway, I need something to put on the table for a hungry man who's been surviving on trail food. Nancy and I'll take a look."

"You do that, ladies. Have a good look around. I got a good selection in the meat department in just yesterday."

"Thanks, Alex!" Before they turned away from the counter, Sandy said, "Did you know Nancy's moving to Vansville to be a nurse at the new clinic?"

"She is? Well, that's great. I'll get another customer, won't I?"

Nancy smiled at the older man. "I can't wait, Alex. I've already put my name on the line for one of Isabel's cabins. It's such a lovely place I'm anxious to move in."

Winking, he said, "So you'll be neighbors with Duncan?"

Acting very prim, she said, "There's a cabin between us, Alex."

He chuckled. "That's hardly anything, Miss Nancy."

Sandy's laughter came to them. "Yes, isn't that so, Alex!"

Several bags of groceries later, Sandy was driving home when they met a delivery truck. Sandy waved and the man waved back, but he only drove passed them enough to turn around in the street. He followed the van to her house and pulled onto their parking lot, off the road. While Sandy turned her van around, opened the garage door and backed in, the man went in the back of his truck. As Sandy turned off the van, the man stepped from his truck with a huge box.

As he walked into the garage, he said, "Hi, Ms Sandy! I have a delivery for you. This sure is big enough, but it's not heavy!"

He carried it to a place that was cleared, obviously where he put other boxes he delivered from time to time. Sandy smiled, as she lowered herself to the floor. "Wow! I guess you do have a delivery for me. Thanks so much, Nelson. Thanks for coming back to bring that in for me. You know I appreciate it."

"No problem, Ms Sandy. It's a pleasure to do this. I guess you still don't have a gallery here in Georgia?"

Shaking her head, Sandy said, "Nelson, I am covered up! The gallery in Philly keeps me hopping. Between the commissions I have and my piano students I couldn't possibly open a gallery. My only gallery here is our office."

After she'd signed his list, she said, "Have time for an iced tea? You know I always keep a pitcher full in the fridge all summer."

He shook his head and took back his clipboard, then said, "Sorry, not today. Sandy, I left the warehouse late this morning because my truck needed a little work and I've been playing catch-up all day. I'll see you next time."

"Sure will, thanks," she called after him.

Nancy helped Sandy with her groceries, as they set things on the counter, she said, "Are you sure you want me here for supper? You have Ramon so little during the hiking season."

Sandy looked at her friend fiercely. "Nancy, don't you ask a question like that! You eat alone and I usually eat alone. Tonight there'll be three of us for dinner and that settles that!"

Nancy chuckled. "Okay, I accept."

Sandy set about putting her groceries away and Nancy helped her with things she knew where to put them. They still enjoyed their 'girl's day out'. They chatted again about their visit with Raylyn and Heidi while they did. It had been sunny and balmy when they were at Raylyn's house, but not long after they were in Sandy's house, dark clouds moved across the sun. Neither of the girls noticed until a branch of the tree outside the kitchen window scraped loudly across the side of the house.

Sandy glanced out the window and said, "Goodness! Are your car windows up, Nancy? It looks like it could rain cats and dogs!"

"I always put my windows up it's a habit, since I live in Blairsville." Nancy went to the window and looked out. "Man! It clouded up fast! It was still warm and sunny at the grocery. If Ramon's hikers don't get back soon they'll get soaked! Duncan has a group out, is Neal out?"

"When Ramon gets in Duncan'll be the only one, Neal's goes tomorrow, he's off today."

"Then it's only Duncan's group that'll have to sleep wet."

Nancy left the window and sat in a kitchen chair, with her back to the window. She didn't mind rain, but this looked like it would be a fierce storm and she'd rather not watch it. As Sandy pulled out her big skillet, she said, "You told Alex that Ramon's group cancelled."

"Yes, they called last evening. They were supposed to go out in two days, but one of the couples who were to go had to cancel and they knew we didn't take less than five. I'm sorry for them, I know people look forward to going on a hike, but at least they were following the rules."

Eleven

"I know about that part, the part about no less than five. I was one of the two that were with Lilly White back in the early spring. I wasn't a close friend of hers, but I'd tried to be her friend. She'd recently moved into my building and I'd met her at the mailboxes. It wasn't until we came out here that I knew her true colors."

Sandy shrugged. "It's water under the bridge, Nancy. We both decided she wasn't worth getting all upset about. You know, Duncan told us she came back and tried to get him to add her to his next hike."

Nancy shook her head. "Did she really? She was such a spoiled brat!"

Sandy had put the skillet on the stove when they heard a loud snap outside. "Uh oh!" Nancy said, "The storm's upon us!" Her last word was drowned out by the roar of thunder, followed immediately by the rain slamming against the window.

Sandy shook her head. "Those poor people will be soaked if they're anywhere close by. I watched the weather last night nothing was said about rain today. But then, nobody ever said weathermen know what's happening for sure."

After another snap and roar, Nancy asked, "Do all your hikes leave from here?"

"Most of them do, but there are a few trailheads that the guys have the hikers drive to. Ramon's left from here, so they'll come back here."

The storm hadn't moved, the lightning and thunder were nearly simultaneous and it was pouring when Nancy heard a car door slam. "I bet the group's back. I heard a car door."

Sandy looked at the clock. "Maybe so. It's about the right time."

Other car doors slammed outside and both women felt a cool draft and heard, "Sweetheart, I'm home!"

"Oh!" Sandy exclaimed.

The skillet on the stove was forgotten, fortunately, Sandy hadn't turned on the heat under it, as the wheelchair whirled around and a smile appeared on Sandy's face. In only seconds the chair disappeared from the kitchen. The door closed and the breeze stopped. Nancy watched and decided she'd let them greet each other without her there to witness. She knew that if she saw her husband only as frequently as Sandy saw Ramon, she was pretty sure she wouldn't want company for dinner when her man came home or a witness when they greeted each other.

From the hallway, Nancy heard, "Honey! You're soaked to the skin! Rush in the bedroom and take a warm shower. It may be May, but you can still catch cold. I don't want even a sniffle from you!"

Ramon's warm baritone reached Nancy as he chuckled. "What, you don't want me to kiss you while I'm wet?"

"Honey, I want your kisses, but I don't want you to get sick." It was quiet for several minutes, but then Nancy heard a door close, so she assumed that Ramon had gone for his shower.

She knew she was right when Sandy came back to the kitchen alone and soon they could hear the water running in the bathroom close by, on the other side of the wall. Sandy poured some oil in the skillet and opened a package of meat she'd bought at Alex's store that afternoon. Soon, she had other things cooking on the stove.

"I try to feed him well for dinner on the night he comes home. He's eaten trail food and some of it can be rather tasteless. I guess you can remember about that."

"Yeah, especially in the rain."

"I guess you can't start a fire in the rain, can you?"

"Duncan got one going that one night, but it was only drizzling, he only found one big log that wasn't wet, so we barely had enough heat to cook our stew. Believe me we had more smoke than heat that night. Of course, the wind doesn't help, either. We all ate granola bars the next morning because we could hear the storm coming and poor Mel didn't get his wake up coffee. It didn't matter, the rain came so fast and the leaves weren't big enough, so even though we ran for shelter under the trees, we got drenched. That storm lasted forever, it seemed. We even saw it later, down in the valley."

"I've never been camping, as you can well imagine. Living in Philadelphia there wasn't a chance, even for my family to go. They never talked about something like that all we ever did was go to the huge park close by. When I came from Philly I stayed a couple of nights in my van on the way down, so that's my total experience with roughing it." Giggling, she added, "Not much roughing, that's for sure."

"I don't know; you still didn't have running water or any facilities."

Stirring her meat sauce, Sandy grinned and exclaimed, "Believe me, I know that! When I stopped at night I tried really hard to be close to some facilities. I didn't travel on the interstates, I wanted to take it slower and see more of the countryside, so there were no rest areas like the interstates have." Nancy turned and looked out the window, but she shook her head. Sandy was such an awesome person there was not an ounce of bitterness in her.

Ramon came into the kitchen in a pair of sweats and a snug T shirt and bare feet. He went straight to his wife and hugged her and gave her several kisses, before he said, "Whew! That feels a lot better. We watched that bank of clouds come up and knew we wouldn't make it back before the storm hit. Believe me, you can't run with a pack on your back. Hi, Nancy, so you had a day off today?"

"Yes, we went to Raylyn's and had a fun day with her and Heidi."

Ramon grinned. "Isn't Heidi cute?"

"Adorable!"

"Honey, guess what!"

Ramon bent over, coming behind Sandy and nibbled her ear. "What, Love?"

"We learned Heidi's part of Raylyn and Roger's secret."

Ramon chuckled. "You did and what was that?"

Her eyes twinkling as she looked at her husband, Sandy said, "Heidi said she's excited because she gets to be a big sister sometime near Thanksgiving."

Ramon straightened up, put his hands on Sandy's shoulders, threw his head back and laughed. "Wow! Of course, that's all you heard, Raylyn didn't tell you anything, is that right?"

Nancy and Sandy both laughed, and Sandy said, "Raylyn wasn't really unhappy that Heidi spilled the beans. I think she and Roger are really thrilled about it. She was most happy to take our congratulations."

Still chuckling, Ramon said, "I can imagine! I must razz that man next time I see him. Imagine that man of the cloth...."

"I knew you would, Honey," Sandy interrupted.

Stan and Duncan were still walking together when the sun went behind a dark cloud. Only a few minutes later a cool breeze swept through the trees around them and only a little while later the cloud had spread to cover the entire sky and the breeze had picked up. Duncan said, "Hmm, the forecast I watched last night didn't call for rain today, but it sure looks like we could be in for a shower before nightfall."

"I guess that's why your literature says to pack rain gear as standard equipment. I had to go buy a slicker, I'm glad I did!"

"Yup, that's true. It's still early enough in the year that showers come up. Later, in July and August we may not get any, even when it's forecast." He turned around and faced the other hikers who were chatting among themselves. "Folks, it looks like we'll get into a shower here pretty soon. We still have another couple of hills to go before we can camp, so you might try to find your rain gear. We'll stop under the trees so you can shed your packs and take a look."

"Oh, great!" the leader grumbled.

One of the hikers looked up at the sky then at the hiker he was beside and said, "Rain? Rain gear?"

"Yeah," Duncan answered. "It does rain in north Georgia in May and our literature clearly says that rain gear is standard equipment."

"Wow! I guess I get wet."

They saw a streak of lightning and shortly after that they heard the thunder. "Yeah," Duncan said, "I guess you will."

"We can't go back?" a young woman whined. "We're gonna have to camp in the rain? How horrible!"

"No, we can't really turn back, we've been hiking all day, we'd get wet either way, if we tried to go back, we'd be still quite a distance from base when it got dark and I'm not partial to getting lost in the dark, since it's hard to see a trail in the dark. If we go on to tonight's campsite, we'll be wet long before we get there."

She sighed, "I didn't bring any rain gear, either. I guess I didn't read the pamphlet Dean gave me too well."

One of the other young men grinned, as he pulled out his rain slicker. "I guess we'll have a wet T shirt contest, won't we?"

As the young man pulled his slicker from his pack, she swatted his arm. "Donald! You are not a nice guy! I swear if you were, you'd lend me your rain slicker so I wouldn't get wet."

Stating the obvious, he said, "Then I'd get wet."

"Yeah, so you would," she agreed.

Not even offering her his slicker, Donald pushed his head into the hole and pulled the slicker down so his hands came through the arm holes. "Since I have my slicker on already, I guess I'll have to enjoy the wet T shirt when it's time." He turned to lift his backpack to put on.

"Humph!" the woman groused.

The sky seemed to get even darker just as a roar of the thunder overpowered anything else Shelly wanted to say. She and Marvin were drenched instantly and the others that had taken their time getting out their slickers were also drenched. The rain beat down on the group, even through the trees, since the wind was blowing fiercely.

Between thunder roars, Stan asked, "Any chance of a tornado?"

"Yeah, there is. Last year Ramon was injured in one. If the sky gets any worse we'd probably better seek shelter. Right now it only looks like a bad thunderstorm." Since he couldn't be heard above the crashing storm and the pelting rain, Duncan raised his hand and motioned the group to start walking. Reluctantly, everyone fell in behind Duncan.

It wasn't long before the trail was completely mud and the hikers were slipping in it. Duncan was glad there was no shale between where they were and their campsite for the night. He wondered if this was a shower or if it would stay with them. He was surprised when he remembered the hike that Nancy had gone on. They'd only had one and a half good days on that hike and the rest they'd survived drizzle and thunderstorms. He sighed, he knew she'd had her fill of hiking with that three days. He wished he could take her on a hike when it didn't rain.

That little imp on his shoulder tapped his ear and whispered, *What are you thinking, man? Aren't you forgetting that you don't like women, you're going to be a bachelor for life, and Nancy..., you've forgotten her, right?*

He brushed his shoulder and muttered, "You're just a drop of rain, so now you're gone!"

On Monday, when Nancy went to the time clock to clock in, there was a note clipped to her card that said, *Come see me this morning, Dillon.* Nancy wasn't late for work, but she only had a few minutes, so she ripped the note from her card, ran it through the clock, pushed it back into its slot and ran down the hall from the clock to Dillon's office in the administrative wing. The door was open, so she didn't knock, just pushed it further open and went in. As usual, he was punching keys on his computer, but he looked up at Nancy with a smile.

"Ah, just the lady I need to see."

Pulling in a breath, she asked, "What's up now, Dillon?"

Handing over a sheet of paper, the young man said, "This was here on my desk when I came in this morning. I guess you must testify and the hearing is set for Wednesday this week."

Nancy sighed, "Dillon, I was really dreading this. I was hoping I wouldn't have to go to court, but I could give a statement or something."

Dillon shrugged. "It doesn't look like that'll be, Nancy. From what I've heard, this may be a sticky situation. You got a lawyer?"

"Some woman from the center's attorney's office came by to take a statement a while ago. She said she'd see what she could do. I guess she couldn't do much. I'll call Miss Osborne and see what I'm supposed to do."

"Better do it today, Nancy, Wednesday's only day after tomorrow."

She sighed again. "Don't remind me!"

Nancy took the paper and saw it was a subpoena from the court requiring her presence at the courtroom of Judge Sanders on Wednesday at ten o'clock. She hurried from Dillon's office to her ward and walked into the head nurse's office in time to take the last seat for morning report. However, the night charge nurse hadn't started report, she was facing the door, obviously waiting for Nancy to arrive, who felt rather conspicuous, since all the others were watching her.

"Hey, girl," she said to Nancy, "this note was on the desk when I came on duty at midnight. The evening charge told me to be sure you got it this morning, I do as I'm told."

Nancy held out her hand and said, "Thanks, I think."

She handed Nancy an envelope, but then turned back to her card file and began report, obviously, now that her mission was accomplished, she was more interested in getting her report finished so she could leave for a comfortable bed than what Nancy's letter said. Nancy quickly slid the envelope under the top sheet of blank paper on her clipboard and pulled her pen from her pocket so she could take notes on the current patients. She'd have time later to read the note. It looked just as official as the subpoena.

Rodney had finished his residential therapy and been released, the patients that Nancy had now were all good patients and she'd been having no problems with them. In fact, she had one empty bed, according to the nurse's report. Maybe she would have a few minutes to get in touch with the supervisor today. She hoped that was true.

After report, she and the other team leaders stayed in the little office, while the CNAs left the room to start their work. It was the usual thing. Looking over her patients, Nancy realized her first treatment wasn't for another forty minutes, so she made her schedule then pulled out the envelope. She was sure it was about the court appearance, even before she slit the seal.

The single sheet inside said:

Miss Nancy Southerland:

Your appearance is required in Judge Sanders' courtroom at ten o'clock Wednesday. You will please appear by nine thirty outside the courtroom to receive instructions. You may have one character witness who should be willing to be called to testify in your behalf. If you so choose, they should be present at nine thirty as well.

For Barnhill, Duncan & Martin Attorneys at Law

Ann Blakestein

"Great! Just great!" Nancy mumbled.

Nancy hadn't left the seat, but the other team leaders had left when Mary Osborne pushed open the door to the office. "Nancy, I was hoping you'd be on. Do you have a minute?"

"Yes, Miss Osborne, my first treatment isn't until nine thirty, so I have a few. I read this note from the attorney and I was thinking of calling you."

Mary held out her hand and Nancy gave her the note. After she read it, Mary handed it back and asked, "Do you have someone who could be a character reference? That does sound like a good idea"

Looking at the older lady, she asked, "That was to be one of my questions. Should I have a nursing colleague, my pastor or a friend?"

"Don't bother with a nursing colleague, I can be that witness. Since the part of the suit against you is religious in nature, I'd suggest not having your pastor, but if you have a close friend who knows you outside of work I'd ask them."

Acting almost relieved at what her supervisor said, Nancy smiled, and said, "Super! I have a wonderful friend, but she's in a wheelchair, will that make a difference, do you think?"

"She was never a patient?"

"No, she's been paralyzed all her life."

"It should make no difference. Yes, ask her."

"So you must appear, too? What should I wear?"

Mary sighed, "Yes, I must appear, just like you, unfortunately. I don't plan to be in uniform, if that's what you're asking. Be comfortable, but not a slouch. At least that's what I plan to do." She shook her head. "I was really hoping the center would settle this out of court, but I guess the Kambro's will not hear of it. From what I've heard their attorney is being very horsey about this, so be prepared for a nasty time."

Nancy swallowed. "Miss Osborne, I hate to hear that!"

The older lady nodded. "Yes, I know exactly how you feel. I really feel like we should make a countersuit, that boy was terrible!"

"I'm scheduled to be working that morning."

"I'll see that the schedule's changed. You should be off all day. I don't want you to think of anything here while you're there. You should be totally focused and not distracted by anything here at the center. I'm hoping that it will be cleared up on Wednesday, but we'll let the chips fall when we get there."

Trying to smile at her supervisor, Nancy said, "Thanks, Miss Osborne. I'll call my friend tonight and see if she can come."

"You say she's never walked? She'll be a good character witness for you?"

"Miss Osborne, she is the most wonderful lady I've ever known!"

"Really!"

"Have you heard of Sandra DeLord?"

Mary's eyes lit up. "Yes! She gave a concert not too long ago here in Blairsville, didn't she? If it's who I'm thinking of, she's remarkable!"

"Yes, you have her right. She is remarkable. She not only plays so beautifully, but she paints and gives piano lessons. I can't tell you all she does, but when I told her about this, she told me fiercely that she will be here for me."

"That is super! If you have no other questions, I'll get down to my office. First thing, I'll change the schedule and call it up, so plan to be off on Wednesday."

Nancy sighed, "Such a fun way to spend a day off. I can easily think of ninety-nine other things I could do."

Mary nodded. "I agree, I'll see you at nine thirty on Wednesday." She stood up and headed for the door.

Nancy sighed, "You know I'm not really looking forward to seeing that spoiled child again, or his parents."

Mary chuckled. "Nor am I! If I never saw that bunch again it would be fine."

Sandy was getting supper for Ramon and herself when the phone rang. Sandy kept on with her task, while Ramon leaned back on the back legs of his chair and reached for the phone on the wall. "Hey, Ramon here."

"Ramon, is your good wife there?"

Ramon pulled the receiver from his ear and said, "Good wife, are you here?" Grinning, he said into the phone, "Yeah, I roused her."

Sandy chuckled and held out her hand. "Hi, this is Sandy," she said, into the receiver Ramon handed her. Since he didn't identify who was calling, Sandy only identified herself into the phone.

"Sandy, it's Nancy. Here comes the big favor I've asked you about. I got notice today I'm to be in court on Wednesday and I need a character witness. Can you?"

"Nancy, I will be there with bells, whistles and fire in my eyes! When I get done with whoever they will know for sure that my friend Nancy is the best person anyone can know. What time should we arrive?"

"I'm to appear at nine thirty outside Judge Sanders' courtroom and I'm dreading it."

Her eyes twinkling, Sandy grinned at Ramon, as she said to Nancy, "Duncan's group gets back tomorrow evening and he's off, shall we bring him with us? You know he can always sit on the back seat in the van."

"Sandy, you'd better not!" Nancy gasped. "Sandy, you will be the death of me yet! I can't imagine how tied in knots I'd be if he was there! I probably wouldn't say a word, or if I did… Oh, my! I mean, I totally embarrassed myself the last time I saw him. Give me a break! In a courtroom…?"

"I was teasing, but Ramon and I'll be there."

"Thanks so much, Sandy," Nancy said, fervently. "I'll see you on the parking lot of the courthouse on Wednesday."

"Sure enough!"

Duncan came in the office after all his hikers had left Tuesday afternoon, to get his assignment for Thursday. He was surprised to see both Ramon and Sandy in the office, and said, "What are you doing home, man? I thought you were out on the trail again with your group that went out two days after me."

With his arm around Sandy's shoulders, he said, "I'm enjoying a rare cancellation with my wife. What's this I hear that you've knuckled under and become a believer?"

Duncan fell into a chair and sighed. "How'd you hear that? I didn't tell a soul!"

Sandy spoke up, "I had to find out how come Nancy threw her arms around you before you left on that last hike."

"You…what?" Instant red flooded his neck and cheeks.

Sandy nodded and grinned. "I was on the phone, but watching for Nancy to come. Only a couple of minutes after she did, you were standing there and she ran to you and threw her arms around you." Tongue in cheek, Sandy added, "You looked like you sort of enjoyed it, really."

Flippantly, he quipped, "What red-blooded man wouldn't like a beautiful woman to throw herself at him? Come on, Sandy, I'm as red blooded as any other man. I may not like women, but…well…"

"Mmm, but that man being you," Ramon said, "who has told us many, many times he won't have anything to do with women... So, spill it! How'd you fall?"

Duncan sighed. "I had a youth group a while back, third week of April, I think it was. The leader brought his son along. The kid was barely old enough to qualify as a 'youth'. That evening, after setting up camp, the boys went off to explore. That's the trail with the pool on the high meadow. Anyway, the boys pushed the leader's son into the ice cold water. He nearly drowned. Anyway, for his devotions, the leader used the first chapter of John and one of the boys asked me to share his Bible, so..."

Sandy chuckled. "So you couldn't be a chicken and run off."

A pale shade of pink crept up Duncan's neck. "Well, yeah, but almost loosing that kid sort of shook me up. Anyway, after the devotions, I went to that pond and... well... I think God spoke to me..." He looked from one to the other. He shook his head and scowled. "Man, I have no idea how Nancy knew, I didn't tell anyone, I didn't tell her, but she kept looking at me, then she asked me what was different, then she guessed and said I'd lost that haunted look, then she threw her arms around me. Sort of took me off guard, you know. I still haven't figured out what haunted look she's talking about!"

"Great! Terrific!" Ramon reached for his friend's hand. "Stay for supper. You gotta be famished, have some real food."

"I got laundry to do and food to buy at Alex's."

"I happen to know from a reliable source that you have a washer and dryer in your cabin now and after you get done with your obligation tomorrow you'll have time to stop by Alex's for your frozen dinners."

Duncan scowled at his friend. "In my place? What obligation? What are you talking about! Being off from the hikes must have screwed your brain!"

Sandy swatted Ramon's arm. "You weren't supposed to tell that!"

"Shucks! I wasn't, was I. Sorry. The obligation? It seems Nancy needs a character witness in court tomorrow..."

Duncan's hands flew up, palms out. "Not me! No way, Jose!"

"You'll come with us, won't you? I mean she needs friends to support her."

Scowling at Sandy, Duncan said, "Maybe she does, but I'm not the man for that! She's a good woman, of course, but I'm not the man for that!"

Ramon said, "Me thinks the man doth protest too much. You'll stay for supper."

"All right, I'll stay for supper! You didn't answer my other question."

"Your other question?" Ramon looked questioningly at Sandy. "Did I forget something the man asked?"

Without answering, Sandy turned on her chair motor and turned toward the door. "I'm on my way to the kitchen to see if the meatloaf's finished and get the vegetables cooked. You two men get the details of Duncan's next hike worked out. I know things are in the computer. Supper'll be ready in about ten minutes."

"We'll be there, Love."

As she pulled the door behind her, she said, "I was sure you would, Honey."

"All right! Spill it!" Duncan said, fiercely, as he slouched into another chair. "What is going on? Being off sure has screwed up your brain!"

Ramon shrugged. "Nancy's to be in court tomorrow for that lawsuit...."

Duncan pulled in a deep breath. "I got that! I won't be there! What about a washer and dryer in my cabin?"

"Oh, that, well, it's just a rumor Sandy told me."

"You, my friend, are being obtuse!"

Ramon shrugged. "All I'm saying is you'd better go home first and check it out before you go to Brad's Washerama." Before Duncan could ask anything else, Ramon changed the subject. "Anyway, seems as though your next hike has a first night by that same pond you mentioned earlier."

"Okay, I liked that trail. Is it a youth group?"

"'Fraid so."

Duncan shrugged. "I'm not afraid of them any more. I took the Bible Isabel put in my cabin with me last time."

"Hey, that's great!"

Duncan grinned at his friend. "You'd better start getting Neal to take some of them now that I'm part of the flock."

Ramon chuckled, his smile spreading. "Yeah, guess I'd better. I'll tell Sandy that. She'll be sure to make that happen."

Through the door, they heard faintly, "Come on, you two!"

The men left the office and with long strides descended on the dining room. Sandy sat at the table with all the dishes in place. She sighed, "I knew I couldn't leave you two and know you'd be here when you said. You can't be trusted together." She held out both hands to the men and said, "Honey, will you?"

The men pulled out their chairs and sat down, but Duncan didn't protest, he took Sandy's hand and bowed his head. Ramon did the same and prayed over the food. As they each picked up something to pass, Duncan said, "I used to resent it when you mentioned my name in your prayers. This is the first time since I asked God to take my sins away that you have and my feelings are so different. Thanks so much for keeping after me."

"Nancy had something to do with that, didn't she?" Sandy asked.

Around a big mouthful of meatloaf, Duncan muttered, "Mmmm."

Sandy's eyes twinkled, as she said, "I thought so."

Buttering a warm biscuit, Ramon asked, "Think she'll chase you now? I mean, she'll soon be your neighbor..."

Duncan slammed down his two thirds full glass of tea. A few drops sloshed over the edge, but his face turned almost blue, as he tried to swallow his mouthful and answer at the same time. Through the last drops, he exploded, "She better not! I mean, give me a break! That woman drives me to distraction! And she'll be living next to me... Maybe I'd better go pitch a tent somewhere!"

Unaffected by Duncan's actions, Ramon calmly took a mouthful of his biscuit and said, "Since she'll be your neighbor soon, I thought you two might get together. You could have Bible studies together when you're home." Thoughtful, he added, "And when you're off, you could go for walks there in the woods behind Isabel's cabins. That's sure a nice area, there's even a lively creek back there a ways."

Looking fiercely at his friend, Duncan said, "Listen, man! I don't know what's got into you today, but you have become no friend of mine!"

"A little thing like that and you'll renounce our friendship? I'm sorry for that."

"By the way," Duncan said. "One of the guys on this last hike I led introduced himself and said he's to be the doctor at the clinic here."

"Really? Did he tell you when the place'll be open?"

"No, not when it'll be open, but he's only going to be here three days a week, at least until they see how much traffic comes through the place. They don't know if the usage will be enough to pay for it."

"We've never had one, so it'll be interesting."

Nancy was in a dither. She had checked her closet Tuesday after work and hadn't decided on anything she felt good about wearing to the courtroom, but she hadn't gone out to buy anything, she didn't have money to waste on clothes. Now it was Wednesday morning and she still had nothing to wear. Around her tiny apartment, on the back of every piece of furniture except the daybed, was a piece of clothing. Even the cushions that were normally on the daybed had something thrown over them. She brushed her teeth and did her makeup, trying to take extra care with it. Her stomach growled, she'd only put a cup of coffee in it, sure she couldn't eat anything else and keep it down. It was nerves making her stomach growl, she was sure.

After her makeup and fixing her hair, she walked around her apartment looking at every piece of clothing laid out. She couldn't decide if she should wear a dress, skirt or pants outfit. Of course, she usually wore her pants uniform to work, but she wore a dress or skirt to church. She hadn't had a date in the memorable past, so that didn't even cross her mind. Nothing lying around struck her as outstanding. She looked at the clock and knew she must make a decision soon; she couldn't appear in her pants and bra in Judge Sanders' courtroom.

Not knowing how else to choose her outfit, she closed her eyes and spun around. Her panty hose slid easily on the wood floor between her two area rugs. When she stopped, she opened her eyes to the outfit in front of her. It was her very best pants outfit. It was plum color with a lilac border around the collar and the sleeves. She sighed, grabbed the pants and pulled them on. As she slid her feet into her Sunday pumps, she pulled the top over her head, being careful not to mess her hair. From the church down the street, the chime started the nine strokes of the hour. Nancy grabbed her keys and her purse. She must hurry; it would take twenty minutes to drive downtown.

She hadn't noticed from her apartment, but as she left the building a gentle breeze moved around her, as the sun shone down brightly on the steps to the parking lot where her car was. Nancy drove to the courthouse and went where she'd been told to park. Already there, with the door open was Sandy's van and Ramon stood on the lot working the controls. Sandy was on the lift coming down as Nancy pulled into a spot. Nancy sighed Sandy was smiling at her, even across the parking lot from the handicapped spot closer to the entrance. She, Sandy and the Lord made a majority then add Ramon and Pastor and they were undefeatable! Because of that thought, Nancy felt more confident, stepped from her car and locked it.

Nancy hurried, but Sandy and Ramon waited beside their car for her to join them before they turned toward the building. Sandy held out her hands and said, "Come on, girl, we're going to pray before we go in there." Nancy gratefully took Sandy's hand, but Ramon took her other hand and also his wife's. "Father," Sandy said, "be in this courtroom today, we pray. Don't let anything be said or done that is not pleasing to You. Keep Nancy's heart calm, give each of us the words we should say, I pray. We pray these things in Jesus' Name, amen."

The pastor recognized Nancy in the little group, so he walked up as Sandy finished, and said, "Could I add my prayer?"

Sandy smiled as she raised her head. "Of course!"

Ramon let go of Nancy's hand and the pastor completed the circle again. After his prayer, the four dropped hands, but Nancy turned to her pastor and said, "Pastor, you don't know my friend Sandy and her husband Ramon. These are wonderful people from the little town where I'll be moving to next month, Sandy and Ramon DeLord. Sandy, Ramon, my pastor."

Ramon held out his hand. "Good to meet you, sir."

"Yes, I'm glad to meet you folks, too. Have I seen you before?"

"Yes, Pastor! Sandy played that concert several weeks ago."

"Ah, yes, that was it. I'm glad you're here for Nancy."

"We wouldn't miss it!" Sandy said, immediately.

The three waited for Nancy to lead them up the ramp to the door into the building. She wished she didn't have to go in at all. Her hand trembling a little she took hold of the handle and pulled the heavy door. Ramon grabbed it and pulled it wide and waited until Nancy, Sandy and the pastor entered the huge, dark foyer, then he came in and the door closed. It was suddenly quite dark in the large room.

Ramon and the pastor checked the directory for Judge Sanders' courtroom, then they all went through the metal detector and headed for the elevator to take them to second floor. When the elevator door opened it was hard to miss the hallway outside the judge's courtroom, there were several people standing around. In the two major groups Nancy recognized several people, but most of those she didn't know.

As Nancy led her little group toward the others, Mary Osborne came from her group of hospital personnel immediately and Ann Blakestein also pulled away from her attorney colleagues. Mary smiled and said, enthusiastically, "Nancy! You look lovely this morning. I must say I've never seen you in anything but your scrub uniforms." She chuckled and said, "That's understandable, of course. I guess we're both out of our element in a courtroom, but we must stretch sometimes and that's good."

"Thanks, Miss Osborne, I guess I've never seen you out of uniform, either. I'd like you to meet my character witness, Sandy DeLord, her husband, Ramon and my pastor. Folks, this is my supervisor, Mary Osborne."

The attorney walked up directly to Nancy and heard her introductions. She looked at the small group around her, then scowled and said, "I didn't think you'd bring a *patient* as a witness, Miss Southerland."

Scowling right back at the attorney, she said, "I didn't, Ms Blakestein. Why did you think I would?"

Ann raised her hand and asked, "Who is this?" even though Nancy had already introduced Sandy to the entire group.

"My friend, Sandy DeLord. She's come to be my character witness. She's been a wonderful friend!"

Rather than speaking to Sandy, Ann continued to look at Nancy and asked, "She's never been your patient? Why is she in a wheelchair?"

Nancy opened her mouth to give the woman a response, but Sandy gave the other young woman a smile and said, "Ma'am, I've been in a wheelchair from birth. Nancy and I've been friends for several months now. Do you have a problem with me being a character witness, since I'm in a wheelchair?"

Finally, looking at the lovely young woman, Ann swallowed and acting very uncomfortable, said, "Ah, no, I guess I was surprised and since Miss

Southerland works at a rehab institution, I assumed you were a former patient. I'm sorry, Mrs.?"

Sandy held out her hand. "I'm Sandy DeLord and you are?"

Taking her hand then dropping it quickly, she answered, "Ann Blakestein."

"Ann, it's nice to meet you. This is my husband, Ramon and Nancy's pastor. They've both come for support."

Ann cleared her throat, still clearly uncomfortable and said, "I see. Mrs. DeLord, there will be several who sit at the defense table, several attorneys from our firm, including myself and several from the rehab center, along with Miss Southerland and her supervisor, but will you please sit behind the rail? I think that would be the best place." It was obvious to Mary Osborne as well as Ramon that the attorney was very uncomfortable with Sandy.

"Of course. Will they ask for my statement from there or will I need to go to the witness box? I understand there is a gate in the rail, is it large enough that my chair will fit through, in case I need to go forward?"

"They'll require you to speak from the witness box. I know they plan to have the boy as a witness, he is in a wheelchair, so they've had to make some adjustments to accommodate that."

"That's fine, thank you."

Ann nodded and said, "Follow me, folks." Mary Osborne motioned to her colleagues, so they fell in with Nancy's group. 'Strength in numbers' did not bolster Nancy's confidence. She knew her hands were shaking like a leaf.

Ann led the group into the courtroom. Straight ahead was the raised dais where the judge would sit behind a large, dark wooden desk. To his right was the witness booth, bordered by the same dark wood. In front of that was an open space with two large tables on either side of an aisle. Behind the chairs at the tables that also faced the judge's desk was a low wooden fence, everything in dark walnut, then there were several rows of seats with an aisle down the middle.

Since the aisle was only about one and a half persons wide, Sandy asked, "Ann, where would you want me to sit?"

"Those seats are moveable I'll have the bailiff remove the one on the aisle on the front row. Will that be enough room?"

"It should be fine." Behind Sandy, Ramon and Nancy's pastor found seats in the rows of chairs for those who came as friends and supporters.

Nancy's insides were tied up in knots. She listened to Sandy talk and wondered how she could be so calm. She followed Ann, through the little gate in the low wall and sat down where she was told. Mary Osborne sat beside her then Dillon Marshall, dressed in a suit and tie, appeared from somewhere and sat down beside Mary. All the attorneys still stood beside the table, talking among themselves.

Nancy didn't know Dillon's position at the center. The plaque on his door only had his name. She leaned forward and asked, "What are you doing here, Dillon? You look sort of prestigious in your suit and tie."

Looking at her surprised, Mary Osborne asked, "You mean you didn't know he's the CEO of Blairsville Rehabilitation Center?"

Her eyes huge, Nancy said, "No! I didn't! Just think; I hiked a trail with the CEO!"

Dillon rolled his eyes. "Nancy, please don't put me on a pedestal!"

She chuckled. "I wouldn't think of it. Not after seeing you look like a drowned rat on that trail, just like all the rest of us."

"Mmm, thanks, I think."

The attorneys separated and Ann pulled the chair the bailiff had removed for Sandy up beside Nancy and sat down. On the other side of Dillon three men sat behind the table. Only moments later, the door at the back opened and several men, two women and a boy in a wheelchair came down the aisle. Nancy and Mary both recognized the boy and his parents. They looked at each other but didn't say anything.

Before the last woman could herd the boy passed Sandy, he put his hands down and stopped the wheels from moving. He looked Sandy up and down and said, "How come you're here? Did she do stuff to you, too?"

Sandy turned to the boy and smiled. "Hi, I'm Sandy, who are you?"

"What's it to ya?"

The room became extremely quiet, since the boy wasn't quiet when he asked his question of Sandy. Everyone wondered what the lady in the wheelchair would say to the insolent boy, also in a wheelchair.

"Nothing at all, young man, except I don't usually answer questions that someone without a name has blurted out at me," Sandy said, pleasantly, but very firmly.

Sullenly, the boy said, "I'm Bill Kambro." He pointed to Nancy. "I was her patient when I was here in Blairsville."

"I see. No, Miss Southerland is my friend I came to speak for her."

"She got friends?"

"Yes, don't you?"

"Not no more. Not since I been in this thing! How long you been cripple?"

Sandy looked at the boy in the eye. "Bill, I'm not crippled, but I've been disabled since I was one day old. A nurse dropped me in the hospital nursery the day after I was born. I have never walked. What happened to you? Was it recent? When you are finished with your physical therapy will you be walking?"

Very uncomfortable now, with everyone's eyes on him and not a sound in the room, Bill put his forearms on his wheelchair armrests and pushed himself up in the chair. "Ummm, I fell off my horse at New Year's. The doctors seem to think I could walk again."

Sandy smiled. "Bill, if I had a chance to ever walk and doing physical therapy would make that possible, I would work my tail off to make it happen. Is that what you're doing, Bill?"

"Come on, Bill," the woman in front of him, said. "It's time for the judge to come in and you must be down here."

"Mom, do we gotta go through this? Can't I just go back to Atlanta and do them exercises so I can get outta this chair and go back to school?"

"We're here now! We're doing this!" she said, impatiently.

Bill's dad turned back and motioned urgently. "Come on!"

Twelve

As the little drama was playing out, no one noticed that the door behind the judge's dais had opened. The bailiff stood silently in the doorway, but the judge stood just out of sight, both of them listening. The bailiff had opened the door before Bill had asked his question of Sandy and they both had been listening to the conversation.

The judge was no spring chicken, but he raised his fist and whispered, so only the bailiff could hear, "Hoorah! Hoorah! Who's the young woman?"

Without turning to draw attention, the bailiff whispered back, "Someone behind the rail on the defense side. I guess she's here for moral support, but not a former patient."

The judge said, "Go ahead; say it! We need to get this show on the road. Besides, I need to see who that young woman is."

The bailiff took a step into the courtroom, and said, loudly, "All present please rise for Judge Sanders!"

Bill's chair still sat behind the gate, but it closed as the woman turned quickly around to face the judge and everyone rose. As the judge entered, only Sandy and Bill remained seated. Ramon and Sandy exchanged looks the judge was a member of the church they attended here in Blairsville. They had spoken with him several times, not really aware that he was one of the judges in the city.

The older man entered the room with a flourish. He swung his gavel and said, "Be seated! Kambro Vs Blairsville Rehabilitation Center is now in session."

The judge shuffled some papers in front of him then he looked up and asked, "What's that boy in the wheelchair doing in the aisle? Isn't that a fire hazard?"

The bailiff, standing behind the judge, said, "Yes, Sir, it is."

Waving his hand, he commanded, "Well, move him somewhere!"

One of the attorneys pushed the gate open and the woman quickly pulled Bill's wheelchair through, then pushed the chair quickly around the table to the far end next to an open seat. As soon as she sat down, the attorney for the Kambro's cleared his throat and said, "He's been moved, your honor."

The judge shuffled more papers then set them down in front of him. He looked up and pointedly looked at the man who had spoken. "Fine, let's hear what this is all about."

That same attorney stood up and said, "Your honor, the Kambro's are bringing suit against Blairsville Rehab Center, ward three and Miss Nancy Southerland."

Before anyone could say anything else, Bill said, loud enough so everyone heard him, "Mom, Dad, why do we gotta do this? Can't we just go back?"

The attorney on his feet looked at the parents and said, "Will you keep that boy quiet? He's being very disruptive!"

The judge held up his hand to keep the man from saying any more. Very sternly, actually with a scowl on his face, asked, "What did the boy say?" Of course, the attorneys all knew that the judge wasn't deaf. The Kambro's attorneys began to fidget, they knew he'd heard the boy plainly enough.

"Umm, your honor, his mother is quieting him."

The judge swung his gavel and thundered, "I didn't ask you that! I asked what the boy said! Is that so hard to answer?"

The man licked his lips, very uncomfortable. He cleared his throat and said, "Your honor, he... he asked if we must go through with this, your honor."

Motioning to the attorney, he said, "Sit down!"

The man sat.

The judge turned toward the boy. Much more kindly he asked, "Son, why do you not want to go through with this?"

Sitting forward in the wheelchair so that he could see Sandy, he said, "Well, see, Judge, that lady over there's never walked. She never could, but she said, if she could do exercises so she could walk she'd do 'em. My doctors, all of 'em, said if I'd do my exercises like they said I should and them nurses were showin' me, I could walk again. I um, ain't done them exercises like I should and that's why I'm still in this chair. I figure if she'd do 'em if she could and I can, maybe I should."

"I see." Without looking at anyone else, the judge looked down the center aisle and said, "Ms Sandy, I don't know why you're here, but I think you saved this court a whale of a lot of time." He looked back at the boy, then at the man and woman seated beside him and said, "Mr. and Mrs. Kambro, I believe?" Uncomfortably, they nodded. "I think you had better take that boy back to the center where you brought him from and get his exercises under way again. This case is dismissed, this court is recessed."

Without another word, Judge Sanders stood, his long robe flowing behind him. He left the courtroom and the bailiff followed. Pandemonium took over.

The Kambro's, both of Bill's parents, started shouting at him. The attorney's started arguing among themselves. The man who had been on his feet, started talking loudly to Bill's parents, but they didn't pay any attention to him. The people for the defense looked stunned for several minutes, but then they began to gather their things and also started talking. This case certainly hadn't gone the way they'd all expected.

Sandy sat quietly in her place, Ramon beside her and the pastor beside him. The attorneys for the Kambro side milled around, the one who seemed to be in charge, picked up his briefcase and slammed it down on the table, shoved his papers together, without looking at them and threw them onto the top of what was in the case.

The man who had nodded to being Bill's dad turned in front of his son and yelled, "Do you see what you've done? You've sent yourself back to that despicable center in Atlanta to do those horrid exercises!"

Sandy was watching the boy. She didn't know how old he was, but she thought perhaps he was less than a teenager. Before anyone could say anything to her, she pulled the gate open and wheeled herself around the attorneys and headed straight for the man and his son. The man had barely stopped talking when Sandy wheeled up. She saw the tears in the boy's eyes, but she looked at the man. "Excuse me!" she said, loudly enough to be heard over all the other noise in the courtroom, which stopped immediately.

The man glanced at her and in the same loud voice said, "What!"

"You would keep your son from doing exercises so that he can walk?"

"What's it to you?"

"Mr. Kambro, I am twenty-six years old. I have never walked. When I was tiny my dad carried me everywhere. When I became too heavy for that, I graduated to a wheelchair that others pushed around. When I became an adult I again graduated to this motorized wheelchair. Mr. Kambro, I will be in this chair for as long as I live because of nerve damage to my spine that could not be repaired. I will be in this chair until I die. Bill told me if he does his physical therapy his doctors feel he will walk again. Do *you* want to be responsible for him being in that wheelchair for the rest of his life?"

The man cleared his throat. "When you say it that way, I guess we'd better get him back to the Atlanta center and get those exercises under way again." He looked at Sandy and asked, "Who are you? Why did what you say have so much weight for the judge?"

Sandy held out her hand. "I'm Sandy DeLord, Mr. Kambro. I'm pleased that you plan to take Bill back to the rehab center to keep on with his exercises."

"Yes, well…" The man stuck his finger down behind his collar and looked extremely uncomfortable under Sandy gaze.

Sandy turned to Bill and said, "Bill, when you're back in Atlanta, you work really hard on those exercises! Will you do some for me? I'd sure like to be able to get out of this chair like you will do real soon."

"Who's that big guy with you?"

Sandy smiled at the boy. "That's my husband."

"Yeah?"

"He's a guide for a hiking service in Vansville. You know, if you're out of that chair real soon, maybe you'd like to go on one of our hikes. Would you like to do that?"

"You mean it?"

"Sure, you find four other folks to go and we'll set it up. But our hikes aren't for wimps! You know those purple mountains outside of the city?

That's where our hikes go, so those exercises you'll be doing have to get you up to par."

"Yes, Ma'am!" Bill exclaimed. "I'd like that! I'll work real hard. Did you say you're name's Sandy?"

"That's right, Bill. I'll be looking for your name to come up."

Bill sent his fist out and Sandy pushed hers against his. "It's a deal, Ms Sandy!"

Everyone in the courtroom still stood around. No one could believe the difference in the boy from the time he'd entered the room and now. He looked at his dad who stood holding the handles on the wheelchair. "Dad, move it! My next exercises are at two o'clock and I don't wanna miss 'em. You heard Ms Sandy; she'll set up a hike for me and my friends. Let's go!"

"But Bill!" his mother cried.

"Mom, you gonna come or stay here?"

"I'm coming!"

"Get the gate and let's go!"

The three Kambro's moved around everyone else, leaving the attorneys standing there with their mouths hanging open, as they nearly ran for the back door of the courtroom. Sandy smiled at the men as she moved more leisurely toward the gate in the low wall. None of the attorneys had moved, but Nancy held the gate open.

"Sandy! You are incredible!"

"Not really, just did what the Lord prompted me to do."

Memorial Day weekend was one of the busiest weekends for the DeLord Hiking and Camping Group. All three guides found themselves on the trails around Vansville over that weekend. Ramon left with his group on Thursday, Duncan and Neal left on Friday, but they were all gone until late afternoon on Monday. They were all glad that it didn't rain for those days and the temperature had been perfect.

Duncan had taken his group on the hike that led to the pool on the high meadow. To him, it was a special place and that evening, even though the group he led there didn't have devotions, he took the red Bible from Isabel's cabin back to the big rock at the pool. The pool and the rock beside it had been the place where he met God nearly face to face. Days were longer now, so he'd spent a good time with the Bible and in prayer, while the others explored. That night, as he crawled into his sleeping bag, he felt refreshed. Now that he was a believer life seemed much more, fuller, happier, he had joy in his heart.

Nancy had the holiday off and had come to Vansville to spend the day with Sandy, so she was there when Duncan brought his group back to base. She watched as all his hikers moved to their cars and Duncan put his huge pack into the back of his SUV. As she had when she hiked, she wondered how he could carry such a huge pack on his back with such ease. She and Sandy were both in the office as Duncan turned toward the house. Nancy turned toward Sandy to say something, but lost her train of thought when she saw the laughter sparkling in Sandy's eyes.

"Will you stop that?" Nancy muttered, as Duncan opened the door.

Duncan came through the door, as Sandy said, "Stop what, Nancy?"

Nancy shook her head and Duncan said, "Am I interrupting something?"

"No, I'm leaving," Nancy grumbled.

"Don't leave on my account," Duncan said, "All I need is my next assignment."

Nancy shook her head and waved a hand in front of her. "I'm on my way to my apartment. I think Ramon's coming home soon and Sandy must fix his dinner. Sandy has your assignment all ready for you, I'm sure."

Duncan scowled. "What's with you? Didn't your case get dismissed and aren't you taking a new job in two weeks? What's the deal? You're as glum as I ever saw you, woman."

"She hasn't seen you since she threw her arms around you that day and she's missed you terribly!" Sandy said, chuckling.

Both Nancy and Duncan gasped so loudly that it almost felt like a vacuum in the room. Finally, Nancy exclaimed, "Sandy! How could you?"

Almost as the same instant, Duncan said, "I'm outta here!" However he couldn't move because Nancy was rooted in the doorway.

Sandy snapped her fingers and said, "Goodness, what's wrong with me! Nancy, Duncan and Neal will be here for supper and I haven't even started the spaghetti sauce! Duncan, you'll have to find your next hike on the computer and Nancy, I'll need your help getting stuff ready for supper.

Now that Duncan's back, both Ramon and Neal should be back soon. I really need your help, Nancy, so come on."

"Sandy, I can't stay! For goodness sake, I need to get to my apartment and get packing! You know I'm moving..."

Ignoring her protests completely, Sandy said, "Nancy, come on, I need your help. I remember Ramon put my last jar of spaghetti sauce on the top shelf of the cupboard and I'll need you to get it down for me." She waved her hand at Duncan. "You'll have to boot up the computer. I forgot and shut it off before you came. Now that you've got that washer, drier in your cabin, you have plenty of time to stay for supper." Without waiting for either of them to answer, Sandy started the controls and headed for the door.

Duncan looked up and sighed, "Ms Sandy, you will be the death of me yet!"

The hum of Sandy's chair nearly covered Duncan's protest, but as Sandy started for the door, she said, "Not me! I'm feeding you! You won't need one of Alex's frozen dinners tonight. How can you say I'll be the death of you?"

Nancy was stuck in the doorway. She looked up at the giant standing right in front of her. Against her many self-lectures her heart gave a little flip as she saw those blue eyes looking down at her. Her cheeks warmed and she was sure she was blushing. Her mouth felt very dry and her tongue snaked out to wet her dry lips. She realized that Duncan's eyes focused on it. Nancy pulled her tongue back into her mouth, but Duncan's eyes still stayed on her lips.

He cleared his throat and said in a voice that didn't really sound like his, "You'd better hop to it, woman! Get on out of here and help Sandy with the sauce."

"Yeah," she murmured, "right on that."

Cheerfully, Sandy said from the doorway, "When the others get here, bring them along, Duncan. You know the drill."

While Duncan was distracted with Sandy's statement, Nancy dashed around him into the house, as Sandy moved down the hall toward the kitchen. Nancy pulled the door closed and whispered, "Sandy, you *will* be the death of me! I mean it! You keep throwing me at that man and he can't stand me!"

"Girl, that is not true at all! You affect that man just as much as he affects you! When you two are together sparks fly. I can't wait for you to move to town and live next door to him. I bet Isabel will be calling Ramon all the time to come referee!"

"That can't be true!" Nancy wailed. "Sandy, he's a bachelor, he's sworn off women for life… He can't stand me!"

"Nope! I think God's up there laughing His head off right now. God has a great sense of humor, you just watch!"

Grumbling, Nancy said, "I shouldn't have taken one of Isabel's cabins, I should pitch a tent on the other side of the clinic and live there."

Sandy threw her head back and laughed. Pushing the knob to make her chair go down the hall, she exclaimed, "Oh, Nancy! Nancy! You can be so funny sometimes. Really! Believe me, that man is coming unglued. Everything about him has changed since this hiking year started. It's great to watch!"

Nancy shook her head. "I don't believe a word of it! I can't see any change in that man at all. He's still as stubborn and sullen as he ever was and he did not like it when I forgot myself and put my arms around him! How can you say he's changed?"

"You don't see him as often as I do, girl."

"Thank goodness!" Nancy muttered.

Sandy started her largest pan filled with water on one burner and then started sautéing onions, ground beef and other vegetables in her large skillet. Nancy found the jar of spaghetti sauce and set it on the counter as several car doors slammed out on the parking lot. That meant that another group had returned. No one came through the door from the office that meant that Neal was back, but Ramon was still out.

"Neal!" Sandy called down the hall, through the door, "You're staying for spaghetti."

Neal opened the door from the office and said, "Sandy I'd really like to stay, but my folks are holding a family picnic at our place and they said they'd be really mad if I didn't come as soon as my hike got back. I'm outta here as soon as I get my assignment. Duncan's printing it off for me right now."

"Okay, have a great time with your family, Neal. See you in a couple of days."

"Thanks for the invite, Sandy. I'll see you."

The door closed between the office and the hall and Nancy grumbled, "You didn't twist his arm like you did Duncan's and mine!"

Sandy shrugged, but she had a twinkle in her eyes, as she said, "He has family close, but neither you nor Duncan do."

Sandy turned back to her sauce and cutting something else into it, as Nancy sighed, "Yeah, I know."

Only a few minutes later more car doors slammed and a few minutes later a voice in the hall said, "Sweetheart, I'm home!"

Nancy found herself alone in the kitchen as the water in the pan began to boil. She looked at the clock and wondered if she should turn off the burner under it or put the pasta in to cook. She looked around the kitchen for something to do and decided that setting the table was something she could do. Now that Neal wasn't staying, she knew how many to set it for. She couldn't very well go down the hall, Sandy and Ramon were probably grid locked in a welcome home embrace, besides, Duncan was in the office and she definitely didn't want to go there.

What was Sandy talking about, sparks flew when she was in the same room with Duncan? What sparks could she be talking about? Yeah, there were sparks every word Duncan said to her was a spark, a spark with a barb. Nancy shook her head surely Sandy didn't know what she was talking about!

Duncan printed out his itinerary and hiking map for his next hike that was scheduled to start on Thursday. He sat staring at the screen that gave him two weekdays to do nothing, or go somewhere. Maybe he'd go see his sister in Atlanta for those days, he hadn't been there since Christmas and he'd like to see his nephew again, once upon a time he had been so little and now was the star basketball player for his school. He was sitting at the desk debating when the car doors slammed outside and then Neal opened the door, walked in and closed it behind him.

"So, what's up?" Neal asked. "You just get back, too?"

"Yeah, about fifteen minutes ago. You want your schedule?"

"Sure, you got it there?"

"I'll pull it up." Duncan hit some computer keys and the printer started humming. He said, "If you don't want to stay for spaghetti, you'd better think up a good reason not to, man. Sandy's friend's here and she's got her and me staying and you, unless you got reason not to."

Neal nodded, as Sandy called. He walked around the desk to the door and opened it, then told Sandy he couldn't come. Sandy accepted his reason, so Neal closed the door and Duncan said, "You lucky stiff! You can always go home to mama."

"Hey! I'm not as old as you, I'm still a growing boy and mama feeds me real good. Besides, I can't resist Dad's bar-be-cue ribs, they are to die for!"

"Humph! Here's your stuff, get outta here!"

Neal looked down at his friend sitting at the computer. "So, your girlfriend's here? Hey, that's great!" Chuckling, he grabbed the papers from the printer and ran for the door. "I'm outta here! Have a good one!" he said, as he slammed the door.

"Too bad that boy lives in Blairsville," Duncan grumbled. "It's good he doesn't live in one of Isabel's cabins! Right now, I think I could seriously injure that boy!" Only seconds later, he grumbled, "Of course, I wouldn't, you understand. That was just a figure of speech." like he was answering his conscience.... or that little critter on his shoulder.

Only moments later more car doors slammed and Ramon came through the door carrying his backpack. He looked at his friend, still sitting at the computer and grinned. "Mmmm, smells good! Hi, man, you're staying for supper? You know Sandy's spaghetti's to die for." Looking back out the window to the parking lot, Ramon's grin widened, as he said, "Hmm, didn't I see Nancy's car out there? I guess she's helping Sandy get the spaghetti ready for supper, is that it?"

Giving Ramon a disgusted look, Duncan said, "My arm was twisted beyond repair to stay for supper, along with that little wench who's moving here soon."

Ramon slapped Duncan on the back as he walked by on the way to the hall door. "Hey! That's great! You haven't seen each other since that day she hugged you."

"Don't remind me!" Duncan grumbled. "I'd forgotten all about that, actually."

Ramon chuckled. "Yeah, right! Uh-huh. Me thinks thy nose is growing, Pinocchio." He opened the hall door and called, "Sweetheart, I'm home!"

Duncan watched as the door closed behind Ramon. On the other side of that door he knew his friend was smiling at, hugging and kissing a beautiful woman - a woman who loved him as much as he loved her. For the first time in his adult life Duncan wondered why he'd been working so hard at cutting himself off from everyone of the opposite sex except his sister. When he'd read the book of Genesis he'd come across the verse where God had said, "It is not good for the man to be alone. I will make a helper suitable for him."(2:18). Duncan sighed. Was he fighting against God when he said he wouldn't have a woman, he'd be a bachelor for life?

He sat staring up at one of Sandy's pictures that hung beside the window. He had seen the picture often in fact it had hung there since the winter. Sandy had painted it while they'd been on winter break, but for the first time he noticed a figure in the picture. It wasn't a large person, not the focus of the picture. There were no features on the person, his back was to the viewer, but although everything else in the picture looked like the sun was shining directly down, the figure was black; everything of the person was black, apparently standing in the shadow. It made him feel lonely.

He was about to rise from the chair when he heard Sandy's voice, "Duncan, come on! Supper's ready and you know you have to eat."

He hit the mouse to click off the computer and stood up. "Yeah, I'm coming, Sandy. I'm shutting down now."

"Hurry all you can, spaghetti doesn't stay hot forever, you know."

"On my way!"

A few minutes later, he walked into the dining room and the others were already at the table. Before he left the office, he speculated about the seating arrangement, he was correct. The seat open was between Nancy and Ramon. Sandy was across the table smiling at him. She already held Ramon's and Nancy's hands. Those two both had a hand on the table waiting for him to grasp them. He sat down and took the hands, but refused to look Nancy's way.

"So," Ramon said, "have you been saying grace on the trail?"

"Yeah, to myself, friend. I haven't graduated to saying it out loud yet."

Ramon winked and said, "No time like the present to start."

Duncan shook his head and let it fall to his chest. "God in heaven thanks for this food. Thanks for another safe trip, amen."

Sandy picked up a bowl of spaghetti and said, "Was that so hard?"

Duncan sighed, "You don't know how much."

"Thanks, Duncan," Sandy said seriously.

As the food went around the table, Ramon took a huge scoopful of spaghetti and said, "So you have two days off, as I recall. Nancy's moving to Isabel's cabin starting tomorrow. You'd be free to help her, wouldn't you? Probably with that big SUV and her car you folks'd only have to make one trip."

Duncan glanced at Nancy, who had a horrified look on her face. It was obvious that no one had checked with her to ask if she wanted his help. Duncan looked back at Ramon and sighed, "You are bound and determined, aren't you? I had thought I'd go visit my sister in Atlanta for the next two days."

Sandy waved his excuse away and said, "You'll have other two days off, but Nancy only needs help tomorrow."

"It's okay, Sandy," Nancy exclaimed. "I plan to move myself. My entertainment center, kitchen stuff and clothes are all I have. I'm sure I can handle that in two trips, it's no problem."

"Your entertainment center! Why, I'm sure that takes up half a wall! Of course you'd need a strong man like Duncan to move that for you. Why, your TV has to weigh a ton all by itself!" Sandy exclaimed.

"How about you helping?" Duncan asked Ramon.

Ramon looked innocently at Duncan and shook his head. "Sandy's got my day all planned out and I only have one day off."

Duncan put another mouthful of spaghetti in his mouth then wiped his mouth with his napkin, perhaps thinking he could stall a bit. He knew he was beat, though, it was a matter of admitting it, but he'd put it off as long as possible. After he chewed sufficiently and swallowed then washed it down with iced tea, he set the glass down and looked at Nancy. With a twinkle in his eye, he said, "So, what time you need me there to help?"

The look on her face told him that she was totally mortified by what their friends had suggested. Trying desperately to keep her voice from squeaking, she swallowed and said, "You don't have to, Duncan!"

"And run the risk of who knows what from these guys? What time, Nancy?"

Looking around at Sandy and Ramon, who were both looking at their food, she looked back at Duncan and said, "Nine o'clock?"

"Great! Give me directions and I'll be there."

Nancy picked up her fork and whispered, "Thanks, Duncan."

Duncan started the water and added the detergent into his washer in his bathroom. His clothes smelled like himself, a bit strong since it was the end of May, but for a change nothing had mud on it. He dumped all the clothes into the washer, only remembering as he saw the red shirt sink beneath the water line that the shirt ran and his white underwear would be pink when it came out. He sighed and watched as it disappeared when the agitator began to move.

The water shut off into the washer, so he stepped into the shower and turned on the faucet. He made sure the running water was comfortable before he turned it for the shower. He remembered the last time he'd done the same thing and had forgotten that the water heater was on the other side of the washer and the spray had nearly scalded him before he had the cold adjusted. He lathered up, washing his hair and let the feel of warm water sluice over his skin. He thought about the chore that awaited him in the morning. He'd only had brief meetings with Nancy since they'd been on the hike in March, but it seemed that each time they'd been together that they'd both been uncomfortable with each other, like at supper earlier. He wondered why Sandy and Ramon had been trying their best to throw them together and come to think of it, Isabel had too at the concert. He shook his head, what was the deal? If they felt so uncomfortable that it showed, why did people try to push them together? It made no sense!

Nancy took her suitcase from her closet and threw it on the daybed. She also pulled out her backpack and put it on the table. She was sure her clothes would all fit in the suitcase, but she had lots of things in her kitchen that needed something to carry them. She had saved several of the boxes for some of her appliances and was glad she had, but silverware and her few dishes would carry better in her backpack. She had a few glasses she especially liked and wondered how she could carry them without them getting broken. Perhaps it would be better to leave an appliance out of the box, wrap her glasses in paper towels and put them in the appliance box. Nodding, she found the biggest box, her paper towels and began wrapping her glasses.

She'd started as soon as she arrived home from Sandy's house, but she knew it would be quite late when she finished packing. Her last day of work had been Sunday and she'd gone to evening church. Sandy had invited her to spend the day today and she had to be out of the apartment by Wednesday, so tomorrow was moving day. She'd been embarrassed when Ramon and Sandy both had insisted that Duncan should help her. She knew he didn't like her, why had they thrown him at her? She was sure they'd be very uncomfortable with each other while they worked at emptying her apartment.

When everything was in boxes, her suitcase or her backpack, she still had the sheets, blanket and pillows from her daybed and the clothes she planned to wear to move. A thought hit her as she pulled the sheet back and lay down. This daybed was a single bed, but the bed at the cabin was a full size and she didn't have sheets for that. It was too late to call someone to ask if she must supply her own or was Isabel in charge of that?

She knew there were only two stores in Vansville, a grocery store and a hardware store. She didn't think either one of them sold sheets. She sighed, looked at the hour on her bedside clock and closed her eyes. Tomorrow was soon enough to worry about the size sheets she'd need and how to get them. She remembered a Bible verse her dad used to quote: "Sufficient unto the day is the evil thereof."

The next thing Nancy heard was her alarm clock playing some tinny tune. She smacked the clock until it stopped making noise but kept her eyes closed for several minutes and savored how comfortable she felt in her bed. A minute later she remembered that this was moving day! Duncan would be here at nine o'clock and she had a lot to do before that. She looked at the clock and bounded off the bed. She had two hours until Duncan knocked on her door. She dressed quickly, put some instant coffee in the one mug she'd kept out and poured water from the tap over it, then stuck it in the microwave she had to leave for the next tenant. She opened the refrigerator and took out the two eggs she'd kept for breakfast. A paper plate would have to do. When the microwave dinged for her hot coffee, she broke the eggs onto the paper plate stirred them together and carefully put the plate on the still warm plate in the microwave. She'd make a sandwich with the two pieces of bread still in the bread wrapper. That was breakfast.

At nine o'clock, after drying her mug on a paper towel and pushing it in her backpack, she heard a knock on her door and her heart went into overdrive. She pushed her Bible into the pocket of her backpack and rushed to the door. Expecting Duncan, she had a huge grin on her face. She forgot to check the one way peephole and flung the door open, it instantly registered that instead of Duncan, there stood her landlord. He was a good looking man, which he knew and capitalized on. She didn't like him. Each month when she paid the rent she made sure it was when the office was open and she'd leave the check with the receptionist and didn't have to deal with the building owner alone. She'd had enough dealings with him since she moved in.

She swallowed and looked up at the man, who was all muscle from his workouts in the basement exercise room and asked, "What can I do for you?"

The man chuckled cynically and said, "Honey, since you asked what *you* could do for *me*, I'll tell you. You can let me in and shed that pretty outfit and let me have my way with you."

The man took one step toward her, his foot on the threshold. Nancy had been so sure the person at the door was Duncan, she hadn't been holding onto the door and the man nearly over-balanced her, as he took that step. She swallowed the bile in her mouth and said, "I don't think so, Mr. Gotlieb, I'm pretty busy, you see, I'm expecting someone to help me move today. He should be here any minute."

"Honey, I don't believe it! You always do stuff on your own. I know you're moving, that's why I stopped, but expecting someone to help you? I don't believe it for a minute."

The man tried to take another step, but Nancy had her balance back and brought her knee up to keep him away. The elevator door opened and the noise brought some sense to the man, so that he took a step back rather than ahead. But even though there was someone on the hall, he said, "Come on, Sweetheart, you're not moving today, surely! I didn't know a thing about that!"

Angrily, Nancy said, "Just a second ago you said you knew!"

The man raised his arms, as if to put them on Nancy's shoulders, but Nancy took a step back into her apartment, wishing she had her hand on the door so she could send it sailing into his face. However the man realized that Nancy had taken that step back, so immediately he put one foot ahead of him and said, "Darling, surely you don't mean to move away, when we're about to get to know each other!"

Duncan stepped off the elevator and was on the hall coming toward Nancy's door when he heard what the man said. He scowled at hearing the endearment he used and his heart nearly turned over. Why was that? He wasn't about to analyze that thought.

However, only seconds later he heard Nancy's nearly frantic words. "No! I'm not your sweetheart or your darling. Yes, I'm moving today and yes, I left word with the receptionist at the desk in your office that today I was leaving, that I'd bring the key back before I left! My help is here, so you need to get out of the way! Now, Mr. Gotlieb!"

Duncan's deep voice said, "Is there some problem here, Nancy?"

The man stepped back immediately, looked at the man towering over him and said quickly, "Ah. No, no! I came to see if Nancy needed any help moving her things downstairs to her car." He smiled at Nancy and said, "I see you have good help, though, so I'll be seeing you. Say don't make yourself scarce, Kitten."

"I most certainly have all the help I need!"

"Yeah," Duncan added, "I think we have everything well taken care of." The scowl he gave the man should have put the fear of God in him.

The man beat a hasty retreat toward the elevator and since it was still there, the door opened immediately, he stepped on and was gone before Duncan had stepped into Nancy's one room apartment. "Was he really coming to help you?"

Nancy was trembling as she stepped back into her apartment so Duncan could come in. "N-no," she stammered, shaking her head. "Before the elevator door opened to let you off he-he told me to s-s-strip off my outfit and let him have his way with m-m-me on my daybed."

Duncan slammed the door and nearly roared, "What! The creep said that just now?"

Nancy took a deep breath, then let it out and said, "It's okay now, Duncan you came at the right time. Actually, I should have looked out the peephole in the door, but I was so sure it was you that I opened it and he tried to push me back in."

Still with a frown on his face, he asked, "Must you take your key to him?"

"No, I'll take it to the receptionist in the office…"

Duncan shook his head. "When we're through moving everything, I'll take the key back, so there won't be any mistake."

"Th-thanks, Duncan."

"Not a problem!" he exclaimed.

The look still on Nancy's face told Duncan things weren't okay. He did something he could never remember doing before in his entire life. He opened his arms and looked tenderly down at the pretty young woman. As he took a step toward her, she nearly fell against him, as she stepped into his arms. Her arms went around his waist and she laid her head on his chest, as his arms closed around her. He could feel her shaking, but she felt so right in his arms. As she felt his steady heartbeat under her ear, her shaking slowed until she rested quietly against him.

Nancy was several inches over five foot, but Duncan towered over her. She was aware that he couldn't even lay his head down on hers without bending over, not that she expected him to, she quickly assured herself. Of course she didn't expect a kiss or even his cheek on her head. She was thankful for the warmth and security of his arms right now, but she realized she could stay right here forever and feel like she was home. When she finally felt steady again, she raised her head and placed a foot behind her to step away, but Duncan wasn't ready to let her go.

She swallowed and said, "Thanks, Duncan. I feel better now."

Duncan cleared his throat and let his hands drop to his sides. "Yeah, I guess we'd better get this show on the road. Has that creep been harassing you since you moved in?"

"I guess I'd have to say yes, but I only had dealings with him rarely. This is the first time he's ever come to my door. I always made sure I paid the rent when the receptionist was there. It was she that took me up here the first time, but when she took me back to sign the lease, he stood in the doorway. He…um… tried to make a pass at me then, but with her there, he didn't do much. I've never let him get close to me and this is the first time I ever opened the door and he was standing there. I guess he found out I was moving and wanted to get one last hurrah in."

"I'm glad I interrupted!"

"Believe me, so am I!"

Standing in the middle of the one room, Duncan looked around at the sparsely furnished room. Even the furniture looked shabby. However he saw Nancy's suitcase, backpack and few boxes on the unmade daybed. "Is this all you claim?"

Also looking at all her possessions, Nancy nodded and said, "Yeah, not much is it? I did get all of my entertainment center back in its boxes, too. They're there beside the daybed. I just have these other few boxes, a couple appliances and my luggage."

Duncan opened the door and looked into the hall. "Why don't you call the elevator and we'll get this stuff moved out there. We'll have the key back to that creep before he can drink his second cup of coffee!"

Nancy smiled up at him and said, "You won't get any argument from me!"

It took them only fifteen minutes to move everything from the apartment, down the hall to the elevator. They filled the floor space and stacked some of the lighter boxes on top of the big ones holding the TV and stereo system. There was just room enough for the two of them when Nancy pushed the button for the main floor.

Duncan was as good as his word, he held out his hand for her key then as Nancy began moving boxes from the elevator, he walked the key to the receptionist's door. He walked in, but kept the door open so he could make sure nothing was going on behind him, since he didn't see the man he'd seen up at her door. "Here's Miss Southerland's key. She's all moved out."

The man who had been at her door when Duncan came, stepped to the door of his office and said, "Susan, don't take it! How do we know it's hers?"

Not knowing anything about what happened upstairs, the older woman said, "Mr. Gotlieb, of course it's hers, it has the apartment number stamped on it."

Still not looking at the key and ignoring what Susan had said, he looked out the door and said belligerently to Duncan, "Why are you bringing it back when it's Nancy's key? What is she, chicken or something?"

"Because, Mr. Gotlieb, she feels it's safer for her if I bring it back." He gave the man a hard look, then said to the receptionist, "You have a good day, ma'am."

"Thanks, sir, I'll do that."

Mr. Gotlieb glared at Duncan, but said nothing.

Duncan was prepared to do something if Mr. Gotlieb had forced him, but nothing happened. By the time Duncan was back at the elevator, Nancy had all her things in the hall by the back door. She was winded, but said to Duncan, "Thank you so much! I heard him! I'd have left the building a long time ago if he'd been the only one there to deal with! I know other people who work at the center live here. I can't imagine they'd take that kind of stuff from him."

"I'm glad you won't have to deal with him any more! Isabel's exactly the opposite, that's for sure!" he said, fiercely.

"Before we leave Blairsville I must ask you something."

"Well, ask."

"I only have sheets for a single bed, but I remember the bed in the cabin I rented from her has a double bed in it. Do I need to buy sheets?"

"She has sheets on the bed, on all the beds, since she does rent them by the day, but you can buy your own if you want, but there's really no hurry."

"Good, I don't have much money right now and my last pay from the center won't come for several days, but when I get it I'll buy some sheets. Thanks so much for your help, Duncan. I can't imagine what would have happened if I'd been doing this by myself and he'd come."

"Mmm, maybe you can't, but I think I have a pretty good idea."

The day after Memorial Day was beautiful. Duncan had filled both her car and his SUV with her things and was now pulling onto Isabel's parking lot. Nancy's heart was galloping in her chest, she was so excited, not just to leave the unpleasant happening at her old apartment, but at coming to Vansville to live and work. Duncan pulled up then backed to the sidewalk into his spot, then Nancy did the same beside him. These spots were the closest to the walk that went in front of the cabins.

Both car doors slammed, but before either of them could reach their storage areas and had a box in their arms, Isabel hurried down her steps and came up to them. Smiling at Nancy, she said to Duncan, "Sonny, I'm sure glad to see you're helping my newest tenant to move in. I knew you had a good bone in your body somewhere."

Duncan sighed, "Ms Isabel! You make it sound like I'm the big ogre!"

The old lady grinned. "Well, if the shoe fits…" Her eyes dancing, Isabel said to Nancy, "Deary, I've been looking forward to you moving in and today's such a beautiful day!"

"It is, Ms Isabel and I'm so excited!"

"Well, you make that big guffer do all the work and get your place just so."

Nancy giggled. "Thanks, Ms Isabel, I'll sure do that."

Thirteen

When Isabel had left them and both Duncan and Nancy had a box in their arms, Duncan growled, "What! You expect me to help you after I get my car emptied? I don't remember Ramon or Sandy saying I had to stay all day!" Nancy didn't know what to say until she looked at the man, she couldn't tell if he was serious or joking. His words were gruff, there was no smile on his face, but his eyes twinkled.

She gave him her best smile and said, "I thought maybe I could bribe you into setting up my entertainment center, before you had to run off."

He walked up on the porch of Nancy's cabin, stood and waited for her to unlock the door and said, "So, what's in it for me?"

Trying to think fast, she said, "If you help me, it'll get done sooner, then I can get to Alex's and get my groceries. I'll fix supper how's pork chops, baked potatoes and green beans sound? Umm, and maybe dessert?"

"I swear you've been friends with Sandy too long! Since you've got your slave labor, I'll take you up on your grub, it sure beats trail fare or a frozen dinner."

"Great!" She looked at the box he held and said, "That's the box with the entertainment center and the hardware. I don't know where my screwdriver is, but that whole thing needs to be put together before the other stuff can go on it."

Setting the box down, he headed for the door and muttered, "Should have figured that. I'll get my tools from my place. You bring in some of the little stuff while I work on this thing."

Giving him her radiant smile, she said, "Thanks, Duncan, I really appreciate this."

"Yeah, yeah," he said, and waved his hand back and forth from the doorway.

Duncan had the entertainment center set up when Nancy heard his stomach growl. "It's lunch time, isn't it!" she exclaimed. "Does Alex have a deli department?"

"Not a department, he's got some subs and things in one of his refrigerators."

"While you bring in the TV and my stereo system, I'll run over there and pick up a couple for us." She grinned at him, "Or would you rather I got a bag of trail mix for you? Would that be enough until I fix the pork chops?"

Duncan straightened up and glared down at her. "Woman! I thought you'd razzed me about that quite enough on the trail! I'll have a foot long beef sub, if you please. Make sure it has everything on it, even the onions!"

Nancy saluted from the door. "Yes, Sir, as you wish, Sir." and she was gone. "One groaning beef sub coming right up!"

Duncan sighed and headed for the door she'd closed. This woman drove him to distraction he knew he was not himself when he was around her. He stayed behind her, as she went to her car to drive to the grocery store, even though he could easily have passed her if he'd wanted to. His eyes strayed and watched as she moved gracefully in front of him. She was obviously not aware he was watching her. He shook himself, what was he doing watching the curves of a woman's body as she moved? He knew right then he was in some serious trouble.

That evening, after Nancy's cabin was set up as she wanted it and Duncan sat in the other chair at her tiny table, she sighed. "You know, I figured it would take me at least to the end of the week to get my place fixed as I wanted it, but with you helping me I'm moved in and I'm happy with the results. All there is to do is go to the grocery and fill my cupboards tomorrow. What'll I do the rest of the week and next week?"

Without thinking before he spoke, Duncan said, "I printed out my next hike and the people who are going. There're only five signed up, you could go if you wanted."

Nancy couldn't believe her ears, her mouth dropped open. Duncan asking her to go on his next hike? "Duncan?" There was no mistaking the question in her voice. "You're asking me to go on a hike with you? The last time I went on a hike you led, I know you were anxious to get rid of me at the end."

Duncan knew he'd stepped in way over his head, but it'd look bad if he took it all back now. "Yeah, well..." He cleared his throat and looked away. "I guess we would need to clear it with Sandy, come to think of it."

Softly, barely in a whisper, she said, "But it would be fun."

Just then the cellphone on his belt boomed out with Bach's Ode To Joy. Duncan snatched the phone from his belt, glad for the reprieve. "Hello?"

"Duncan!" Sandy exclaimed. "I've tried your land line all afternoon! Where are you?"

"Um, Nancy's paying me for helping her, she fed me pork chops."

With all seriousness, Sandy said, "Ah let me get this straight. Did you say you've been with Nancy *all day*?"

"Well, yeah, it took till now to get stuff arranged. Oh, um, could we squeeze another hiker into my next group?"

"Duncan? You don't like big groups, as I recall."

"Um," he puffed out his cheeks before he said, "When I printed out the names it was a group of five. One more isn't too many to handle."

Pretty sure she knew, she asked, "Duncan? Who is this one who's wanting to add on?"

"Um, well, it's Nancy." Quickly he added, "She said she doesn't have much to do before her first day at the clinic in two weeks."

In awe, the words came over the phone waves, "Duncan, something has happened to you! Are you sure it's Duncan Roads I'm talking to?"

Duncan was looking at the pretty lady across the tiny table from him. It was a good thing he was secure in the chair, because he'd be a puddle on the floor otherwise. There was a crimson blush on the cheeks of the lady at the table that emptied his brain. He had to swallow and even then, his voice came out on a husky note. "Yeah, Sandy, I'm still Duncan Roads. Is it okay to add another hiker so close to the time?"

"Duncan, I wouldn't keep Nancy from going on your hike for a million dollars, you can count on that! Say, I tell you what! Ramon'll be gone on his hike, I hate eating alone you two come for breakfast. Let's do like we used to before everything got so hectic. We can share a meal before you get on the trail. Okay?"

Duncan looked at Nancy and knew the crimson wasn't only on her cheeks. His face flamed, but he swallowed and said, "It's okay for you to go and she wants us to come for breakfast. Is that okay?"

Overwhelmed, Nancy could only nod.

Duncan cleared his throat again. "Yeah, Sandy, it's good. We'll be there for breakfast, what, about seven?"

"Sure! That'll be great! I'm looking forward to it already. See you day after tomorrow at seven o'clock sharp."

With the blush crimson on her face, Nancy murmured, "I can't believe this!" Nancy realized they had finished eating, so she jumped up, as Duncan closed his phone. "I bought a custard pie at Alex's today. Could you eat a piece, Duncan?"

"Nancy, I may enjoy leading hikes on rugged trails in the lower Appalachians, but when I'm off the trail I have no qualms about eating sweet stuff."

Nancy turned to her refrigerator and pulled out a small pie. She found her two small plates and cut two wedges and slid them onto the plates. She pulled Duncan's dinner plate from in front of him and placed his dessert in its place, then did the same with her own. When she slid the pie back in the refrigerator, she pulled out her pitcher of tea then filled their glasses. It was very obvious how nervous she was, there were waves in the pitcher as she poured.

When she was seated again, Duncan said, "Thanks, this looks great, Nancy! Custard pie with whipped cream is one of my favorites."

"I'm glad," she murmured.

Nancy had put the last piece of pie in her mouth and rested her fork on the plate, when Duncan placed his hand over hers. Nancy felt the heat rise onto her neck, but Duncan didn't move until she looked at him. When she finally raised her eyes from looking at their hands, she realized he was looking at her.

"Nancy; thanks for dinner. You're a good cook and I enjoyed the company right along with the meal. In fact, today was a great day."

"Really? Really, Duncan?"

"Yes."

The hold on her hand became stronger as he stood up, bringing her up with him. Before she realized what he was doing, he turned her and brought her into his arms for the second time in one day. She looked up at him and couldn't read the look in his eyes, but when he lowered his head, she was sure she knew his intent.

Gruffly, he asked, "May I?" At her nod, he kissed her.

Duncan left soon after he helped Nancy with the dishes. It was a warm end-of-May day, the air conditioning in the cabin had been good to work in, but instead of going down the walk to his cabin, he walked straight ahead from Nancy's door. Isabel's house was off to his right, the clinic to his left, but straight ahead was an open field and a long way off were the beautiful mountains the area was known for. He knew he needed to clear his head before he went back to his cabin, so a long walk was in order.

He never looked behind him to see that Nancy had pushed the curtain slightly away from the edge of the window so she could see him, but she wondered where he was going. She stood at the window holding the lacy curtain back enough so she could see his tall, athletic body striding along. His dark blond hair was pulled back in a three inch ponytail, but that didn't bother her. She sighed the man was definitely in tune with the earth.

She put her arms around herself, savoring the day they'd spent together. Maybe he'd felt as uncomfortable as she had at first, but after they'd left the apartment building and arrived at Isabel's cabins, things had settled into a good routine. In fact, as the day wore on, they'd almost anticipated each other's actions. He'd been totally a gentleman and she couldn't recall a harsh word that had passed between them.

Dreamily, she sighed, "He invited me to go on his hike with him! It'll be neat, but I sure hope it doesn't rain."

When he was a speck in the twilight, she turned from the window and looked around her new home. The dishes were done and put away her entertainment center was in perfect shape, with her TV on top. She loved the fireplace and had hung Sandy's picture over it and on the table next to the couch sat an open Bible. She walked over and sat on the couch beside it, then looked to see where Isabel had left it. At the very top, the reference was Proverbs 3:33. The verse had started on the page before but she read, "…but he blesses the home of the righteous."

At the same time tears came to her eyes, but a smile spread on her lips. "Yes, thank You Lord! I am so happy here! Thank You for all You've done for me," she murmured.

After a time of reading and prayer with lots of thanksgiving, she turned off the light and went again to look out the window. It was too dark now to see much. Isabel had one security light on her parking lot, but where the cabins were there was no light. The clinic that was beyond the last cabin hadn't been there long enough to get its own security light, so it was a huge hulk in the darkness. Besides, the part she could see was the back of the building it had one small door with only a foot path to it. The parking lot was on the other side of the building. She turned the lock in her door out of habit and smiled, as she headed for her lovely bedroom, a luxury she'd never had since she'd left home. When she left for college she'd shared the dorm room with another girl and since then she slept in the same room as she lived. Now she not only had a lovely bedroom, but also a full size bed to sleep in.

Instead of going down the walk to his cabin, Duncan took himself from Nancy's cabin across the meadow to the thick pines beyond. He had some deep thinking to do and probably the solitude of the little forest would do. He found a rock beside a quiet brook that moved lazily along and sat down. The sun was behind the mountains now, only the long shadows of evening found him in the woods. Since he was so quiet, the tree toads soon started their evening choir practice and upstream a bullfrog grumped out his evening solo. There were some birds in the trees making short flights from branch to branch and twittering their evening lullabies to their babies. There was a slight breeze that sighed through the pines around him and he felt at peace. He knew God was in this place.

He'd been with a woman all day, not his sister, either. In fact, he hadn't even thought of his sister, even though yesterday he'd planned to go see her today. Things had changed in his life since Christmas when he'd last seen her. He wondered if she would know him. He'd had his beard altered twice since he'd seen her. Once he'd had it shaved off for Roger's wedding and recently he'd cut it back himself because.... well, just because. His hair wasn't near as long as he'd worn it when he saw her, again a victim of Roger's wedding, since he'd had to escort a city slicker down the aisle.

He'd met Nancy in March it was probably the second week of March, now it was the last week, actually almost the last day of May. He'd felt a stirring in his chest the very first time he'd seen her, in fact, she'd put a stop to his forward movement for a minute and he'd been fighting everything about her ever since. Today he'd spent the day with her, from nine this morning until after seven tonight. He had to admit, reluctantly, of course, he'd enjoyed every minute, except, when he'd seen that man trying to force her into her apartment, then he'd seen red instantly.

When the sky he could see through the bows of the trees had turned black, he sighed and stood. He'd walked nearly a straight line to get to this rock, so surely he could walk that same line and get back to the cabins. He set out, now the birds were quiet, the bullfrog was still and only a few tree toads were still screeching. What he now heard were the scratchy noises of night-time insects calling to each other across the meadow. He loved the sounds of nature they changed from hour to hour through the day, but also through the night.

He moved noiselessly through the trees and off in the meadow ahead of him, faintly at first, then more boldly he heard a whip-poor-will call. Only a minute later another answered from across on the other side. He also heard an owl. Finally, he came out onto the meadow and saw ahead of him Nancy's cabin. He couldn't believe he'd walked that straight a line! While he looked, the light went off in her living room, now all the cabins were dark. None of the other cabins except his and Nancy's were rented right now. They had been full over the weekend, including the one Nancy now claimed. When they'd entered it this morning, Duncan had been surprised how quickly Isabel had gotten it back into pristine condition for Nancy's move in.

He turned onto the walkway in front of the cabins and soon walked up the steps onto his porch. This cabin was his most favorite place he'd ever lived. He'd like to think he could live here forever. He went inside and closed the door behind him, then turned the bolt, something he hardly ever did. The place was dark, but he knew right where his couch was. He went to it, flipped the light switch for the lamp beside it. Just as he knew it would be, the red Bible was there waiting for him to pick it up. He went to his refrigerator and pulled out a can of soft drink, then went back to the couch and picked up the Bible. He sat down and opened it, then soon found the passage he looked for.

> "The Lord God said, 'It is not good for the man to be alone, I will make a helper suitable for him.'
>
> "But for Adam no suitable helper was found. So the Lord God caused the man to fall into a deep sleep, and while he was sleeping, he took one of the man's ribs and closed up the place with flesh. Then the Lord God made a woman from the rib he had taken out of the man, and he brought her to the man.
>
> "The man said, 'This is now bone of my bones and flesh of my flesh; she shall be called 'woman,' for she was taken out of man.'
>
> "For this reason a man will leave his father and mother and be united to his wife, and they will become one flesh." (Genesis 2: 18, 20-24)

Duncan sighed, "Maybe I could do a little thinking about this, one of these days. After all, she's not hard to look at…" He sat quietly for a minute, not really looking at the Bible, but not seeing anything else, savoring the events of the day he'd spent with Nancy. He had to admit, he'd enjoyed it all.

Finally, he closed his eyes, but he knew there was a long-standing problem he and the Lord had. Finally, he murmured, "God, I guess maybe I've been fighting what You really want for me. I think You're telling me I should…" He cleared his throat. "Do I really have to… God, do You really mean I need to forgive Mom?"

In the stillness he almost heard it *Yes, Son, that's what I mean.*

He sighed, closed the Bible and turned off the light. He'd finished his drink but the can could sit on the table until morning. In the darkness, he sighed again. He'd held the anger and frustration against his mother for a very long time and God knew how his life had been filled with those emotions, he wasn't quite ready to let go of them yet. Maybe someday… He sighed again, he knew God wanted him to deal with it now

He went in his bathroom and turned on the night light, then washed his face and brushed his teeth. He made his way through the closet to his bedroom. Slowly, he undressed and stretched out on the bed, then pulled the sheet over him. He looked out the east window and saw the bright evening star and knew it was Venus. It seemed like God was watching him through that bright heavenly object.

Before he closed his eyes that same voice said, *Son, you need to forgive your mother.*

He turned his back on the window, bunched his pillow under his cheek and closed his eyes. "But God, she neglected me, she used all the money she should have used for food and clothes and gave it to her church..."

Son, you will never have true peace, you can never love a woman as your mate until you forgive her of all those things. Remember what Sandy said? Not all believers, not all churches are like that or even believe that way.

Continuing to roll, Duncan found himself beside the bed on his knees. "Okay, God, You win! I forgive Mom, but You need to help make it stick. I'll tell her the next time I see her."

That's good, Son, that's a start.

When the sun shone in the window the next morning, he hadn't slept too much. He certainly didn't feel rested. He'd had a long time of wrestling with God about what he should really do about his mom. He pulled the covers up as far as they would go and buried his head in them. Finally, when the warm sun made it uncomfortable to stay in bed any longer he pushed the covers back and sat on the edge of the bed for several long minutes. Finally, he heaved a sigh and stood up, then went back through the closet, collecting clean clothes on his way to the shower. From there he stopped in the kitchen and made a mug full of instant coffee, heating it in the microwave. Before he sat in his chair at the table, he picked up the cordless phone and took it with him. He dialed the number from memory. He didn't dial the number often, but it was a number he'd learned as a child.

Hoping that the voicemail would kick on before anyone answered, he swallowed a sigh when a voice said, "Hello?"

"Hello, Mom, it's Duncan." Quickly, before she could say anything, he said, "There's something I have to say. Mom, please forgive me for resenting you for giving all that money to your church. I realize now that it was wrong of me."

"Son?"

"Yes, Mom, it's me."

After a very long silence, when his mom was trying to fathom what her son was saying, she said, "But… but… we're supposed to give all we can to the church!"

As kindly as he knew how to say it, he pressed on. "According to my friends here in Vansville, who are Believers and go to church regularly, we are to give to the Lord. It's not how much we give it's Who we give it to. God doesn't expect us to give so much that we deprive our families of things they need. He…"

"Well!" Loudly, the connection broke in his ear.

When the dial tone hummed, he pulled the receiver from his ear, switched it off and murmured, "God, I tried, but she didn't listen."

That's all I asked, Son.

Nancy spent a happy day browsing through Brad Thomas's hardware store, finding many things that wouldn't be in a big city hardware store. She didn't have much money, but she did buy a few trinkets for her new home. After paying for her purchases, she took them back to her car then went to Alex's store for some essentials she'd forgotten yesterday. Then, she'd been distracted by the man who was still working in her cabin, now, she could think more clearly, so she picked up what she needed. She found another sub in Alex's refrigerator and bought it for her supper, but she knew she'd have to be more conservative, her money wouldn't last until her first paycheck from the clinic if she splurged on subs all the time. She had resigned from the rehab center mid-pay-period, so her check from there wouldn't be large, either. A thought hit he, she had lots of vacation and personal time that would be added.

After supper and watching the sunset from her porch, she found her backpack, her sleeping bag and her one man tent. Excited, she started loading her backpack. It wasn't until she had everything in, including her Bible, and still had room, it hit her. "What about food! When I went in Dillon's group we filled the rest of the room with food packets."

It was night, but she grabbed her sweater and as she pushed her arms into the sleeves, she jerked the door open then ran down the walk to the second cabin. Duncan couldn't imagine who could be pounding on his door at this hour. He set down his book and went to the door.

A very agitated lady barged passed him, then turned and looked at him while he closed the door. "What about food?" she blurted out.

Scowling, he said, "What about it?"

She took a deep breath to calm herself a little, Duncan always seemed to do that to her. After another deep breath and realizing Duncan had no clue why she'd blurted out what she did, she said, "Duncan, I'm one of the hikers who's going on your hike tomorrow. When I went with the group from the rehab center I had to pay Dillon so much extra for the food. I never thought to buy anything today at Alex's and I haven't paid any fee to DeLords."

He came to her and put his hands on her shoulders. He looked down at her, his eyes twinkling. When she finally looked up at him, he said, "Will you stop dithering, woman! Don't worry about the fee, I won't and I'm ninety-nine and nine tenths percent sure that the DeLords won't accept a fee from you, so just give it a rest. About the food,…" He couldn't help it, she seemed so agitated, he grinned as he looked at her, "…you don't have any of those dry packets hidden away somewhere?"

She let out a long breath. His hands on her almost took away any coherent thought. She licked her lips and said, "Duncan, you know I don't. You saw what I put in my cupboards. I went back today for more staples and never gave food for the trail a thought." Then her eyes twinkled as she lifted her head and looked back at him. Raising her hands in a helpless gesture, she sighed, "I don't even have a bag of trail mix."

He did something he never remembered doing in his life before. He threw his head back and pulled her to his chest at the same time. After a good laugh, he said, "You will never let me live that down, will you! I tell you what I have two bags of trail mix that I'll put in my pack. We can each have one for lunch the first day."

"Humph!"

His athletic heart was pounding out a constant rhythm under her ear and his strong arms around her felt absolutely wonderful. She realized that she was content and wouldn't mind staying right here for a very *very* long time. In fact, she almost forgot what they were talking about until he put his hands on her upper arms and pulled her away from his chest far enough that he could lower his head and kiss her.

Then she did forget everything.

She melted against him and her arms stole around him, holding him tightly. She kissed him back fervently. When they were both nearly out of breath, he reluctantly released her lips, but rested his forehead on hers and said in a husky voice, "Where were we?"

Licking her swollen lips, she murmured, breathlessly, "I think… I think we were talking about food for the hike tomorrow."

"Yes, maybe we were." He sighed and murmured, hardly loud enough for her to hear, "But that was a whale of a lot better."

She didn't answer, but she had to agree.

He dropped one arm, but kept the other around her, as he walked to his own cupboards and opened one of the upper ones. "Usually, I carry a packet of coffee for each morning, because sometimes the group I lead is young people who don't drink coffee." He pulled out six packs and set them on the counter. "One of the requirements in the literature is that the hikers bring enough food that the guide doesn't have to supply his own and so far this year every group has done that. I still take enough that in case I need some I have my own supply." He pulled down a stack of dry rations and chuckled as he set the last pack on the counter. "I started that habit after some feisty lady caught me out with a bag of trail mix for lunch one day."

He looked down at her, moved his hand over the two piles on the counter, his eyes twinkling, he asked, "Think that'll be enough for us, Miss Nancy?"

She looked up at him and giggled. "Yes, I think that'll be plenty."

"Good. My pack's full now with cooking utensils, but when I come up for you in the morning, we can put all these in the top of your pack, how's that?"

"But I can take them now!"

Duncan shook his head. "Nope. Won't happen. Now I'm walking you back to your cabin and kissing you goodnight. You're going in and go to bed for a good night's sleep. I'll come for you about six-thirty and bring your pack back here where we'll load all this stuff in it and then get in my SUV and head over to DeLord's for breakfast, like Sandy wants."

Snickering, she said, "We will, will we?"

"Yup, that's how it's going to work."

He looked up at his kitchen clock and turned with her still in his arm toward his door. He grinned, as he opened it and led her out. He knew, with his much bigger size that there wasn't too much she could do but come along. He closed the door on the crisp night air, wanting to keep what little warmth he could in the cabin, and walked down the steps to his walk then they turned as a unit on to hers. When he reached her walk, light was spilling from her open doorway and he scowled.

"Why's your door open?"

Instantly, she could feel her cheeks getting very warm, but she had to be honest. "I... umm... forgot to close it when I came to ask you about food."

He threw his head back again and laughed. "Lady, I knew you were agitated, but to forget to close your door at night? I know it's not Blairsville, but you never know what wildlife is out and about in these parts. Not just two legged varmints either. Who knows, you may have an unwelcome visitor in there waiting for you."

"Duncan," she cried, "surely not!"

He walked her up the steps, across her porch and inside then deliberately closed the door. He stopped and she looked up at him, but before she could speak, he put his finger across her lips and looked around the cabin. "You're lucky it seems nothing came in while you were gone."

She let out a long breath and said, "Good!"

He pulled her to his chest again and put his other arm around her. "Now, in keeping with what I said at my house, it's time for your goodnight kiss."

As he was lowering his head, he felt her arms stealing around him. He couldn't decide if that made his heart speed up or stop, but it felt right to hold her. Again she yielded against him and put her head back for his kiss. Just as they were running out of breath, they both heard a scratching that seemed to come from the kitchen. They broke apart, her eyes wide, she murmured, "Oh, no! Something did get in!"

"Yup, sounds that way."

"Oh, Duncan!"

Duncan spun away from her toward the kitchen. They both looked and saw the cupboard door under the sink was open. A little bandit had Nancy's new package of paper towels open on the floor. He was busily shredding the wrapping and several layers of towels onto the floor around him. He looked like he was having loads of fun.

Duncan bent over and whispered to Nancy, "Go open the door and stand behind it. I'll try to shoo him toward it."

She nodded and silently went to the door. When she had it wide open, she stood back while Duncan went toward the sink. Before he reached the little beast, he saw her broom and grabbed it. The raccoon was still shredding towels when Duncan pushed on his back with the broom, intending for him to head across the living room, the way he had come. The little animal looked behind him, saw the big man and made a dash, not for the open front door, but the open bathroom door. Duncan was hard on the tail of the little creature, but when he arrived at the bathroom door, he nearly lost his religion when he saw that the door into the closet was open and the door beyond into the bedroom was also open. However, the raccoon ran behind the toilet, so Duncan took advantage of that and reached to close the door into the closet.

"Little monster," he muttered, "get on out the door and leave for your own place." However, the little creature seemed to like the lighted, warmer place he was in. He left the bathroom and lumbered under the back of an upholstered chair.

It was an hour later the furnace had been running constantly to try to warm a place where the front door stood open. Both Duncan, with the broom and Nancy with her mop, chased the little furry beast from under or behind all the furniture in the kitchen and living room. Duncan was closest to the door when the critter finally ran out and he quickly slammed it behind him.

The couch was the closest piece of furniture to her and Nancy collapsed onto it, her chest heaving from running around her cabin. Duncan soon joined her, but he wasn't panting, nor had he broken a sweat. Letting the mop slide from her hand to the floor, she murmured, "I can't believe what that wretched little creature did to my place! I never had something like that happen in Blairsville!"

"No, I imagine not," he said with a twinkle in his eyes. "But must I remind you, this is not the city, not even close."

Nancy's hands were spread out on the cushion and her legs out in front. She had her eyes closed, she was panting, her hair was wild curls all over her head, some of them even stuck to her forehead, but Duncan was sure he'd never seen a woman so beautiful. He leaned over and kissed her. "Goodnight, Beautiful," he whispered and stood up.

Her head popped up immediately, as she exclaimed, "Duncan, how can you say that! For goodness sake! I'm a mess!"

From the doorway, he said, "I'll see you at six-thirty." Then he was gone.

"*Six-thirty!!*" she screeched.

Nancy jumped up, ran to the door and locked it, then looked at the clock as she turned around. It was nearly midnight. She was still breathing fast and her heart was going in double time. Quickly, she went to all the lights they'd turned on to see the raccoon and turned them off. She went in her bathroom, brushed her teeth quickly and went through to her bedroom. She hardly remembered stripping off her clothes before she fell onto her bed. Her eyes were nearly shut when she remembered she needed to set her alarm. With the last bit of energy she had she made her hand push the button to make the alarm sound in the morning.

"*I'm so tired, Lord...*" A sigh left her lips, "*Goodnight...*"

There was a little light in the eastern sky when Nancy's alarm went off. The station was playing some loud song. Before her hand snaked out from under the cover, she remembered why it was going off so early. She scrambled from the bed and raced into the bathroom. She took a shower and washed her hair, then combed it, glad that she didn't have to style it.

After dressing in her jeans, a T shirt and a flannel shirt and lacing up her hiking boots, she reached for her backpack to make sure she had everything she needed. She had just zipped it closed again when heavy footsteps came across her porch. She grabbed the doorknob and yanked the door open, as Duncan had his hand raised to knock.

She grabbed up her pack and said, breathlessly, "I'm ready."

He grinned at her. "No more unwelcome visitors last night?"

She made a face at him. "If there were, I didn't hear them. You closed the door as you left and I locked it. I fell into bed before midnight and only woke up with the alarm."

"Good." He grabbed her pack in one hand and her hand with his other. They went down the steps together, headed for his cabin.

Nancy pulled in a deep breath and said, "WOW! Look, there isn't a cloud in the sky!"

Chuckling, Duncan shook his head and said, "I can see where Mel got his name for you, Merry Sunshine."

She couldn't help it, she swung their hands and exclaimed, "But it is! It's the day the Lord has made we should rejoice and be glad in it!"

Inside his cabin, he began stuffing the piles from his counter into the top of her pack and said, "As soon as I get my first cup of Sandy's coffee in me, I'll rejoice and be glad with you."

"Okay, that's great!"

He zipped the pack closed over the last dry ration, picked up her pack and went to the door, where his pack waited. With both packs in his hands, he said, "Push the lock on the door and pull it tight. I don't want any unwanted visitors to greet Isabel when she comes to clean my place while I'm gone."

Nancy did as he asked, then hurried down the steps and caught up with him on the walk before he reached his SUV and said, "Duncan, you won't ever let me live that down, will you!"

He had his remote aimed at the back of his Jeep. He chuckled as he pressed it. After it beeped at him, he said, "Nope, probably not, at least not until you quit reminding me about that bag of trail mix."

She sighed, as he slid the two packs inside, "Thanks."

"You're welcome, I'm sure." He grinned at her and took her to the passenger side of his vehicle and opened the door. He blocked her way, but his eyes were twinkling and he lowered his head. "Good morning, Sunshine." Then he kissed her.

On Sandy's parking lot, Duncan parked in his spot, turned off the ignition and pulled out the key. Before they left the vehicle, he pushed the button on the remote to unlock the back. He didn't go there however, he circled the cab and went to Nancy's door. As he pulled it open he raised his face and took a deep breath through his nose, appreciating the smell on the slight breeze. "Ah, Sandy has the coffee ready!"

"It does smell good, doesn't it!"

Through an open window, they heard Sandy's cheery voice call, "Come on up the walk and let yourselves in breakfast's almost ready!"

Nancy shook her head. "She is something else, isn't she?"

Duncan nodded. "The best."

"Yes, I agree."

Inside, Nancy found the coffee carafe full and poured the mugs full on the table. Duncan carried two of the serving dishes to the dining room table then waited for Nancy to come back. Sandy wheeled herself to her place and Nancy came to the place beside her. Duncan pulled out her chair and seated her. She looked up at him and smiled. He tried not to show it, but his heart skittered in his chest with her smile.

"Thanks," she murmured.

"Yup," he muttered.

As was customary, they held hands while Sandy said grace. Smiling, she looked at Nancy and asked, "So how've you slept since you moved?"

Nancy had her mouth open to answer, but Duncan beat her to it, by saying, "I don't know how she slept that first night, but last night she had a visitor."

Sandy scowled, "You didn't keep her up, did you? Last night, you didn't have stuff for him to do still in your cabin, did you?"

Duncan shook his head. "It wasn't me, it was her own doing. Can you imagine, she left her front door open and this little bandit came in."

Looking from Duncan to Nancy, Sandy asked, "What do you mean?"

Nancy sighed, "I packed my backpack and then I remembered I didn't have any food for the trail. I never thought about critters, I ran out the door and ran to Duncan's to ask what I should do. Later, when he brought me back, this raccoon was ripping up my paper towels in the kitchen. It took over an hour to get him back out the door."

"He didn't bite you, did he?"

"No, Duncan used my broom and I used my mop."

"The little guy seemed to like Nancy's cabin, though, he went from her kitchen to the bathroom and then all around the living room, including the fireplace before he finally ran out the front door."

"You must have been exhausted!"

"Not me," Duncan said and stuffed his mouth full of eggs. "Just another day in the little town of Vansville."

Nancy had a fork full half way to her mouth, but she sighed and said, "Yes, I almost didn't remember to set my alarm for this morning."

"My goodness! What excitement!" Sandy exclaimed. "You had a raccoon in your cabin and he shredded you towels! Wow!"

They finished eating and cleared the table, but the clock showed they only had a few minutes before the group should arrive. Sandy shooed them from her kitchen, so Duncan and Nancy left for the office. Duncan booted up the computer to print off the information he needed for the hike and Nancy stood behind him watching the screen. The printer had barely shut off when they heard two cars pull on the lot. He clicked off his page, but left the computer on so Sandy could use it after they were gone. Holding the papers in one hand, he opened the outside door and ushered Nancy out ahead of him. She smiled and walked out.

A man left his car and walked over and said to Duncan, "I'm Jim Freeze; I presume you're our guide for our hike?"

"Yes, I'm Duncan Roads. I hope you don't mind that I'm bringing a friend along. This is Nancy Southerland she's from here in town."

Jim looked the pretty girl up and down, enough that Duncan was almost sorry he'd invited Nancy. However, Jim didn't comment, he nodded and said to Duncan, "No, that's okay."

A woman joined Jim then another couple and a young teen came up too. Jim turned to them and said, "Guys, this is our guide and his girlfriend, Duncan and Nancy."

Nancy swallowed a sigh. This whole thing was so new, she didn't know if she was Duncan's girlfriend or what. She had to admit to herself that she wished it was true, but she wouldn't say anything if he didn't. Duncan looked at the group and said, "Time's wasting, let's get our packs on and get on the trail." He turned to Nancy then headed for his SUV, so she followed. She was determined not to give him a hard time on the parking lot.

Duncan wasn't about to touch the man's sentence with a ten foot pole. Maybe he thought of Nancy as a good friend, or maybe he had deeper thoughts than that, but unless she denied it, he wouldn't. He pulled her pack from his storage area and held it for her to put her hands behind the straps, then shrugged into his own pack. The other hikers talked among themselves as they shouldered their packs.

As the group from the rehab center had done, the two couples and the child waited for Nancy to take the place behind Duncan as they left the parking lot and headed up the trail. Of course, they were sure she was his girlfriend, so they didn't come between them. This time, she wasn't reluctant to take the spot she smiled at the group and started up the trail right behind Duncan. He didn't have to look back, he knew where she was he could smell the faint scent of her shampoo. It had twitched his nose for several months.

Duncan knew this part of the trail by heart, most of the hikes left on this trail, but several trailheads went off out of sight of the parking lot. As soon as they left the blacktop he turned and walked slowly backwards. When Jim realized Duncan's intent, he motioned to his group to move closer. When they were close, Duncan said, "Everyone keep together. As soon as we leave this first part and take our trail, we'll be walking some fairly steep grades before lunch and we don't want to lose anyone."

Jim nodded. "We'll be sure to keep our line close behind you. Believe me we don't want to get lost, especially on the first day."

Nodding, Duncan said, "That's good. If anyone has to stop for any reason, be sure to give a holler, so we don't get out of range."

"Fine."

Nancy's face glowed as she looked up at him. He had the hardest time keeping his hands to himself. In fact, he grabbed the waistband of his pack with both hands to keep from grabbing her hands to pull her against him. He cleared his throat and spun around then headed down the trail for the hike they were going on. She was about to question his actions when she glanced at his back, but saw his hand motioning her up beside him. At the beginning of this trail it was wide enough, so she took several running steps and was beside him.

His voice was gruff, but he said quietly, for her ears only, "Woman, you'll be getting a kiss pretty soon if you don't stop looking at me like that."

She giggled. "You don't want any of them to think I really am your girlfriend, Duncan?"

"Cut it out," he grumbled.

Several hours later he stopped in a clearing and said, "It's lunch time, folks."

"Do we build a fire now?" Jim asked.

"No, we don't take time for that, get out your filters, cups and dry rations. There's a stream over yonder, filter some water into your cups and add the rations. When we stop for the night I'll build the fire for a hot meal."

The other man whined, "We have to wait for supper to have some coffee? I almost always have a cuppa in my hand."

Duncan scowled at him. "Yeah, seems so."

Fourteen

Looking from Duncan to Nancy, Jim's wife said, "We brought extra rations that we thought would be enough for our guide, like the literature said, but we didn't think there'd be another extra."

"That's no problem, Nancy brought some for herself."

Nancy didn't dare look at Duncan she shed her backpack and started unzipping the top to pull out her cup, filter and rations. As the others reached for their filters and cups and headed for the stream, she went along with the rest. Duncan sat down beside her to eat his arm brushed hers several times while they ate. After he had done it a few times, she looked at him and he winked at her. Her heart jumped in her chest and her cheeks felt like they'd been scorched.

When everyone was finished and they were getting ready to move on, Duncan picked up Nancy's backpack and held it for her. Jim saw him, lowered his own to the ground and picked up his wife's and held it for her. The look on her face was priceless, it was obvious that he didn't usually help her in any way and was only doing it now because of Duncan's example.

Before he took a step, Duncan said, "Across this meadow and beyond those trees is an incline down over shale. I'm not sure any of you is familiar with shale, but it can be treacherous." Looking at the young boy, he said, "No one should try to cross it alone. When we get there, we'll send you two together, then you three next. Nancy and I'll bring up the rear. Wait until everyone is across before moving on."

Jim nodded. "We'll follow instructions."

"That would be a good idea, thanks."

Duncan had anticipated that the boy would give them problems on the shale. Jim and his wife were half way across when Duncan said, "Okay, you three go. Be very careful, that shale can be very unstable under foot."

"Should we hold hands?" the lady asked. Her voice was shrill, almost like a scared child, as she looked from Duncan to the ten feet or so before her.

"If you want, the main thing is to stay together so if one steps on pieces that move, there are others close by to stabilize him."

Duncan was silently hoping that the adults would flank the boy, but they let him go onto the shale first, then the woman took a tentative step, with the man going last. The boy was obviously not nearly as afraid as his mother, before she had taken her second step the boy was three steps ahead of them.

"Ben, come back!" she squeaked.

Taking another step, the young teen sighed, "Ah, Mom, it's not so bad! Just put one foot ahead of the other, come on!"

The boy took several steps then waited for his mother to come more cautiously. She held tightly to her husband's hand, but to her credit, she kept moving. Duncan watched the boy until it was his and Nancy's turn. Nancy remembered the shale they had crossed in the rain back in March. When Duncan silently motioned for her to step on the shale, she took a deep breath and stepped out. It didn't look nearly as bad as when they'd walked that wet shale on their hike.

Duncan had barely stepped onto the shale when there was a thud and a grunt in front of them. Nancy stopped and looked up and Duncan stepped up beside her. Just as he had figured, Ben had been moving his feet as he waited for his parents and one foot came down on an edge that broke away. The boy lost his footing and landed on his rear.

"Oh!" his mom exclaimed, "Are you okay, Ben?" She tried to take a step toward her son, but her husband held her firm. She looked back at him and said, "Alex, he could be hurt!"

Nodding to the boy who was on his feet already, he said, "Look, Maryann, he's already on his feet, he's okay." Sternly, he said, "Ben, don't be jumping around so much! If you walked more slowly you wouldn't get so far ahead of your mother."

The boy sighed, "Yes, Dad."

Maryann whispered, "Oh, my, this is scary!"

Duncan watched and listened to the family exchange and was glad the boy's dad seemed to have his head on straight. They were half way across the shale, but Duncan couldn't have reached him right away. Nancy was doing fine, but the question Maryann had asked didn't sound like a bad idea. With a wink, Duncan reached down and grasped Nancy's hand and they walked across the shale together.

"What's the deal?" she whispered, looking at their hands.

"Nothing, I hadn't really thought about it until Maryann mentioned it. It sounded like something I wanted to do. Do you mind?"

"Duncan! Of course not!" While they whispered back and forth Duncan laced his fingers with hers. Nancy had to admit, it felt wonderful!

"Good."

Much later, Duncan led them onto a meadow with a lively stream running at the edge of the trees. In the middle of the open area he stopped and said, "This is our camping place for the night, folks. I'll start the fire and maybe Ben can help me gather dry wood and brush to burn. Jim, you and Alex set up our tents and you ladies get the stew fixed up so it can go on the fire as soon as the wood's burning well."

Jim and Alex unhooked their two man tents from their backpacks, but Jim said, "You want us to set up yours too?"

"Yes, if you don't mind. Nancy's and mine are hooked on our backpacks. Ben has his own, too. They need to be set up before dark. Make a circle about ten feet back from the fire pit, so we can sit and chat while we eat. The smoke and the fire help keep the mosquitoes away."

Jim nodded. "Okay. I guess you've had lots of practice on building fires for the hikers. We'll let you get to work."

Duncan gave him a grin. "You could say that."

Nancy had brought several cans of vegetables to contribute to the stew, one for each night, as they'd done for the hike she'd gone on in the spring. She'd also slipped in a box of granola bars she thought would taste good for dessert. Before Duncan started the fire, he brought out the spit and his large pan that the cooks used for the stew. Nancy set her can down beside it and waited for the ladies to collect cans from everyone's backpack.

However, when Maryann and Cindy came back to the firepit, they didn't have cans of vegetables, they had two cans of canned meat in gravy and several packages of biscuits that needed to be oven baked.

Looking at the large pan Duncan had set beside where he was starting the fire, Cindy said, "Umm, don't you have a Dutch oven to cook the biscuits in?"

Duncan had just struck the match under the brush. He rocked back on his heels and looked at the packages in the ladies hands and said, "Ladies, I think the literature asked that you bring ingredients for an evening stew, I have room in my pack for the spit and two pans that fit inside each other. We use the larger one for the stew and the smaller one to heat water to wash up our dishes. A Dutch oven is much too sophisticated for our hikes. I'm sorry if you brought things like that because we can't use them."

The women looked at each other and Cindy sighed, but Maryann said, "See, I told you I didn't think we should bring stuff like that, Cindy."

Cindy looked at the large pan, then back at Duncan. "So we can't use these?"

Duncan looked at the woman's hands as they held the two tubes of soft dough. "Not unless you can think of some way to keep them from sinking into the meat and vegetables and maybe cook them on top."

"We didn't bring vegetables enough for all the nights."

The fire was going well, but Ben was slow at bringing back enough wood. Duncan stood up and dusted off his hands above the fire. Just before he turned to find more wood, he said, "Improvise, ladies. That's what camping's all about."

Nancy sighed in the darkness and looked at the clock on her bedside table again. She didn't need to get up until after sunrise, but she was awake again and had looked at that clock nearly every hour all night long and it had been long. She sighed, four thirty was still too early to get up, there was nothing to do around her cabin that could keep her busy so she pulled the sheet and light-weight blanket up to her chin and closed her eyes. She'd been anxious for this day to come for well over a week. Obviously she didn't realize how anxious. Once this morning came, she could walk in the new clinic and start her new job. Today was the day for the staff to start their orientation at the site.

Over the last few days she'd watched many delivery trucks back off the road on the other side of the building and then leave from ten minutes to an hour later. She was sure after they had introductions that each one of them would get an assignment to start stocking shelves and move furniture to make the place usable by this time next week when the clinic opened for business. Her eyes popped open again and after reading the illuminated digits on the clock to see that only five minutes had passed, she went to the bathroom and had a drink, then lay down and turned away from the clock, pushed the corner of her pillow under her cheek and closed her eyes. Much to her surprise, the alarm went off at the proper time and she had slept until it went off. She left the radio on to listen to the news and headed for the bathroom.

Yesterday, she and Duncan had spent the day together. It was his day off between hikes and they'd enjoyed an all day walk and picnic not far away, but in some of the beautiful mountains close by. It had been at the overlook where Sandy had snapped four pictures of the awesome views, then painted the four beautiful paintings she'd recently sold to a couple who had hiked the trail close to it. Sandy had confided to her that that sale alone would keep them in groceries all winter or make several mortgage payments.

After coming home from their hike together a few weeks ago, Nancy had taken over fixing breakfast for Duncan before he left on a hike. He was coming this morning then go to DeLord's and soon after he left, she'd go to the clinic. She was excited for both things. She and Duncan were very close now and she missed him when he was gone on the trails. Starting today, she'd have something to take up the time while he was gone, at least for eight hours a day. When she'd left the rehab center she'd gotten vacation time, so now she felt rested to start out.

After her shower, she combed out her hair and decided to let it air dry. It didn't need to look perfect today they were to come in jeans and 'T' shirts ready to work. She knew the building would be air conditioned, but she was sure there'd be plenty of dust and dirt flying around in the building. There was always dust in a new building, but she was sure those delivery men hadn't been careful when they made deliveries and probably brought in dirt on their feet or on the boxes, since it had rained several of the days when deliveries had been made. They'd have floor mops going as well as plenty of boxes to open. Still she was excited to see this new facility ready for its customers.

After she entered her kitchen, she filled her carafe with water and dumped it into the top of her coffee maker. No matter the temperature outside, Duncan liked his coffee for breakfast. As the aroma filled her tiny kitchen, she pulled out her skillet, the eggs she'd bought from Raylyn and the bacon and bread from Alex's store. She smiled, it was fun to know the people personally where she got her food.

She'd popped the bread in the toaster and lifted the bacon from the skillet when she heard heavy steps on her porch. She smiled again, a giant was coming for breakfast, but he was a gentle giant, at least with her. "Come on in!" she called cheerfully, "The door's unlocked." She didn't dare tell him the door was open, he'd remind her of her encounter with the raccoon not even a month ago. That episode she would gladly put out of her mind, but Duncan liked to remind her any chance he could.

"So," Duncan said, as he closed the door behind him. "have you got that coffee recipe from Sandy down yet?"

With a sigh, Nancy said, "Duncan, my coffee may not taste just like hers, but you know it's good. Anyway, it's better than that stuff we made on the hike."

Letting out a long-suffering sigh, Duncan took the carafe from the warmer and filled his mug, the one he had commandeered from her cupboard the very first time he'd come to her cabin for coffee, then took it to the table and sat down. He'd learned that first evening that there wasn't room in Nancy's tiny kitchen for both him and her, so he got out of her way as fast as he could. Besides, he liked watching her move around her kitchen.

She brought the plates, silverware and juice to the table, then went back for the eggs, while he sipped his coffee. "So how is it today?"

Nodding, Duncan said, "Surprisingly good," he said to goad her.

"Duncan, you know it's fine! I make good coffee. I've had to I made it at the rehab center because nobody drank coffee anybody else made."

Giving her a wink, he said, "Like I say, surprisingly good."

Nancy set down her own mug, along with the platter of eggs, but Duncan was on his feet and pulled out her chair. She sat down and he helped her pull into the table. He sat back down and reached for her hand, but before he lowered his head, he grinned and grabbed her other hand.

He squeezed both hands and said, "Father, thanks for this food Nancy's prepared for our breakfast. Bless her as she goes to the clinic for her first day and help me lead a safe hike today. In Your Son's Name, amen."

Silently, to herself, Nancy said, *Thank You, God for the change in Duncan's life.*

The clock read the far side of seven thirty when Duncan took his dishes to Nancy's sink and swallowed his last mouthful of coffee. Nancy was right behind him with her own, but he took them and put them in her sink. Before she could move away from him, he snagged her arm and spun her against his chest. "Listen, young lady, it's time for me to leave and you're not getting away without a genuine hug and kiss. It'll have to last me for almost a week, you know."

Looking up at him, as she slid her arms around his waist, she grinned. "I didn't intend to go far. I'll take one of your kisses anytime you're free to give it."

His one arm lifted her to her tiptoes, while he put his other hand behind her head and brought his face down. His eyes twinkling, he murmured beside her lips. "That's good." They savored a kiss, but finally, he pulled away and said, "Save that thought for when I get back. I'll honk; you'll know when I'm home."

She squeezed his waist and said, "I sure will! Have a good hike." She made a face at him. "Maybe you shouldn't work on your tan any more, though. I'll be inside most of the time from now on, so I can't work on mine too much."

He chuckled. "Too bad for you! See you!"

Nancy went with him onto her porch, where he stole another kiss then she watched as he walked to his SUV. When he reached it, he turned and they blew kisses to each other. She grinned and watched him get behind the wheel of his big machine then waved again as he left Isabel's parking lot. She missed him already, but he'd be back on Friday and she'd fix dinner.

She stood for a minute to enjoy the lovely day. The sun was out, birds were singing merrily and off in the distance dark evergreens were swaying in the gentle breeze. Even further away were those awesome hills and mountains that Duncan hiked in all the time. Finally, she spun around and hurried back inside and started cleaning up, she was to be through the little door in that impressive concrete wall in only twenty minutes.

With only minutes to spare, Nancy grabbed her purse and rushed to the door. She flipped the lock and pulled the door closed behind her, then hurried to the end of the walk in front of Isabel's cabins. She dashed across the narrow grassy area to the concrete walk leading to the little entrance door on the back of the building. The door opened easily and as it pneumatically closed behind her, she heard voices at the front of the building, so she hurried toward them.

There were four people there, three she had never met before. Dillon Marshall grinned at Nancy and said, "I see you're still Merry Sunshine here in Vansville! Welcome to your first day of Nurse Jane Fuzzy Wuzzy." He cleared his throat and said, "Although, that part will surely have to wait until next week."

Giving a huff, she said, "Dillon, will you cut that out! It is a beautiful day, what's not to smile about?"

Dillon turned to the other three and said, "We're still waiting for our doctor, when he arrives I'll make the introductions so I only have to do it once."

"So are you transferring out here?" Nancy asked Dillon.

Grinning again, he answered, "Me? Move out here to the back side of nowhere? You can't be serious, Nancy!"

She shrugged. "Thought I'd ask. I never like being in the dark if I can help it."

Only a few minutes later the front door opened and a young man walked confidently in and crossed the large waiting area toward the group. Nancy looked at him, he had dark hair cut to his collar and his face was clean-shaven. He was well built, possibly six feet tall. However, there was no stirring in her chest as with another man who was bigger, taller, had a blond beard, a blond ponytail and blue eyes.

Dillon said, "Hi, Stan, meet your crew."

Stan joined the circle and looked at all the faces. "Hi, folks."

Dillon said, "This is Nancy Southerland, the RN. Next is Dan Whitaker, the phlebotomist, Angie Lamont, the LPN who can do pharmacy if needed and Jill Simpson, who'll be the receptionist and office manager. Folks, this is Doctor Stan Miles."

Stan worked around the circle as Dillon spoke the name, shaking hands. At closer inspection, Nancy noticed that Stan was a young man he was probably just out of his residency. He had straight dark hair in a military cut. His eyes were dark brown and he was probably five inches taller than she. It was also obvious he kept himself in good shape, but he was nothing like Duncan, as far as muscles were concerned. He had a nice tan she had to give him that.

Dillon slapped Stan on the shoulder and said, "I'm out of here! Whip these guys into shape, Stan and get this place ready for opening day next Monday! See you all some other time. Don't let me hear you're sloughing off now that you're here in the boonies."

"I'll do what I can, Dillon. Thanks for coming out."

After the front door closed behind Dillon, Stan said, "Let's start with the furniture and at least slide the boxes into the proper rooms. That'll probably take most of today. Tomorrow we can start with the supplies."

Nancy eyed the huge boxes that were haphazardly pushed together near the main entrance. It looked like the delivery men had only pushed the articles once inside the doors. After a glance around at the others on her crew, she wasn't sure how many of those boxes she and the other two women could move. All three of them were slim she thought perhaps she might be the strongest of the three, since she'd worked at the rehab center for three years. Angie had probably only graduated from her nursing program and Jill couldn't be much older. Dan was a big man, bigger than Stan, maybe they should team up, Stan take Angie and Jill and she and Dan work together. Maybe, just maybe, the five of them could get those huge boxes moved.

Looking at the huge boxes, Angie said, "How do we move those? It's the five of us who get to do all the work?"

Stan also looked where she did and said, "Dan takes you and Jill and I'll take Nancy. Surely with a man on each team we can get this place whipped into shape."

Jill sighed, looking at Stan, "Yeah, I guess we can only try."

Nancy grinned, it was obvious which team Jill wanted to be on.

Stan was eyeing the women, a bit more subtly. He was glad Nancy was the RN and she'd be working with him more closely than the others. She could easily take the place of his girlfriend who'd ditched him several years ago. He knew she'd been working for several years, so she was more his age. Jill and Angie were hardly out of diapers, as far as he was concerned. He decided that Nancy would start off with him as one of the teams. He'd noticed immediately that she didn't have any rings on her left hand. He was pretty pleased with that.

Dan was a man of action. As soon as Stan told him who he'd be working with, he said, "Ladies, let's get this job moving. The boxes are together lets see what they say on the outside."

As he herded his two woman crew toward the far side of the reception area, Stan said, "I guess that's our hint to not slack off either."

Nancy chuckled. "I'd say. Where do we start?"

"Same place, I guess."

When all five people were standing among the boxes, Angie said, "Here's a bunch that says reception. This one says exam room."

"There should be four that say exam room," Stan said. "I was told those are the exam tables, but chairs and such for those rooms come from the reception bunch."

"Peachy," Jill said.

Getting behind a box marked exam room, Dan said, "Come on, girls let's get this one into one of those rooms down the hall. It won't move itself and there's nobody here but us to get the job done, you know."

Grabbing Jill's arm, Angie moved to Dan's shoulder and said, "We're on it, boss. We'll get 'er on the move in seconds."

Dan grinned. "I like your spunk, Angie!"

"Mmm, well…"

They moved it about two feet, but then the edge of the box snagged on the carpeting and nearly tipped over, but then it bounced back. That wouldn't have been so bad, but the instructions on the box showed them that the box was upright and the instructions were to keep the box with the top up. Jill had been pushing so hard that the resistance of the box sent her unceremoniously down onto the floor with a thud and a grunt.

As she rolled from her bottom to her knees, to stand, she grunted, as she put her hands down, "That was graceful."

Nancy and Stan had begun to open one of the boxes that said, 'reception' but she looked up and said, "I was in the hardware store a while back. He has dollies we could maybe borrow to move those heavy things across the carpet."

"Is he a nice guy, would he loan us one or would we have to buy it?" Stan asked.

Nancy shrugged. "He seemed nice enough when I was there."

"You keep on opening these I'll go see what I can come up with." He looked at the other crew, while Jill was still on the floor and said, "Guys, see if you can find some lighter weight stuff to work with until I get back. It's obvious we can't scoot those things across that long space by pushing. I'm going to see what there is to use in this little place. Surely since we're so close to that store he'll trust us."

Twenty minutes later Stan came back pushing a dolly in front of him. He came inside and grinned at his staff. After the door closed, he said, "Here we go, guys! Brad was nice enough to loan us this for the day. He closes long after we should be done, so lets get those babies moved and in position."

By five o'clock, there was lots of cardboard on the parking lot outside the main door and the big room inside didn't look quite so much like a forest. In fact, the reception area looked like they could open for business but of course, the rooms behind the reception desk were still in chaos. Nancy knew it would take at least until Friday to get everything still in boxes put into their rightful place. There were still a lot of smaller boxes and during the afternoon another truck backed up to the door and added many more boxes to the mess.

Stan looked at his watch and said, "It's five o'clock, folks, I guess we must knock it off. Tomorrow's my day at Blairsville Hospital ER, so you four'll be on your own." He grinned. "I'm sure you four can handle what's left or a good part of it and I'll see you on Wednesday."

Dan's stomach growled. "What's in this town? Are there any drive-thru's?"

The other four knew by now that Nancy lived in Vansville, so she spoke up, "I think the closest one is on the highway a mile or so the other side of the pull-off."

Heading for the door, Dan exclaimed, "Dillon was right! This is the boonies!"

Angie and Jill were close behind Dan, but as Nancy turned toward the back door, Stan said, "Why are you going that way, Nancy?"

She shrugged. "I live a couple of doors down in one of Mrs. Isaacson's cabins. Since you work part time in Blairsville, I guess you'd live there."

Feeling the emptiness in his own stomach, Stan had his hand on the door bar, swallowed a sigh and said, "I live in an efficiency close to the hospital. Could I interest you in going for dinner with me after work on Wednesday? If you live so close, it wouldn't take much to change and be ready." Thinking about it, he added, "I guess you'd need to drive so you could come back when we're finished."

"That's kind of you for asking, Stan, but I'm working with a friend of mine after work for several days, so I've made plans for Wednesday."

Stan's stomach growled, so he said, "Okay, it'll be another time, see you Wednesday."

"Okay," she called, as she headed for the back door and he out the front. She wasn't really upset that Sandy had asked for her help this week.

Duncan met his group on the parking lot at eight o'clock with the papers warm from the printer in the office. A woman came up to him and said, "Are you Duncan?"

"Last I checked."

The woman held out her hand and said, "I'm Patty Greene and these are the members of my youth group. Our youth pastor had planned to go with us, but he had something come up, so it's thee and me against the world of teenagers."

Duncan took the woman's hand, but before he could say anything, one of the strapping teens, said, "Ahh, Patty, we aren't so bad!"

After one shake, Duncan dropped Patty's hand and said, "That remains to be seen. How good are you at following directions?"

One of the girls spoke up, "Real good, Mr. Duncan, real good!"

Nodding, he said, "Actually, I'm Duncan, this mister stuff is too sophisticated for me. We'll hold judgment on the directions part until we come to our camping site tonight or one of those hand over hand places on the trail."

"Wow!" one of the boys who looked a bit like a couch potato said.

"So we do rappelling?" the first boy asked.

"No, nothing like that, but some of the inclines are a bit steep."

Shouldering into his pack the boy said, "Piece of cake! We're onto it!"

"Okay, let's get out of here!" Duncan said and reached for his backpack. "We've got a few hills and hollows to cover before lunch."

"Yes!" two boys smacked high fives then reached for their backpacks. Duncan noticed that none of the boys helped any of the girls into their packs.

He looked at Patty and said, "You made sure everyone has a place to sleep inside and everyone has rain gear, plus hiking boots?"

As she buckled her waist belt, she said, "They all assured me that they did. I had the rules posted in our meeting room at church for the last month."

Buckling his waist belt, Duncan said, "Okay, let's get on the move. We have about four hours of trail before lunchtime."

Patty moved up beside Duncan on the wide trail and said, "What do we do if it rains? We all have slickers, but doesn't the trail get bad?"

"Yup. The trail can get pretty muddy, even treacherous if we get a thunderstorm or a gully washer. It doesn't matter, once we're on the trail, we keep on until we get back to base at the end of our hike. We try to keep up to schedule, because the camping place for the night is a certain distance from the last camping spot. It's a matter of being more careful."

"Wow! So we can't come back if it rains tomorrow?"

"That's not in the plan. We don our rain slickers and keep on. We warn the crew to be as careful as possible, but to keep going."

"I guess I never really thought about it. I figured if we were caught in rain we'd put on our slickers and try to get back to our cars as quick as we could."

"Sorry, nope," Duncan said, shaking his head. "When you set up a hike and tell Sandy how long you want it, she works on the computer and matches your choices with a trail."

Patty shrugged. "I guess that's why you're the leader and I'm not."

Duncan chuckled. "Could be."

It was late June and there wasn't any rain in the forecast through the end of the week, so Duncan hoped that was what would happen. He was pretty sure Patty and Nancy weren't made from the same mold. Nancy put on her rain slicker and went on, her hair in ringlets all over her head. He wasn't sure how Patty would do in the rain, maybe she was a youth leader, but he wasn't impressed with her outdoorsmanship. All he could do was hope for the best and lead the group all the way back to the starting point.

It had been a beautiful day and there was a good breeze in the hills as the sun worked its way toward the mountains in the west. Duncan wondered if youth leader Patty would have devotions after supper, since she wasn't the true leader of the teen group. He led the noisy group out of the trees onto a meadow and turned around. "Folks, we seem to have reached our campsite for the night. While I get the fire going for supper, you boys get the tents up and you ladies get supper going."

"We all gotta do tents?" one boy whined.

"That's what I said. Unless you want to gather wood and brush for the campfire. We need a good supply, since it's our only source of light after the sun goes down and we'll need water heated in the morning."

Looking at the other guys, he said, "No, I'd better help with the tents."

Duncan nodded and said, "Girls, while some of you gather the ingredients for supper, a couple of you'll need to fill a pan with water for clean up. The water must be hot as soon as supper's over, because daylight fades soon after that and it's hard to see if everything's clean."

One girl left the group and wandered to the rushing stream. After looking at the water, she turned back and asked, "We gotta use that stuff for washing dishes and stuff?"

"That's it and you'll have to use your filters to fill your canteens for the trail tomorrow."

A shudder went up the girl's back, as she said, "But I saw fish in there!"

"Yeah, so?"

"How can you get stuff clean with fish in the water?"

Duncan threw a log in the firepit and shrugged. "You push the pan so the top is barely under the water and let the water flow over the top to fill it up. With the filter, you do the same then you pour the water into your canteen. It's not hard, ladies, really."

Looking at the deep blue sky that made a huge dome and the stately evergreens around them, wide open space where she could see for miles in any direction, another girl turned to Patty with tears in her eyes and said, "I wanna go home, Miss Patty! It's not that far, is it?"

Helplessly, Patty turned to Duncan and said, "How far is it, Duncan?"

Duncan struck the match and the pile of wood and brush caught. Duncan sat on his heels and looked at the leader and the girl. "We've come about five miles, ladies. We left the parking lot this morning it took us all day to get here. This is a five day hike, which means we won't see the parking lot with your van until Friday afternoon. That's when you'll get to go home."

"There isn't a road close by?" the girl asked, anxiously wringing her hands.

"No, we head into the hills. If we cross another trail it's unusual, but when we set up these hikes, we try to steer clear of any roads."

"Oh," the girl whispered.

The boys had finished setting up the tents and since the girls hadn't finished cooking the stew, the guys gathered around Duncan and one asked, "Is there any wildlife? Can we see any bears or stuff like that? Our youth pastor said he came on one and heard some wolves one night. Will we see stuff like that?"

"I know there are bears in the Smokies and these hills lead up to those mountains, but none of us from DeLord's has ever seen or encountered any evidence of bears. Yes, we sometimes hear wolves off in the distance and sometimes they visit during the night. That's why we must clean up right after supper, but usually they don't bother us if there's nothing out for them to get. Of course, there are skunks, raccoons, opossums, rabbits and deer, but usually they come and go without a problem."

"Skunks!" Patty exclaimed.

Duncan shrugged. "You leave them alone, they leave you alone."

"I wanna go home!" the girl cried.

As each teen was cleaning his utensils, one of the boys said, "Miss Patty, are we gonna have devotions tonight?"

Patty scowled. "I guess not, Junior, how could we?"

The boy shrugged. "We pull out our flashlights and our Bibles. Pastor Jim said we probably would."

"He never said anything to me. I figured we'd say grace at meals and let it go at that. You brought your Bible?"

"Yeah, so did the other guys."

Patty looked at Duncan. "Devotions?"

Duncan nodded. "Most of the youth groups I lead have them. It's a bit natural out here in God's out-of-doors."

"Wow! I never thought." She stood up and walked away from the group. After several minutes she came back and said, "I guess if somebody wants to lead it we could have devotions. Somebody want to do that?"

None of the kids looked at her. They all lowered their heads and stared at the ground. Finally Duncan said, "I have a favorite. You all get your Bibles if you brought them and we'll read it. I was going to do that anyway for myself."

Several of the kids scrambled for their backpacks, while Duncan opened his and pulled out the red Bible and a flashlight. When the kids came back with their Bibles, he said, "I guess not everyone has a Bible, so why don't those of you that do find someone who doesn't and share so everyone can read the Psalm with me. Someone needs to share with your leader, too."

When they were all settled, Duncan said, "Let's open our Bibles to Psalm 19."

> "The heavens declare the glory of God; the
> skies proclaim the work of his hands.
> Day after day they pour forth speech, night
> after night they display knowledge.
> There is no speech or language where their voice is not heard.
> Their voice goes out into all the earth, their
> words to the ends of the world.
> In the heavens he has pitched a tent for the sun,
> which is like a bridegroom coming forth from his pavilion,
> like a champion rejoicing to run his course.
> It rises at one end of the heavens and makes its circuit to the other,
> Nothing is hidden from its heat....
> May the words of my mouth and the meditation
> of my heart be pleasing in your sight,
> O LORD my Rock and my Redeemer." (vs. 1-6,14)

One of the girls looked up at the sky and reverently said, "Wow! Awesome!"

"Think about it, guys, everything declares the glory of God. I haven't been a Christian very long, but I couldn't help but see God in everything I saw around me."

"Yeah, that's awesome!" one boy murmured.

As the sun set and discussion died down, Patty asked, "Duncan, when should we be up to get on the trail?"

"My alarm goes off at six. We need to be on the move by seven thirty."

"Man, six o'clock! That's before the birds, isn't it?" one boy groaned.

Duncan chuckled. "No, not really. A few days ago was the longest day of the year. Dawn is a good while before six o'clock. Remember we must heat water for clean up again and take down all these tents. See you in the morning."

"Miss Patty, will you sleep with me?" the scared girl asked.

"Linda, it can't happen. I have a one man tent and so do you. You'll be fine, there's somebody on either side of you. Nothing's going to happen."

"I'm scared," she whispered.

"Linda, get over it," one of the boys said.

Duncan sat by the fire, as the kids found their tents. He loved this time of day and he had a lot to think about. He wondered how Nancy had made out her first day on her job. Before his thoughts took him back to a cabin in Vansville, Patty sat down, stretched out her legs and held her hands out to the fire. She had on shorts and a wispy top, obviously she had no sweatshirt. She hadn't shivered... yet.

"Duncan thanks for rescuing me tonight with the devotions. I never thought about having devotions on the trail, but I guess it's one of the best places."

Setting his Bible beside him, he said, "I think so. That's what got me thinking about spiritual things, really. A lady on one of my early hikes this year had her own devotions. I asked her questions and she answered them. It got me thinking. Tell me, you're the first woman youth leader I've ever taken on a hike. Why is that?"

"Our youth pastor was to be the leader for this hike if he'd come as we all thought, but I'm single and I love teens so my church asked me to help. At first that's all I did, but then the youth pastor got really busy and his wife had a baby, so it's kind of fallen on me." They sat for a few minutes, but then Patty turned, looked at Duncan and said, "I guess you're single, Duncan?"

"Yeah, it's sort of hard to be much else with a job like this." He didn't feel like telling everything, what he did off the trail wasn't a youth leader's business that he'd never see again.

"I suppose that's so. You don't get to date much."

Chuckling, Duncan said, "I never aspired to being a lady's man."

Patty patted his hand and rolled to stand up. "When the right woman comes along, you'd better gobble her up."

Duncan rolled the other way and headed for the stream. Over his shoulder, he said, "I'll think about that, Patty, sleep well."

Duncan decided he'd think about it, but it wouldn't be Patty whom he thought about. Actually, he was already thinking about a lovely lady whom he ate breakfast with this morning. She'd gone on his hike just weeks ago she'd told him she loved it. He'd spent a lot of time with her, especially since she'd moved to Vansville. He felt comfortable in her company; she seemed to be comfortable with him. He still wasn't convinced she'd be content to spend the rest of her life with him, especially since he didn't have any real skills other than computer skills and loving the out-of-doors. He sat down on a rock close to the stream and put his hand into the cold, running water. As the stream gurgled on its merry way, thoughts bombarded his mind. He watched a stick bob its way around rocks on out of sight. Why should Nancy want to spend any time with him? She was a nurse, a good one, for all he knew. She had a profession, she'd gotten higher education he had high school. What was he thinking?

On Friday, Duncan saw the hikers off then went in the office. Sandy was behind the desk typing in some information into the computer, then she hit the mouse and the printer kicked on. She said, "Duncan, your stats for your next hike are printing, but it doesn't go out until Monday at eight. Can you handle two full days off?"

"I'll get to go hear Roger preach, that'll be good."

"Has Nancy started going here or is she still going back to Blairsville?"

"I don't know, I'll have to look into that."

Sandy looked up at the clock. "You go on, she'll be finished for the day real soon and I know she's planning to fix dinner for you both. Take her some wild flowers from that field, why don't you? She'll love them."

"Mmm, I'll have to think about that. See you Monday."

Cheerfully, she said, "Have a good weekend!"

Duncan grabbed his papers, rushed to his SUV, and grabbed a piece of paper from his notepad. Quickly, he scribbled a note, then drove to Isabel's parking lot, left his Jeep running and ran up the walk to Nancy's door. He slid the note under the frame around the window; then rushed down the walk back to his Jeep. He breathed a sigh as he glanced at the clock on his dash, pulled the stick into reverse, backed around and gunned his machine out of the parking lot. He left town as the front door of the clinic opened and four people left the building for their cars.

By Friday, the clinic was set to open. Everything was in its place, the exam rooms were fully stocked, the exam tables were covered with the paper sheets, just as they were supposed to be. The drawers were full, the cabinets were lined with everything they should have and Nancy was counting the minutes until she could leave and go home to fix a nice dinner for her and Duncan. He should be home about the time she walked out the back door of the clinic.

With a smile on her face, Nancy hurried through the back door of the clinic and ran the few yards to the walk in front of the cabins. Duncan should be home soon. She went on by the row of cabins to the mailboxes Isabel had put up soon after she moved in. She opened hers, found one piece of junk mail and hurried back to her door.

From the walk she noticed the white paper stuck under the window frame, so she hurried up and retrieved it. It said, "Nancy, sorry, but something's come up, I can't come for supper. See you sometime, D."

The smile left Nancy's face; in fact she felt tears sting her eyes. She blinked quickly, to keep them from falling. She pulled the note from the door, pushed her key into the lock and let herself in. She'd fixed a crock-pot of delicious smelling meat and vegetables, something that was easy after a day's work, but also nutritious and something Duncan really liked. She went to the electric cord and pulled it from the wall. If he wasn't coming, she wasn't that hungry.

She couldn't help herself, she whispered, "A big old chicken!"

Her air conditioning was off, since it had cooled some after the sun went down when she heard Duncan's Jeep drive across the gravel and stop. She wondered if she should find out what had come up, but she looked at the clock and saw it was ten o'clock. Surely tomorrow would be soon enough, unless, of course, he came to her door. She listened intently, but there were no heavy boot sounds on her porch, all she heard was a door closing two doors away.

Her heard sank. Was he telling her something?

Nancy had talked to Sandy last evening and she'd said that the leader was a woman. Tears pooled in Nancy's eyes as she turned the door lock and headed for bed. Tears streamed down her cheeks, as she shed her clothes. She let them fall and was glad she always kept her nightie under her pillow. She threw the cover and sheet back and fell across her bed. Yanking the pillow under her face, she let the tears flow. Maybe the youth leader was much more poised or beautiful than Nancy Southerland. She probably had her life altogether, too.

Fifteen

Duncan saw the lights shining through Nancy's windows when he returned late. Had she been waiting for him? Surely she had better things to do with her time now that she was working. He'd met Doctor Stan Miles he was a much better match for Nancy than him. He sighed and closed the door, she probably hadn't even thought about him once she started work.

In the darkness he went to his bedroom. He'd gone to Blairsville, ate supper from a drive-thru and made himself watch a movie. The food had tasted like cardboard. He was exhausted, usually, he came home from a hike, threw his clothes in his washer, hibernated with a cold soft drink and a microwaved frozen dinner, his Bible and the bed. Tonight was supposed to have been different, Nancy was cooking dinner, but he'd beat a hasty retreat. After his decision on Monday, he must leave town, he couldn't look her in the eye, not when he was so vulnerable.

Leaving his dirty clothes on the floor beside the bed, he managed to pull the covers back before he collapsed onto the soft mattress. It was an effort to pull his legs up and slide them under the sheet. He let out a deep sigh and was asleep about the time his head hit the pillow. However, it wasn't a restful sleep. Around midnight he woke up after a dream. He was wrapped up in his covers and as he tried to straighten them, he stared at the black ceiling, but he could still see the lovely face with the curls around it that he'd seen in his dreams for many nights. This time, however, there was no sunny smile, there were tears running down her cheeks. He sighed, he knew he'd put them there.

He got up and made his way through his closet to the bathroom. He flipped on the nightlight and filled a glass for a drink. He had to do something, her face in his dream was much too vivid for him to close his eyes and go back to sleep. His body was still craving sleep, but his mind was working overtime and his heart felt like a big chunk of ice in his chest. On the way back to bed he convinced himself he'd go see her in the morning and explain that things were off. He was sorry that he'd led her on. She needed to set her sights on somebody more worthy of her than him. With that thought he fell on his bed again and turned his back on the window to try to sleep again. One other time he'd tried to sleep looking at that window and it seemed like God had talked to him about a problem He had with His child.

Nancy slept late in the morning. They'd been working hard all week. All the furniture deliveries had been made by last Monday, but all week long the delivery trucks brought more supplies and by yesterday afternoon, they'd been running, all five of them, to get everything put away. Besides, if Duncan was being scarce, what was there to get up early for? Finally, the sun coming in the bedroom window was warm enough that she had to throw off her covers, so she decided to get up. As she headed for the bathroom, the air conditioning kicked on, so she knew it would be a warm day. What should she do? Last time she'd been off, Duncan had been off, too and they'd gone for an all day hike and picnic. She thought they'd had a wonderful time and that he'd enjoyed the breakfast she'd fixed for him, but maybe he was biding his time, knowing that a woman was the leader of his hike on Monday.

Her stomach growled reminding her she hadn't had but a sandwich for supper. She started her coffee and threw some bread in the toaster. She found some orange juice and a jar of jelly in the refrigerator and decided that was good enough for breakfast. After pouring a second cup of coffee and leaving it on the table, she dressed then took all her dirty clothes from the week into her bathroom. As she sorted, she knew it would take her three loads to get everything washed. She'd be busy all morning.

That was a good thing. Surely it was it would take her mind off the man from the cabin only two doors away. Maybe after she had her laundry finished she'd go to Alex's store for some groceries and maybe to Raylyn's for some eggs. She'd gone back to the kitchen for a swallow of coffee when she heard heavy steps on her porch. Her heart skipped a beat then settled into double time. She picked up her mug and went to the door as she heard the knock. She turned the deadbolt and opened the door to Duncan's dear face.

She couldn't help it, a grin spread across her face, but it faded when she saw there was no answering smile. "Umm," he muttered, "could you come out on the porch for a minute?"

She pulled the door open and stepped out. "What's up, Duncan?" she asked, as she slid into one of the wicker chairs on the porch.

Just the way she said his name made his insides churn, but he had to ignore it and say his peace. His heart was beating double time as he gazed at the lovely woman. "Umm, we need… Well, I guess I…" He sighed, "I won't be coming for meals any more. I'm sorry I led you on, Nancy, but we, umm, need to break it off."

"I see." She was proud at how strong her voice sounded. "Care to tell me why?"

Duncan looked straight ahead across the meadow he'd walked that night she'd moved in. "Well, it's like this." Some minutes later, he said, "You're not my speed, see. I'm a country bumpkin, a hiking guide, sorta want to be out in the woods a lot. It's not what you need, see."

Nancy stood, but much to Duncan's surprise, she threw her tepid coffee right into his face and hurried to her door. Before she closed it, she said, "I'm *so* glad you know what's best for me, Duncan. I'll keep that in mind when I talk with the Lord and ask Him to show me if I'm to stay single or look for some other fool who'll have me." Just before the door closed completely, she said, "By the way, have a good life in your stubborn bachelorhood!"

Wiping his hand down his face, his thoughts hit him. He'd done the right thing, hadn't he? Of course he had. Having settled that monumental question he shook his wet hand and stood up. He left Nancy's porch slowly. He knew he'd done the right thing! The new doctor at the new clinic had to be a better choice! Didn't he? He left her porch very slowly. His feet dragged and instead of going back to his cabin or his vehicle, he wandered toward the woods. He always got such inspiration from walking these woods.

It was Monday of Fourth of July week. The clinic would open for business at eight o'clock and DeLord's three camping guides were to lead three hikes out on different trails. They were also to leave at eight o'clock. Neal and Duncan had descended on DeLord's at seven, but there was no coffee smell coming through an open window as Duncan and Neal left their cars.

The two men looked at each other and Neal said, "It looks dead around here!" He raised his nose and sniffed. "No coffee's going at this place!"

Duncan nodded. "My thoughts exactly. What'll we do? We only have an hour before the groups come packing in."

Neal scowled and said, "You're here awful early, aren't you? I thought you didn't eat breakfast here any more, that your neighbor fixed your breakfast on days you left for the trail."

Uncomfortable, Duncan looked away and said, "We parted ways, you know? She's working at the clinic now."

"So?"

Wishing his friend would drop his inquisition, Duncan said, "You know how it is, we're gone a lot and she works with a doc there."

"So?" Neal repeated himself. "She told you to take a hike?"

"Well, no…"

Shaking his head, Neal said, "You're a fool, man! *You* wanted to be rid of her? She doesn't interest you any more? Who you got in the wings?"

"Well, no, not exactly."

Setting his backpack down next to the back wheel of his car, Neal crossed his arms over his chest and said, "So tell me exactly what the problem is."

Duncan shrugged, taking a long time to answer. Actually trying to think why he'd told Nancy he didn't want to be with her any more. "Well, see, she's educated, got a nursing degree, I'm a hiking guide, you know. They don't fit."

"Really! Who told you that?"

"Well, nobody, exactly."

"Like I say, you are a first class fool!" He looked the big man up and down. "Geeze, I thought you were smarter than that!"

They had reached the door to the office when it opened and a haggard Ramon looked at the men on the outside. "What is it, man?" Neal asked, reaching out immediately to his friend. "You look beat!"

Hardly waiting for Neal to ask, Ramon blurted out, "Sandy's sicker than a dog! She has been for a few hours! I've never seen her sick before, but she can't get her head off the pillow! I can't leave her like this!"

"'Course you can't!" Neal exclaimed. "What's the scoop?"

Ramon shrugged helplessly, pulling his hand down his face. "I can't leave her, not like this! She got sick this morning, so I couldn't call my group to cancel. I'll have to give them their money back when they get here."

"So how many people are we talking about?" Duncan asked.

Ramon stepped away from the desk and said, "I gotta get back to her, boot up the machine and see. I don't remember." Ramon ran, not waiting for the men to say or do anything.

When they stepped in the office and had the computer running, had the screen showing one, then another of the groups, Duncan said, "Ramon's got five in his group, you got six and I have seven. How about you take some of his and I take some?"

Neal shrugged. "I'd say if we don't want some unhappy hikers that's what we do. Let's see if we can divide his up that way."

Duncan sighed, looking at the screen then flipping it to another. "Doesn't look like we can his only wanted to go from today through the holiday and mine's to run to Friday. You could take them."

Neal sighed, "I guess eleven's no worse than some church youth group."

Duncan slapped his friend on the back. "They're harmless, believe me. I've had a few of them since I started here."

Neal's stomach growled. "What'll we do for breakfast? I figured since we're all going out the same day we'd all eat here."

Looking at the closed door into the house, Duncan said, "Yeah, same here. Come back to my cabin, I got coffee and some pop tarts."

Neal followed him back outside and grumbled, "Real nourishing, that'll last me all the way to lunch time, for sure."

Duncan nodded. "Better than nothing, man."

"I guess if you say so."

Ramon poked his head out and said, "What'd you find?"

"I'm taking your group with mine. We're going to Duncan's for coffee and pop tarts now. Tell them all to wait for us."

"Hey, I'll do it, guys! Thanks for the rescue."

"Hey," Duncan said, "you take care of Sandy, that's most important. We can manage this little bump in the road."

Ramon scowled, realizing something for the first time. "Hey, Roads, how come you're here so early and you're taking Neal back to your cabin for breakfast? Pop-tarts? Really?"

"Umm, it's a long story, man. It's kind of hard to explain."

"No, it's not!" Neal exclaimed, glaring at the other man. "He told Nancy to take a hike!"

"What! What's wrong with you, man?"

"Nothin'" Duncan growled. "We parted ways, is all! She went her way, I went mine. It's better that way."

"Oh, sure, got it!" Ramon muttered. "Hey, break a leg, if I don't see you when you're back and ready to go."

Nancy was in her kitchen finishing breakfast when she heard Duncan's SUV come back onto the lot. They hadn't spoken to each other since she'd thrown the coffee in his face Saturday morning. Sunday she'd gone back to Blairsville to her old church, she didn't want to run the risk of going to Roger's church and running into Duncan in the small place. Her heart felt like a block of ice, but she was afraid if she saw the man it would snap in two and she didn't want to make a scene. She was glad the people at her old church welcomed her with hugs and blessings.

Just as she snatched up her purse and headed for the door, she heard men's voices and decided Duncan and Neal had come back for breakfast. She wondered what was wrong at DeLord's house, but she waited behind her door until she heard Duncan's wheels crunch on the parking lot before she opened her door. She didn't care what brought Duncan back to his cabin, she'd put the louse out of her mind! Of course she had! She didn't ever think about him at all! Whatever his problem, he could handle it!

The sun shone as she ran across the grass to the back entrance, it would be a hot day, but this was July first, so it should be hot. Maybe Duncan would roast to death, it'd serve him right! She pushed that thought away, she wasn't thinking about him any more, not today, not any day! She yanked on the handle to the clinic back door. Dillon and several others from the Blairsville Hospital board were coming to cut the ribbon for the opening ceremony this morning at eight o'clock. Today she was in uniform for the first time in almost a month. It felt good. Shorts and tops, jeans and T-shirts were okay, but a uniform felt right for work.

She wondered how many people they'd have visit the clinic today. She shrugged, probably several would come with minor problems just to see what the inside of a new clinic looked and smelled like. She hoped there would be a steady stream of people who came she wanted this job to last for a very long time. She loved Vansville and when they had recently looked at a map they discovered that there was quite a large area that they could service, because there was no other clinic close by.

She glanced at the clock over Jill's desk and realized she was a few minutes early, but all the crew had decided to come in the back door so as not to mess up the pretty red ribbon strung across the front door. Several of the staff were there, but as usual, Stan wasn't there yet. By last Friday she'd decided that some doctors thought they could be high and mighty and come when they chose. Stan Miles was apparently one of those. Several of the dignitaries hadn't arrived yet either. She looked up at the clock over Jill's desk and saw that they had all of three minutes to arrive before eight. She heard a vehicle on the parking lot and out of curiosity looked out. She scowled, what was Sandy's van doing here?

She was sure Ramon was leading a hiking group and Sandy hadn't mentioned that she'd be coming to the opening ceremony. As she watched, she scowled harder as Ramon ran around the back of the van and put the key into the lock to activate the big door. She kept watching, becoming more concerned, as he brought the lift partway down, climbed on then took himself back up. Momentarily, he brought Sandy's chair onto the lift and brought both of them down to the ground. Sandy didn't look right.

As Ramon leaned over to reach the controls, Sandy's head lolled to the side. "Who's that?" Jill asked. Nancy jumped, she had not been aware that others had gathered behind her to look out the glass door.

"That's my friend, Sandy!" Nancy gasped.

"Get the door!" Dan's big voice boomed.

"But the ribbon...!" Nancy answered.

"So? The woman's in a wheelchair, she needs help! Forget the ribbon!"

Nancy pushed on the door, just as Ramon noticed the ribbon across in front of it. As Nancy pushed the door farther open, the ribbon snapped and the two parts fluttered slowly to the ground. "What's wrong?" Nancy asked.

Breathless, Ramon said, "She woke me up retching and she hasn't stopped! She's hardly responding now. You're not open yet?"

"Come on in, our doctor's running a little behind, but he should be here any minute. We'll take her to an exam room. You can put her on a table, right?"

"Of course!"

"Follow me!"

Everyone moved out of the way and turned silently to watch as Nancy hurried across the reception area with Ramon pushing the control of Sandy's chair right behind her. Nancy pushed the door of the first exam room open and went in to hold the door open so Ramon could get Sandy's chair into the room. Inside, he picked her up from the chair and tenderly laid her on the table. Nancy was right there and pulled out the extension so Sandy's legs wouldn't fall over the edge. When she was on the table, Ramon maneuvered the chair out of the way, but went immediately back to Sandy.

The door had closed, of course when Nancy let go of it, but only moments later, Stan appeared in the doorway and exclaimed, "What have we here?"

"These are Ramon and Sandy DeLord..." Nancy said.

Ramon was so anxious about Sandy he interrupted, "Sandy woke me up retching about four-thirty. She only stopped before I put her in the van because she passed out! I brought her I didn't know what else to do!"

Stan had never met Sandy, so he scowled and said, "She's a paraplegic?"

"Yes, she's never walked. Really, she's healthy as a horse! She's never been sick since I've known her; she didn't even get a cough last year when everyone in town had the flu. Several of her students coughed all over her and she never caught anything."

Stan pulled a sheet of paper from the desk in the room and took his pen from his pocket. "I guess she can't give us a specimen, can she?"

"If she was awake, but it's hard for her even then. I can't help her much."

"We'll get a blood sample," Stan said. He pressed a button on the intercom on the desk and barked, "Need a blood drawn in here now!"

"Yes, Doctor," Jill answered. Dan heard the exchange and whirled around to rush back to get his supplies.

By now, all the dignitaries had arrived and one of them said, loudly, "Who came in the front door and broke the ribbon?"

Not liking the pompous questioner, Dan called over his shoulder, "We have our first patient who's very sick and had to come in the front door!"

"Well," the man said, "What was the sense of coming all the way out here when the ribbon's already been broken?"

Stan opened the exam room door a few inches and called, "Dan, I need a blood drawn!"

Dan left the back room with his phlebotomy tray and said to the arrogant man, "Sick people come first, Mister, sorry you had to make such a l-l-o-o-n-n-g-g trip for nothing." He pushed on the closed door and disappeared into the exam room.

Dan readied his syringe then washed off Sandy's inside elbow with an alcohol swab. She wrinkled her nose, but instantly started heaving. Stan saw her action and said, "Nancy, pull up two cc's of that anti-nausea medicine." He turned to Ramon, "Is she allergic to anything?"

"I don't know, as I say, she's never been sick."

As Nancy turned toward a cabinet, Stan said, "Go ahead and draw the blood, Dan. We need to see what's going on as quick as possible."

"Sure, Stan, I'm on it!"

Out in the reception area several had come for the ceremony and were milling around. Nobody knew what to do, since the doctor and the staff were already busy. Since the ribbon had been broken, everyone came inside, thinking the cutting ceremony had already taken place. Dillon was one of the last of the hospital dignitaries to arrive, but he looked around for Stan.

Finally, he leaned on the counter and looked at Jill. "Where's Stan?"

"We have a patient, he's in with them."

"A patient! Nobody was supposed to get in for service before we officially opened the place. What's with you guys?"

Jill shrugged, but a bit intimidated by the CEO. "I guess when somebody's really sick they come in to get helped."

Dillon turned away and grumbled, "Best laid plans..." He turned back to Jill and asked, "Who's the sicky?"

Jill shrugged. "Nancy knew her, but she's in a wheelchair."

Dillon's eyes grew wide. "Sandy DeLord? What could be wrong with her?"

"We don't know yet."

Dan left the exam room with his tray and headed for the lab at the end of the hall. Dillon took advantage of the open door and hurried into the room. He saw Sandy on the table with her eyes closed, her upper body heaving. "What's wrong?" he whispered.

Stan shook his head. "We're not sure. Dan took a blood sample we'll have to wait for his results to know for sure."

Dillon shook Ramon's hand. "She just get sick?"

Nodding, Ramon said, "Yes, this morning." His voice cracked, as he said, "No warning, she didn't complain, just started retching and then after several hours of that, she fainted."

Patting Nancy and Stan on their backs, Dillon smiled at the frantic young husband and said, "I guarantee she's in the best of hands."

A tear slid from Ramon's eye, as he choked out, "I hope so, I love her so much. She's the best thing that's ever happened to me!"

"I know, man, I'm sorry for you."

About twenty minutes later, Sandy stopped heaving and lay still. A few minutes later, she opened her eyes and looked up into the eyes of her husband. "Where are we?" she whispered. She looked around. "Honey?"

He leaned over and kissed her tenderly, then said, "I brought you to the new clinic because you were so sick this morning, Love."

Stan stood up and moved to the head of the table. "Mrs. DeLord, have you any idea what's caused this?"

"N-no, not really. I can't remember ever feeling like this before. I've had some infections before, but never anything like this."

Nancy looked at the men in the room, as a feeling checked through her mind. Dillon had left and Dan had rushed away, but still there was a frantic

Ramon and a puzzled Stan. She wished it was her and Sandy. She walked close to the exam table, bent over Sandy's head and whispered, "You do have your periods, don't you?" Sandy nodded. "When was the last time?"

A light came on in Sandy's eyes and a smile spread across her face. "You think I'm pregnant!" she exclaimed.

Nancy nodded. "We can't be sure until he checks out your blood sample, but I think it's a good possibility."

Sandy reached for Ramon's hand, grabbed it and squeezed it hard and exclaimed, "Honey! Oh, Honey!"

"What, Love?"

The grin firmly in place, she pulled his head down to her and whispered, "Nancy thinks I may be pregnant!"

Dan pushed the door open enough to look in and said to Stan, "First results give a reading that there might be a pregnancy, Doc."

Stan looked from Dan to Ramon, to Sandy to Nancy and blindly felt behind him for his exam chair. As he sank into it he finally whispered, "Wow! Oh, wow!"

Ramon had Sandy in his arms and danced around, until her head fell onto his shoulder and she moaned, "Oh, Honey."

Quickly, he set her back on the table as Nancy reached for a small pan. Ramon groaned, "Darling, I'm so sorry! I didn't mean to make you sick again."

Sandy kept her arms around Ramon's neck and kissed him, before she said, "It's okay, the feeling's passed now." Turning her head, she looked at Stan. "We're going to have a baby? Really? My paralysis won't be a problem?"

The new doctor really had no idea if her paralysis would be a problem, he'd never had dealings with a married paraplegic before, but he said, confidently, "Ms Sandy, I've never had anything like this happen in my practice. Believe me, I'll find out today how I can take you through this. Do you have a family doctor?"

Shaking her head and shrugging at the same time, Sandy said, "My family in Philadelphia had a doctor, but I never went to him much. Unless Ramon has one he hasn't told me about, I don't have one here."

"We'll have this figured out before the end of the week," Stan vowed.

"Thanks, Doc, we'll count on that!" Ramon exclaimed. "Wow! Amazing! We're going to have a baby!" All his consternation had turned to pure joy.

Duncan's group had seven people, three couples and a single woman. That's what the print-out showed him. However, the other two groups came before his, so he was waiting with Neal on the blacktop when first Ramon's group, then Neal's group arrived. Neal and Duncan walked together to the first group, but of course, no one else came from the house.

The leader looked at the two men and said, "Where's Ramon? Is he running behind?"

Duncan being the big man that he was and much more imposing than Neal, said, "We're sorry, but Ramon left with Sandy for the new clinic a few minutes ago. She got really sick and then passed out. We decided that Neal, here, would take your group with his, if that's alright with you folks."

The man turned to Neal with a smile and his hand out. "Sure! Ramon's a good man, so I know anybody who works with him is a good man. So it's Neal?"

"That's right; I'm pleased to meet you, sir."

Moments later Neal's group arrived, they introduced themselves and headed down the trail, as the last van full of people drove onto the lot. Duncan was glad, he wouldn't have time to think about the little neighbor with the sandy blond hair and sparkling blue eyes who churned up his heart. He'd done the right thing, sending her on her way. After all, she'd be working with a doctor, he was more her stile than a hiking guide. Neal didn't know what he was talking about.

By the time the group left their van, Duncan was the only one left on the parking lot. The group gathered at the side of their van and Duncan walked up. "I suspect that I'm the man you're looking for, I'm Duncan, your guide for this hike. Welcome to our Fourth of July hike, it's to be a nice week for our jaunt into the woods." *Was that a cool touch or what!*

One man from one of the couples opened his mouth, but the woman standing alone sidled up to him and in a husky voice said, "Hi, there! It's so good to meet you, I'm Rosie." She took his hand and immediately wound her fingers with his, then led him to the man who'd opened his mouth. "Duncan, this is Sam, he's the man who got this group together, but he's my brother." Patting Duncan's hand, she said, "We're glad to be going with you, Duncan."

Duncan tried very hard not to make a face, at least he ducked his head, but Rosie did nothing for him. He shook Rosie's hand off then held out that hand to Sam. "I'm pleased to meet you, Sam. I guess if we all get our backpacks in place, we can be on our way. We have four hours of hiking before we stop for lunch."

Sam nodded. "Yes, that'll be good." He grinned at the big man. "I think that's what we came for, isn't it?"

Duncan went to his SUV, opened the back and hauled out his backpack. He checked the pocket where he always put his phone and saw that it was there and charged. He didn't know for sure, but he had a feeling he'd be the one who needed rescue before Friday evening arrived. He pulled in a deep breath and swung the heavy pack onto his back. Only moments later, he left the asphalt parking lot for the wide trail.

He hadn't reached the trail head he was aiming for when a breathless female voice behind him, said, "Duncan, wait up!"

Duncan whirled around and saw that the hikers were scattered out behind him, so he stopped. He let out a long sigh maybe it was the demons of hell that were chasing him down the trail. Rosie reached him first, but he put both hands on his backpack belt but looked out beyond her until the rest of the group gathered around them. "Okay, folks, listen up. We have four hours of hiking ahead of us before lunch. I plan to get there a few minutes before or after twelve. If that's not your plan, let's get it out now and head back to the parking lot. I'll give you your money back and you can go home. If you want to go on this hike, then you keep up with me. I'm not setting too fast a pace."

He looked at each couple and said, "None of you are old, you all look like healthy young people, there should be no problem maintaining my stride. So what'll it be?"

"I wanna go," Rosie said, immediately.

Sam looked at the others. "Let's hear it, folks, go or not?"

"We're with you," another of the men said. The women silently nodded.

"Fine, then get your feet in gear and let's go!" Duncan whirled around and started down the trail. Noisily, the rest of the people set off behind him.

Much to Duncan's displeasure, Rosie kept up, walking beside him on the wide trail and behind him when it was single file. The little creature that usually sat on his shoulder tapped him on the ear and said, *So why are you mad that Rosie's after you? You told Nancy to scram and she threw coffee in your face and told you to have a good life. Isn't that the way you wanted it? Didn't you want to be free? To be free means you can have any woman you want! Right?*

Duncan kicked a stone - hard - down the bank to the side. It was a good thing Rosie was behind him, he'd probably have to call the MEDIVAC; he'd have broken her ankle, even with her boot, if she'd been beside him. He pulled in a deep breath he couldn't keep on this way. He glanced over his shoulder; he must have put fear into the group they were practically on each other's heels trying to keep up with him.

Late that afternoon, Duncan walked out onto the meadow. Close to the middle he stopped and said, "Folks, we've reached our camping place for the night. While I get the fire going, ladies gather your food for this evening meal and get it ready. Men, your job is setting up the tents; all of them. Our water source is that pool over there. On the far side is the source, it's a spring that comes from under the rocks. This water is very pure and very cold. If any of you run out of things to do, you can gather wood and shrubs for the fire. We'll need a good supply, since it takes quite a hot fire to warm the cold water for dishes and we'll have to have a fire in the morning. Usually, we have a campfire here after supper."

Rosie looked at the other women and said in her sultry voice, "Do all us girls have to fix supper, Duncan?"

Duncan looked at the other women, then at Rosie. He shrugged, nodded and said, "It seems to me there's plenty to do. Here are the pans someone needs to get water heating for cleanup. If you're not getting water, gathering the ingredients for supper, you can gather wood from the trees around."

"You don't need help with the fire?"

"No, Ma'am, I don't!" he said, emphatically. "I've been building fires this whole hiking season and I've done just fine without any help from the hikers."

Rosie let out a dramatic huff.

"Rosie," Sam said, as he unhooked her tent from her backpack. "Listen to what the man said he's quite capable of doing his job by himself. Besides, I think he has a girlfriend. When did you plan to see him again?"

Her ears burning, Rosie swung around, grabbed the large pan and without a word, headed for the pool for water. When Rosie was gone, Duncan said, "Thanks, Man, I needed your help."

"No problem, I've been doing that most of her life."

After supper and cleanup, the group sat around the fire, but Duncan went to his tent and found his Bible in his backpack. It was obvious that this group was not from any church. This camping place was his favorite. This was where young Alex had nearly drowned and where he'd come face to face with God. Every time he took this trail he went to his favorite rock by the pool and God met him there. He realized it had been a week or two since he'd been here. It was obvious to him that he needed to meet God, really needed to meet God tonight!

It took a bit of maneuvering to get to the most comfortable place on the rocks, so he put his Bible on top, close to where he planned to sit then started to climb up to sit beside it. Much to his surprise, when he brought his leg up and turned to sit down, the Bible was already open, so he looked where it was. His heart skittered in his chest, because it was open to a place he'd been avoiding for several days. It was open to Genesis, the second chapter. Duncan sighed, he knew what Genesis 2:18 said, "The Lord God said, 'It is not good for the man to be alone.'...."

Duncan squirmed in the spot to get more comfortable and slammed his hand down on the page. He dropped his head to his chest and mumbled, "But I screwed up. I told her to get lost. She threw coffee in my face and told me to have a good life."

Being very persistent, the little critter on his shoulder said, *It's not good for man to be alone...Duncan. You're brave, right?*

Duncan shuddered and muttered again, "I'm not sure I'm that brave."

You might be surprised.

Just as Duncan picked up his Bible to open to another place to read, he heard, "Duncan is there room up there for me?"

"Rosie, I'm about to have my *devotions* for the day. You probably don't have your *Bible* with you, do you?"

The look that crossed Rosie's face was one Duncan wished he could capture on camera. She swallowed, after she closed her mouth and finally croaked out, "Are you one of those?"

Duncan smiled at her and said, "I'm not sure what you mean by 'one of those', but I am a believer in Jesus, He's taken my sins away, so that I'm a new man and I can go to heaven. Are you a believer, Rosie?"

"NO! I'M NOT!" She raced away before Duncan could say anything else.

Duncan watched her for several minutes. He couldn't remember a woman her age run so fast unless they were in a race. He wondered: were the bats of hell after her or the hounds of heaven? A minute later he opened his Bible to another passage to read, but as he thumbed through the pages, he said, "I guess I don't have to worry about her bugging me any more. I guess I'd better concentrate on getting back on Nancy's good side."

The wind sighed around him and he was sure it said, *That's a good plan.*

When Duncan arrived back on Friday evening, Ramon greeted him at the office door. "Howdy, how'd your hike go?"

"Not bad, once I got that woman with the long talons off me, I rather enjoyed it. So is Sandy all fixed up? Over being sick?"

Duncan had never seen Ramon's face so full of excitement and joy before, as he said, "No, she's not over being sick, at least in the mornings, but man! We're going to have a baby! Can you believe that! Us! Sandy and me!"

Incredulously, Duncan looked at his friend. "You're excited?"

"Excited!! You can't imagine!"

Duncan held out his hand and Ramon grabbed it. "If you're excited, then I'm happy for you, Man! Congratulations!"

"Thanks! Nancy was the one who figured it out, even before the blood test came back and the doctor knew."

Duncan nodded. "She's a smart woman."

"Yeah, and you, my man, had better get over there and claim her. She's been complaining to Sandy about the doctor trying to make time with her."

Duncan dropped Ramon's hand, looked down at the ground then looked back up to look in Ramon's eyes. Earnestly he said, "But isn't that right? I mean, he's educated, she's educated. They work at the same place..."

"So?"

"But... I don't know, Man..."

Ramon scowled at his friend. "You love her, don't you?"

"Lo..." Duncan didn't finish the word. He looked into his friend's eyes and asked, "What did you say?"

Ramon's face burst into a grin again. "You, man, are in denial. You heard what I said and you know exactly what I meant. Get your tail down the street and knock on Nancy's door."

Shuddering, Duncan said, almost whined, "Man, I can't! She threw coffee in my face the last time I saw her."

"Did you deserve it?"

"Probably."

"Get out of here!" Just as Duncan reached the back of his SUV Ramon called after him, "Hey, man, break a leg!"

Reluctantly, Duncan climbed into his SUV, fumbled with his key and sighed. "God, help me. I'm scared spitless!"

Nancy was walking across the grass toward the walk in front of the cabins when she looked up and saw Duncan's SUV turn into his space. Her heart skittered around in her chest, but she visibly raised her chin and kept on toward her cabin. She was almost there when Duncan opened his door and called, "Nancy!" Nancy, of course, didn't so much as slow down or act like she saw him, she kept on to her walk and hurried up to her door, opened it and went inside.

Duncan's heart took a nose-dive. It wasn't hard to read Nancy's body language and that was all he had to go on. He slowly pulled the keys from the ignition and left his car. He sighed, as he heard Nancy's door close. "God, help me to keep my hands and nose from getting smashed in her door when I go to knock, please?"

He pulled his backpack from the back of his SUV and started up the walk. He dropped it on the walk that led to his cabin, but with slow steps he walked on toward Nancy's cabin. He couldn't see her, but Nancy had stopped inside her door and was watching his progress toward her door through her gauzy lace curtains. A tiny grin swept across her mouth as she noticed how much slower he came from his cabin to hers. But he was coming, maybe, just maybe… Was there, could there be a chance?

Just to be sure he didn't see her; she stepped back from the curtain covered window as he turned onto her walk. She went in her bathroom and flushed the toilet as he walked onto her porch. When he knocked she walked into her closet, and since the door from it into the big room was closed she was sure it was muffled, as she called, "Coming!"

She walked on into her bedroom and waited several minutes, until Duncan wiped his forehead with one hand and knocked again with the other and said, "Nancy, I'm sure you're in there, come on, please open the door!"

Duncan had his hand raised to knock again when Nancy finally opened the door. "Hi, Duncan! I guess you're back from your Fourth of July hike?"

"Umm, yeah, I am…"

"It's good to see you're still in one piece. I'm about to change into more comfortable clothes. You can see I still have my uniform on…."

As the door started to close, Duncan moved his foot onto the threshold and said, "Umm, Nancy, after we both change, could I, umm, take you to Blairsville for a burger or something?"

"Me? You wanna take me?"

"Yeah, I wanna take you!"

"But why? Why take me?"

Letting out a really long sigh, Duncan swallowed and said, "You're gonna make this really rough, aren't you?"

She smiled sweetly at him, her hand still on the door and said, "What do you mean, Duncan?" She meant for him to spell it out.

Duncan cleared his throat. "I mean, because I was a real jerk the other day. I've missed you a lot and I'm sorry."

Nancy started to close the door. "I'll think about it while I change clothes. Come back in twenty minutes and I'll tell you if I'll go or not. After all, I've worked really hard all week with *Stan*. I was going to relax this evening. Eat one of my frozen dinners, put my feet up, you know, that sort of thing."

Duncan saluted and pulled his foot from the threshold. "Yes, Ma'am, I'll be here in twenty minutes." He said the last few words to the closed door.

Nancy watched him through the curtained window as he jumped from her porch to the ground. He never touched her walk, took two strides to the main walk and was picking up his backpack three strides later. She heard his door slam and a smile slid across her face then she turned and raced into her bathroom, stripped off her clothes and nearly jumped over the side of the tub into the shower.

After a quick rinse, she pulled her comb through her curls to get them settled where she wanted them, then dashed into her closet to find the right outfit. She pulled on a pretty blouse, walking shorts and white sandals She stuffed some money into her purse and was applying lipgloss when she heard a knock. Grinning at herself in the mirror, she called, "Coming!"

She immediately slowed her pace and walked sedately to the door. When she opened it, she looked into a clean shaven face except for a mustache. There was a tiny smile on his face, but his blue eyes were pleading. "Miss Nancy, would you go with me to dinner in Blairsville?"

She looked him up and down for several seconds before she finally said, "Yes, Duncan, I guess I'll go with you to Blairsville."

The breath whooshed out of him, as he stepped back for her to pass him. "Thanks, Nancy. I'm happy you consented."

He realized he had to touch her. He took her elbow and escorted her all the way down the walk to his SUV. He opened the passenger door and helped her in. When her purse was on her lap, he gently closed the door and walked around to his side. Of course, Nancy's hungry eyes followed his every movement.

After he opened his door, he looked up to see that she was looking at him, so he gave her a tentative smile. "Thanks for coming," he murmured as he closed the door.

"Sure, I'm happy to get away for a little."

"No, I'm happy you consented, after I was such a jerk the other day."

"Yeah, that's true," she murmured.

Some time later, Nancy turned so she could look at him and asked, "What made you change your mind, Duncan?"

Duncan took a deep breath and let it out slowly. "The group I had was three couples and one single woman. She started right off by taking my hand, introduced herself then led me to the group leader. She stuck to me like glue all day that first day until after supper when I took my Bible to the rocks for my devotions. She asked if she could come up and sit with me, but when I asked her if she was a believer, she ran. Right then I knew I was dead wrong and that I wanted to come back to you in the worst way."

"I see."

He took his eyes from the road and looked at her, as he asked, "Will you have me back, Nancy, please?"

Trying to hide her smile, she said, "I'll have to think about it, Duncan."

Seeing her smile, he asked, "How long?"

Looking out the side window she said, "Oh, maybe until we get to Blairsville, we'll see."

"I'll be waiting for your answer."

Rather than go to the fast food place outside Blairsville, Nancy realized Duncan was driving on. A few minutes later he turned onto the parking lot of a nice restaurant. They would have to wait for a few minutes, there was a line to the door and several couples were ahead of them, but Nancy's heart took a leap and it caused a smile she couldn't hide. Duncan had never taken her out on a date! They'd eaten together at DeLord's or at her cabin, but go out to a restaurant? Wow!

The line moved quickly and soon the hostess led them to a quiet table for two with a light hanging over it. There was a red and white checkered table cloth and a small vase of silk flowers in the center, but to Nancy's eyes it was beautiful. Duncan smiled at the hostess as she placed menus at the places, but he went to a chair and pulled it out. Nancy looked up into his eyes and smiled, she had never felt so special in all her life.

After Duncan sat down and before anyone came to take an order, he reached across the table for Nancy's hand and said, "Nancy, I've been miserable all week without you. Will you have me back?"

"Yes," Nancy whispered. "I'll gladly have you back."

The waiter came and asked, "What'll you have to drink?"

Without hesitation, Duncan said, "Two iced teas, please."

After a delicious meal that Duncan ordered for them both and Nancy couldn't have eaten another bite, he pushed their coffee cups out of the way and reached for Nancy's hands. He cleared his throat, then swallowed, very nervous. "Nancy, love. I love you with all my heart. Will you honor me by consenting to be my wife? Really, I think I've loved you since that first time we met, but I wouldn't own up to it."

Looking at their hands and therefore not looking into his dear face, she pulled one hand from his and put her index finger beside her mouth. Pulled in a deep breath and said, "Well..."

Duncan still watched her, but also pulled in a deep breath and whispered, "Please, Love?"

After another pause, that almost killed her to make, she looked up into his dear eyes. "Soon?" He nodded. Nancy's grin stretched across her face. "Yes, oh, yes, Duncan!"

There was a nip in the air, late fall was upon them. Sandy had finally gotten over her morning sickness and the phone had stopped ringing incessantly. The people from DeLord's Hiking Services who lived in Vansville had said goodbye to Neal for the winter, but he was looking forward to the spring. There were already groups signed up who wanted hikes starting in March. He and Duncan both knew that for a while, they'd be leading all the hikes, because there would be a little DeLord coming to stay.

It was the first Friday in November, the clinic had closed its doors for the day, but there were many still milling around inside and several cars were on the parking lot, including Sandy's van. She, Isabel and Raylyn were busy fixing the meal and Ramon, Alex and Roger were standing on ladders and chairs decorating the large waiting room for the rehearsal dinner, but also for the reception taking place after the two o'clock wedding tomorrow.

Nancy had gotten off work at five, but she was in her cabin changing clothes and Duncan was putting the last touches on the log house he'd built on his off days since July. Somehow he'd talked Brad Thomas into selling him part of the field behind Isabel's cabins and the clinic.

After their honeymoon, Duncan would take his bride to her new home. He was very much looking forward to loving his wife for the rest of their days. Life was good. Duncan had finally become a believer that the love of a woman was much, much better than life as a free, unattached man. Duncan had come to realize that all roads lead home and home was where his heart.... and Nancy were.

www.ingramcontent.com/pod-product-compliance
Lightning Source LLC
Chambersburg PA
CBHW021439070526
44577CB00002B/218